# This book is presented to:

_____

## on this day of:

_____

## by:

_____

# Here's What Sunday School Teachers Are Saying

This is wonderful. I really like the short synopsis of each story. I don't think it's too easy or too hard to read. The questions really do a great job of recapping the story and I like the fact that each day you ask the kids to write down what they learned. I think this part will allow the older ones to express themselves and the younger ones will only improve their writing and analytical skills through doing this.

**Richelle Muth**, Pre-K Sunday School Coordinator, *Millwoods Pentecostal Assembly,* Edmonton, Alberta.

---

The devotions were brief and had direct messages that a child could understand. The questions were not too many and allowed child to express her own understanding of the passage read.

**Dr. Bayo Adams,** Bible Study Leader & Coordinator of International Fellowship, *Woodvale Pentecostal Church,* Ottawa, Ontario.

---

Structure is okay and understandable. Time it takes is just right. Child enjoyed reading it and learned something. Will be a good devotional book for children who want to know more about God by reading on their own.

**Dr. Kwamena & Gifty Quagraine,** Sunday School Teachers, *First Assembly of God,* Pine Bluff, Arkansas.

---

I really enjoyed reading the devotions. They were a blessing to me and a ministry to my son. I like that the devotions were based on Jesus' life and ministry. I also like the way they encouraged a natural and relaxed context to discuss spiritual concepts with my son. I can hardly wait until my son can begin reading the entire devotion book.

**Mettie Jane Wiskar,** Vacation Bible School Director, *Cambrian Heights Baptist Church,* Calgary, Alberta.

---

I found the daily devotions to be very educational yet inspiring at the same time. The new stories every night had my child learning every day while receiving an inspirational message that stayed with her throughout the week. The stories were bite sized enough to be comprehended by her young mind yet filled with just enough spiritual content to relate to her day to day walk with the Lord.

**Emmanuel & Nicole Pobee,** Junior Church Coordinators, *Bramalea Christian Fellowship Open Bible Church,* Brampton, Ontario.

---

It is concise and targeted to the correct age group. The scripture selections are excellent and cover the basic requirements of our role as salt and light of the world. Parental involvement will be enriched ....

**Dr. E. Dapaah-Afriyie,** Director of Christian Education, *Victory Assembly of God,* Providence, Rhode Island.

# *My Daily Walk*

## *Discover The Life of Jesus*

Flora A. Trebi-Ollennu

edited by
Reverend Peter Barker

Amerley Treb Books
Canada

My Daily Walk: Discover The Life of Jesus
Text Copyright © 2004 by Flora A. Trebi-Ollennu

**Library and Archives Canada Cataloguing in Publication**

Trebi-Ollennu, Flora A. (Flora Amerley), date
My Daily Walk: discover the life of Jesus / Flora A. Trebi-Ollennu; edited by Peter Barker: illustrations, Jan Vandenberg.
Includes bibliographical references
ISBN: 1-894718-04-6
1. Jesus Christ – Person and offices – Meditations – Juvenile literature. 2. Christian children – Prayer – books and devotions – English. I. Barker, Peter II. Vandenberg, Jan III. Title.
BT306.53.T73 2004  j232  C2004-904725-6

First Amerley Treb Books hardcover edition: October 2004

Scripture quotations marked (NIV) are taken from the Holy Bible, New International Version®. NIV®. Copyright © 1973, 1978, 1984 by International Bible Society. Used by permission of Zondervan. All rights reserved.

Scripture references indicated NRSV are from the New Revised Standard Version of the Bible, copyright © 1989 by the Division of Christian Education of the National Council of the Churches of Christ in the USA. Used by permission.

Scripture references indicated KJV are from the King James Version of the Bible.

Edited by Reverend Peter Barker
Illustrations copyright © 2004 by Jan Vandenberg
Clip Art copyright © 2004 Dream Maker Software
Cover Design by John Deheer Adjaye
Book Design by Amerley Treb Books

Printed in Canada

# Here's What Young Readers Are Saying

Well, I thought it was great. It took less time to do the devotion. I learned a bunch of stuff from the bible that I really did not know. Some of the miracles are unbelievable like feeding many people with a piece of bread. I think the people were fed with crumbs but now I know Jesus can do impossible things.

**Damaris,** *Age 9, Pine Bluff, Arkansas*

---

It was the right length. The examples fit my age group and I could understand the lessons. The devotions were suitable and appropriate. They helped me to think about what I was reading and learning from the Bible. I think I could do the devotions on my own but I like having help from my Mom with the questions and discussions.

**Ethan,** *Age 9,* Calgary, Alberta

---

The lessons are very much applicable for now and in the future. I am thrilled by the fact that humble people will inherit the earth- that is very cool. The lessons will prepare me for life and teach other people when I become a missionary trying to convince people to turn away from their wicked ways. I enjoyed knowing so much more about what Jesus said in the beatitudes.

**Ahiney,** *Age 10,* Ottawa, Ontario

---

I enjoyed the devotion as I learned new things about the return of Christ and what to expect. I found the devotions interesting and will like to do it more often.

**Toluwa,** *Age 10,* Ottawa, Ontario

---

Easy to understand and interesting. The time it takes to complete each day's devotion is just right.

**Philbertha,** *Age 9,* Caledon, Ontario

# ACKNOWLEDGEMENTS

I owe my greatest debt of gratitude to God for leading me in his wisdom to serve him in this way.

I am also indebted to Reverend Peter Barker for his passionate commitment in editing this work. In addition, I am grateful for his tireless effort, time and advice to ensure accurate information and teaching, passing along much valuable insight from his experiences as a missionary, pastor and author. His inspirational comment as we neared the end of this project has been more than energizing - "I hear the angels cheering us on ...."

I am also grateful to Mettie-Jane Wiskar who spent countless hours reading through the manuscript and also passed along valuable suggestions. Her friendship and spiritual support is ever appreciated. Thanks to Ray Suchow who scoured parts of the manuscript for errors.

Thank you to my Christian brethren who helped evaluate this book by participating in surveys across various cities in North America. I also want to thank my dear friends who faithfully upheld me in prayer.

Deep appreciation goes to my brother, Ashitey, for his encouragement, prayers, technical assistance and for checking scripture readings carefully.

I am especially indebted to my children (Fraikua, Trebi, Essilfua, and Papa-Ollennu) who were not only eager to use the preliminary notes of this book for their quiet time, but contributed ideas, pointing out omissions and putting a much needed kid-flavor into the book.

Finally, my most heartfelt thanks go to my husband and best friend, Kwaku Deheer, for spiritual and moral support. His technical assistance in various ways is also much appreciated.

This book is dedicated to my son, Trebi Deheer, the inspiration behind it all.

# CONTENTS

**The Parables of Jesus**

## The Arrest and Trial of Jesus

# A Word To Mom, Dad or Guardian

Please assist eight-year-olds and slow readers in using this devotional. The strategy is to wean children from this assistance when they are ten years old or thereabout. The goal is to develop in children a high interest to investigate the truths in the Bible for themselves, becoming well versed in the teachings of the bible as they grow up. Familiarity with the words of Jesus is sure to deliver children from extremist and false doctrines.

It is suggested that parents assign particular periods in the day for this project, preferably before children leave for school in the morning. The whole point is to teach children to start the day with the Lord. We encourage you to ask children what they read from the Bible as well as lessons learned. Children should be encouraged to go over portions of the devotions once or twice to reinforce lessons learned (e.g. over every three month period). This way, children will not be overwhelmed with too many lessons.

Most of the text in this devotional is based on the New International Version Bible. However, children may use Bible versions they are comfortable with. A few memory verses are taken from the King James Version and the New Revised Standard Version for clarity.

Be a shining example yourself – let the children know you also read the Bible and pray daily, and share your devotions with them. We hope children would realize that their parents appreciate and value time spent with the Lord in prayer and in the WORD. Parents who dedicate themselves to this will find it a double blessing as they themselves acquire more discipline with regards to their daily devotions or quiet times.

## Use It For Family Bible Study Too
This book is a useful tool for family Bible studies. It is dedicated to the life of Jesus – his birth, his ministry, his death, resurrection and ascension, all of which make for a good family bible study. There are questions to be addressed for each passage; there are memory verses and points for further discussion.

# Dear Young Reader,

## Here's How You Can Use This Book

Keep it with your Bible and use it everyday to find a Bible passage to read. It takes between five and twelve minutes to read the Scripture suggested and the comments in this book. Talk to adults and they will tell you they sometimes struggle to do their quiet time everyday, because they never acquired the habit when they were young. Start now and you'll be glad you did.

### What you will need
- A Bible
- A quiet room or personal place
- A desk or table to sit behind comfortably
- A pen or sharp pencil
- A note book to record answers and thoughts for the day

### Here's how you can start
- Thank God for a new day and commit the day into his hands.
- Pray to God to help you understand and enjoy reading the Bible.

### When you finish
- Remember the lessons you have learned and thank God for them.
- Ask him to help you put those lessons into practice.

# John's Birth Is Announced

*Today is a very special day, because you are joining a worldwide family of people young and old who are reading the Bible in many hundreds of different languages. It won't be easy to keep it up, so let's pray together right now, that God will help you to read again tomorrow, and the day after, and every day from now onwards. Yes, Lord, please help us all to do that. Amen.*

**Now read Luke chapter 1, verses 5 to 13**

In Bible times, God's people called their church a Temple. They went to the Temple to worship God. Zechariah was a priest who worked in God's Temple. Zechariah and his wife, Elizabeth, loved God. They were old. They had no children. But one day, while Zechariah was working in the Temple, he looked up, and he saw a messenger from God, an angel! He was surprised and afraid. The angel said, "Don't be afraid! You and Elizabeth will have a baby! This baby will make you glad! You are to name this baby John."

Whatever God gives brings joy and gladness. Be glad for the things you have been blessed with – parents, sisters, brothers, home, games, friends, and many other things too.

**Dig Out The Answers**

1. Zechariah and his wife Elizabeth loved God very much but did not have child. *Children*

2. Zechariah worshiped God in the Temple by offering prayers in the form of incense. Write down two things you do at church to worship God. *Sing, Plisten to the word of*

3. God's angel appeared to Zechariah in the Temple and told him *God* _____. *He and his wife will have a baby*

**In Your Own Words:** Write down what you learned today.

**My Prayer:** God, I thank you that you know my needs and will supply them just as you did for Zechariah and Elizabeth.

**Today's Wise Words:** God knows and meets my needs, so I am not afraid.

# John – A Special Baby

Today, we will continue to read about what the angel told Zechariah the priest in the Temple. You remember that the angel told him not to be afraid. He also told him that he and Elizabeth were going to have a baby. And they were to name him John. This baby John was going to be special because:

1. He would make his parents very happy
2. Many people were going to be happy because of him
3. God would use him for great things
4. John was not supposed to drink alcohol or any strong drink
5. He would be filled with the Holy Spirit

## Dig Out The Answers

Can you remember these five things without looking at the paper? Try to write them down from memory.

**My Prayer:** Pray that God will fill you with his Holy Spirit like John.

**In Your Own Words:** Write down what you learned today.

## Today's Wise Words:
1. I am special
2. I can do great things for God when I'm filled with the Holy Spirit

18

# Zechariah Doubts God's Message

After the angel finished talking to Zechariah in the Temple, Zechariah asked, "How can I be sure this is true?" Zechariah did not believe the angel. The angel told Zechariah he would not be able to talk until baby John was born. And it happened as the angel had said. When Zechariah stepped out of the Temple, he could not talk to the worshippers waiting for him outside, so he made signs to them with his hands.

The angel spoke God's word to Zechariah. Today, God speaks to us through the Bible. It is good to believe the Bible and do what it tells you. When you do what the Bible says it makes you wise.

### Dig Out The Answers

1. How did God talk to Zechariah?
2. How does God talk to us today?

**In Your Own Words:** Write down what you learned.

**My Prayer:** God, help me to believe all that I read in the Bible because it is your word; help me to obey it too, in Jesus' name.

**Today's Wise Words:** We believe everything the Bible tells us because God's Holy Spirit is speaking through it.

19

## An Angel Sent To Mary

Day 4

An angel from the Lord appeared to Mary. The angel's name was Gabriel. The angel told Mary that she was going to have a baby and she should call him Jesus. Jesus is the Son of God, a king and our Savior. Mary believed the angel. The angel also told Mary that her relative Elizabeth, Zechariah's wife, who was thought to be too old to have children, was also expecting a child. The angel also said, "no problem is ever too difficult for God to solve". Remember that God can solve all problems, so tell him about yours.

**Dig Out The Answers**

1. What were the first words the angel spoke to Mary?

*You are going to have a baby*

2. Did Mary believe the angel's words? *yes*

3. What was the name of Mary's relative who had a baby even though she was quite old? *Elizabeth*

**In Your Own Words:** Write down what you learned from the story.

**My Prayer:** Ask God one thing you want him to do for you, and look forward to the answer.

**Today's Wise Words:** God is able to do everything I ask Him

# READ

**Luke 1:39-45**

Day 5

## Mary Visits Elizabeth

After some time, Mary visited Elizabeth, her relative, who lived in a town in the hill country of Judea. She wanted to share the good news from the angel with Elizabeth. But before she could say anything the Holy Spirit filled Elizabeth. And Elizabeth praised God that Mary had believed what the angel told her about the baby Jesus. We can praise God when the Holy Spirit fills us.

**Dig Out The Answers**

1. Why did Mary hurry to Elizabeth's house? *To tell her the good news*

2. What did Elizabeth do when she saw Mary? *She praised god that mary had believed what the Angel said*

3. What do you think God wants us to do when he does something good for us? Remember what Mary did, and Elizabeth, too. *Obey what he says.*

**In Your Own Words:** Write down what you learned today. *I learned that you should always obey Gods word.*

**My Prayer:** God, fill me with your Holy Spirit so I can praise you and tell others the good things you do for me every day, in Jesus' name, Amen.

**Today's Wise Words:** The Holy Spirit fills me so I can praise God and tell others about Jesus.

21

## READ

**Luke 1:57-66**

Day 6

# John Is Born

After some time, Zechariah and Elizabeth's baby was born just as the angel had said. Friends and relatives came to see him. They wanted to name the baby Zechariah, just like the baby's father. But Elizabeth said, "No, his name is John." The relatives and friends were surprised. They asked Zechariah what the baby's name should be. Zechariah wrote, "His name is John." Suddenly, he could talk. Zechariah was so happy. He praised God. Did God do things for you in the past? What is God doing for you now? Remember to praise him for all he does for you.

**Dig Out The Answers**

1. What did Zechariah do when he was able to talk again?

2. What did the relatives and friends do when they heard Zechariah praising God?

3. Did God do what he promised Zechariah through the angel?

**In Your Own Words:** Write down what you learned today.

**My Prayer:** God, help me praise you like Zechariah. Help me know that you keep your promises. And you will do everything you promise in your word. Help me also to keep my promises to my family members and friends.

**Today's Wise Words:** God keeps his promises.

22

# Jesus Is Born

**Luke 2:1-7**

**Day 7**

A long time ago, Caesar Augustus was Emperor of Rome. The people of his land were called Romans. The Romans conquered many countries and ruled them. Jesus' country, Israel, was also conquered, and the Romans ruled them. One day, Caesar Augustus, the Roman emperor, issued a decree that all people living in the Roman Empire should be counted. Everyone had to go to his hometown to be counted. The emperor wanted to know how many people he ruled. Joseph was from Bethlehem. That was his hometown, so he took Mary, who was expecting, along with him to Bethlehem. But when they got to Bethlehem, there was no place for them in any of the inns (or hotels). Do you have room in your heart for Jesus?

Finally, they found a place in the manger. Mary gave birth to baby Jesus in the manger. She wrapped him in clothes and placed him in the manger. Jesus was born in Bethlehem, just as the prophets of God had said. Mary had a baby boy just as the angel had said. God keeps his promises.

**Dig Out The Answers**

1. Why did Joseph take Mary along to Bethlehem? *because she was expected*
2. What happened to Mary when they got to Bethlehem?
3. Why was Jesus born in a manger?
4. Do you have room in your heart for Jesus?

**In Your Own Words:** Write down what you learned today.

**My Prayer:** I make room in my heart for you today, dear Jesus. Help me obey you always so you can live happily in my heart .

**Today's Wise Words:** Every day there is some part of my life where I can make room for Jesus.

23

## Shepherds Hear the Good News

**READ**

Luke
2:8-20

**Day 8**

The night Jesus was born, there were shepherds taking care of their sheep in fields near Bethlehem. An angel of the Lord appeared to them and told them the good news of Jesus' birth. Many other angels joined that one angel and they praised God together. The good news is that Jesus brings peace to all who believe in his name. The shepherds went to the stable to see Jesus. After, they hurried back to town and told others the good news of Jesus' birth.

**Dig Out The Answers**

1. Why did the angels appear to the shepherds?

2. What did the shepherds do after they had seen Jesus'?

**In Your Own Words:** Write down what you learned today.

**My Prayer:** Thank you, God, that Jesus brings peace to all who believe in him. Amen.

**Today's Wise Words:** Jesus was born to bring peace to all.

# READ

## Simeon and Baby Jesus

Luke
2:21-28

Day 9

When Jesus was eight days old his parents, Joseph and Mary, took him to the Temple to present him to the Lord. This was something every parent whose firstborn was a boy was supposed to do according to the Law of Moses. God gave Moses that law. Mary and Joseph also took along a pair of doves as an offering to the Lord.

An old man named Simeon used to spend a lot of time in the Temple. The Holy Spirit had told him he would not die until he saw Jesus, the baby born to save the world from sin (that is why we call him "Christ", which means a person anointed like a king for a special job). The moment Mary and Joseph went to the Temple, the Holy Spirit told Simeon also to go the Temple because Jesus the Christ had been brought there. On reaching the Temple, Simeon took the baby in his arms and praised God.

### Dig Out The Answers

1. Why did Joseph and Mary take baby Jesus to the Temple?
2. Who told Simeon he would not die until he saw the Christ?
3. Who told Simeon to go the Temple because Jesus had been brought there?

**In Your Own Words:** What did you learn from the story?

**My Prayer:** Lord, let me keep reading the Bible so your Holy Spirit will help me understand it, and give me power to do what it says too, in Jesus' name, Amen.

**Today's Wise Words:** The Holy Spirit speaks into my heart.

**Day 10**

## Simeon Praises God

Simeon praised God when he saw baby Jesus, because God had kept his promise. Simeon told those present that Jesus would save the world.

Jesus is the light of all the people of the world. We cannot see without light – Jesus will make us see God as he is and love him as we ought.

Simeon blessed the parents of Jesus and told them some of the things that would happen to Jesus and his parents. Simeon could tell what would happen to Jesus because he had read the Old Testament Scriptures many times, and the Holy Spirit helped him understand how what he read would happen. Scriptures is another name for the Bible.

**Dig Out The Answers**

1. Why do you think Simeon praised God when he saw baby Jesus?

2. Write two other things Simeon said about baby Jesus.

**In Your Own Words:** Write down what you learned today.

**My Prayer:** Holy Spirit, please teach me about Jesus, just as you taught Simeon. Amen.

**Today's Wise Words:** The Holy Spirit teaches about Jesus

# Anna and Baby Jesus

**READ** Luke 2:36-40

Day 11

There was an old lady called Anna. Anna loved God so much that she lived in the Temple. She loved talking to God through prayer. She also fasted a lot – that meant she did not eat food some days, so she could have more time to pray. She was a widow – that meant her husband was dead. When she saw baby Jesus in the Temple, she praised God. She thanked God she'd seen Jesus, the promised Savior of the world. When Joseph and Mary finished presenting Jesus in the Temple, they left for home.

Jesus grew and became strong. He was filled with wisdom and the power of God. God fills all his children with wisdom and power so they will become strong to serve him.

### Dig Out The Answers
1. What was the name of the widow who lived in the Temple?
2. What did Anna do day and night in the Temple?
3. What did Anna do when she saw baby Jesus?
4. What happened to Jesus as he grew?

**In Your Own Words:** Write down what you learned today.
**My Prayer:** God, like your son Jesus, help me grow and become strong. Fill me with wisdom and the power of your Holy Spirit, in Jesus name. Amen.

**Today's Wise Words:** God fills his children with his wisdom and power.

27

**Day 12**

# Wise Men in Jerusalem

Some wise men from the east saw a strange star. They saw that this was no ordinary star. The star was the star of a king born in Israel. So, they hurried to Jerusalem, the great city of Israel, to find out about this baby king so they could worship him. King Herod, who was the king of Israel at that time, was very angry that another king had been born. He wanted to find out the town where the baby king had been born. The chief priests who studied the Bible (the Old Testament) told where the king was to be born – "Bethlehem," they said. King Herod told the wise men to go to Bethlehem and search for the baby king. King Herod pretended he would soon follow to worship the baby king. He was lying – really *Kind* Herod intended to kill Jesus.

**Dig Out The Answers**

1. Why did the wise men travel all the way to Jerusalem?
2. Who found out for them where the baby king had been born?
3. What is the name of this baby king?
4. Did Herod actually want to worship Jesus?

**In Your Own Words:** What did you learn today? Write it down.

**My Prayer:** God, let me search your word to know more about Jesus. And let me worship you more and more as I see how wonderful you are.

**Today's Wise Words:** Seek Jesus to worship him.

# Wise Men Worship Jesus

The wise men left Jerusalem and went on their way to Bethlehem. Then, something wonderful happened. The star they had seen in the east appeared once more in the dark sky. They were very happy. The star led them to the house where baby Jesus was. When they saw baby Jesus, they worshipped him. Worship means praising God and blessing him. They also gave gifts to Jesus – gifts of gold, incense and myrrh.

Giving is part of worshipping God. These days most people give money as gifts to God during worship at church.

God knows everything. He knew the evil that King Herod was planning. So he warned the wise men in a dream not to go back to King Herod. The wise men obeyed God and took another route back to their own country.

**Dig Out The Answers**
1. How did the wise men find where baby Jesus was?
2. Write the two things the wise men did when they saw Jesus.
**In Your Own Words:** Write down what you learned.
**My Prayer:** God, help me give to you because it is part of worship. I believe that you know everything, so you can deliver me from evil men like King Herod, in Jesus' name. Amen.

**Today's Wise Words:** Giving to God is part of worship.

# Joseph Takes His Family to Egypt

**READ**

Matthew: 2:13-18

**Day 14**

An angel of the Lord appeared to Joseph in a dream. The angel told Joseph to take baby Jesus and Mary and go 300 miles to a country called Egypt. Joseph obeyed immediately. He took baby Jesus and his wife Mary during the night and they started off to Egypt.

King Herod had given orders to kill all the babies living in baby Jesus' town, Bethlehem. His soldiers killed many babies in Bethlehem. King Herod was furious because the wise men had not come back to tell him where to find the baby Jesus. Joseph and his family stayed in Egypt until king Herod died.

God knows everything and can protect us from evil people like King Herod.

**Dig Out The Answers**
1. Why did an angel appear to Joseph in a dream?
2. What did King Herod do in his anger?
**In Your Own Words:** Write down what you learned today.
**My Prayer:** Father God, Joseph believed you and obeyed what you told him in the dream. So baby Jesus wasn't killed along with the other babies. Joseph, Mary, and baby Jesus were already on their way to Egypt. Father, help me understand that the only way to keep out of trouble is to obey your Bible, in Jesus' Name. Amen.

**Today's Wise Words:** God has a way of steering me away from dangerous situations.

30

# Joseph and His Family Go Back Home

**Day 15**

Joseph, Mary, and baby Jesus escaped from Bethlehem as the angel told them to, because Herod wanted to kill baby Jesus. Now they were all living safely in Egypt. When King Herod died, an angel of the Lord appeared to Joseph again in a dream and told him to go back to their home country, Israel. Joseph obeyed and took his wife Mary, and baby Jesus, back to their country Israel. He went first to Judea with his family. But when he heard that King Herod's son was reigning as king in the region of Judea, he was afraid and took his family to live in the town of Nazareth, which was in the region called Galilee. Joseph obeyed whatever the angel told him to do. Do you also obey what you read in the Bible?

**Dig Out The Answers**

1. How did Joseph know that it was safe to go back to Israel?
2. Which words in these verses tell you that Joseph obeyed what he was told by the angel of the Lord?
3. If Joseph hadn't obeyed, what do you think could have happened?

**In Your Own Words:** What did you learn? Write it down.

**My Prayer:** Lord, help me obey all that I read in your word because it will save me from trouble, in Jesus' name. Amen.

**Today's Wise Words:** I must obey the Lord's word at all times. It will save me from trouble.

31

# Jesus in the Temple

When Jesus was twelve years old, he went to Jerusalem with his parents to celebrate the Feast of the Passover. When the celebration was over Jesus' family started out back home, not knowing that Jesus had stayed behind in Jerusalem. They had traveled for one day when they noticed that Jesus was missing. So they began looking for him. They found him in the Temple in Jerusalem. He was in the company of the teachers. He listened to them and asked questions. Jesus' answers surprised the teachers. He showed a lot of understanding for a child. His parents took him back home. And Jesus continued to obey his parents. And he continued to grow strong and wise. Even Jesus, who is God, obeyed his parents while here on earth and you must too.

### Dig Out The Answers
1. What was Jesus doing in the Temple?
2. What was Jesus' answer when his mother found him in the Temple? What does it teach you?

**In Your Own Words:** Write down what you learned.

**My Prayer:** Lord, teach me to love my church, to listen to your word, and to ask questions. Help me gain more understanding of your word even as I listen and obey, in Jesus' name. Amen.

**Today's Wise Words**: I must meet with other believers to talk about God's word.

**READ**

**Matthew: 3:1-6**

**Day 17**

John the Baptist was a prophet. The prophet Isaiah had written about John a long time ago. Remember that Zechariah and Elizabeth were John's parents. John was now a grown man and a prophet of God. He wore clothes made of camel's hair and a leather belt around his waist. He ate locusts and wild honey. God sent John to come and make the people ready for Jesus.

How did John prepare the people? He preached to them. He told them to stop sinning and come near to God. Many people flocked to him, telling of their bad and sinful ways. John then baptized them in the Jordan River. John was doing what God told him to do.

Do you know Jesus is coming back to earth one day? God has called all Christians to tell others about Jesus just as John did, to prepare them for his second coming. That way many will be saved and escape hell. Start telling people about Jesus, too.

**Dig Out The Answers**

1. What was John preaching to the people who flocked to him?

2. What did the people have to do before they were baptized?

**In Your Own Words:** Write down what you learned.

**My Prayer:** God, teach me to get people ready for Jesus' second coming by telling them about him.

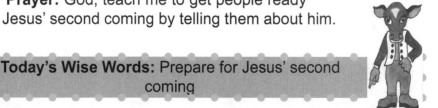

**Today's Wise Words:** Prepare for Jesus' second coming

33

# John the Baptist Preaches

**READ**

Matthew:
3:7-12

**Day 18**

Some of the Pharisees and Sadducees also came to listen to John the Baptist. The Pharisees were a religious group who strictly kept the Law of Moses, which is found in the first five books of the Bible. The Sadducees were also a religious group but did not believe in the resurrection, angels and spirits.

John knew that they did not want to turn from their bad ways. John told them, warning them that people who were sorry for their sins and still didn't do what was right were liars, and God was about to punish them. God punishes sin. God wants us to tell him about our sins but he also wants us to stop doing those same bad things. John also told them about somebody, who would come and fill or baptize people with the Holy Spirit. John was talking about Jesus Christ.

**Dig Out The Answers**

1. What did John tell the Pharisees and Sadducees who came to listen to him?
2. What does God want us to do after we have told him to forgive us our sins?
3. John said someone would come and fill us or "baptize" us with the Holy Spirit. Who was he talking about?

**In Your Own Words:** Write down today's lessons.

**My Prayer:** Father, I ask you to forgive me for doing the same bad things. Help me stop them. Let your Holy Spirit give me power to say 'no' to sin and 'yes' to doing right all the time, in Jesus' name. Amen.

**Today's Wise Words:** I must do what is right after I've asked God to forgive me.

# READ

**Day 19**

**Matthew:**
**3:13-17**

## Jesus Is Baptized

John was baptizing the people who were sorry for their sins in the Jordan River. Jesus also came to John to be baptized. Jesus was now a grown-up. You must remember that Jesus never sinned, so John was very surprised when Jesus asked to be baptized. John told Jesus that instead, he needed to be baptized by him. Then John agreed to baptize Jesus because it was part of God's plan for the work of Jesus on earth.

When Jesus was being baptized the heavens opened and the Spirit of God in a form of a dove descended on Jesus. Then a voice from heaven said, "You are my Son whom I love, and I am very pleased with you." That was the voice of God.

**Dig Out The Answers**

1. Why was John surprised when Jesus asked to be baptized?
2. What happened when Jesus was being baptized?
3. What did the voice from heaven say?

**In Your Own Words:** Write down what you learned.

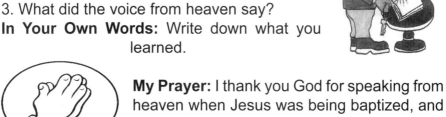

**My Prayer:** I thank you God for speaking from heaven when Jesus was being baptized, and saying that he *is* really your Son. I believe it. Amen.

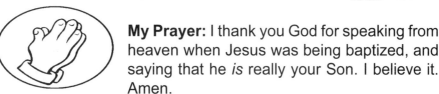

**Today's Wise Words:** God spoke from heaven and said that Jesus *is* his Son.

35

# READ

**Matthew:
4:1-4**

As soon as Jesus was baptized, the Holy Spirit came down on him. The Holy Spirit filled him with power to do God's work on earth. The Holy Spirit *led* Jesus into the desert. A desert is a very dry bare place because there is very little water and few plants. Jesus fasted (went without food) for forty days, so he became very hungry.

The devil came to tempt Jesus. The devil is called the tempter here. Because Jesus was very hungry, the devil told him to turn stones lying about into bread to eat. But Jesus knew better. God does not want us to use the power of the Holy Spirit to perform wonders to show off and impress others. Rather, God wants us to allow the power of the Holy Spirit to help us *understand* his word and *obey* it. That was what Jesus meant when he told the devil that "we don't live just on food but also on the word of God". Jesus spoke the word of God to overcome the tempter.

**Dig Out The Answers**

1. Who tempted Jesus? And who tempts you?
2. Who led Jesus into the desert?
3. So when the Holy Spirit fills you or comes on you what does he do?
4. How did Jesus overcome the tempter?

**In Your Own Words:** Write down what you learned.

**My Prayer:** Lord, lead me by your Holy Spirit and help me speak your word and obey it when I am tempted, in Jesus' name. Amen.

**Today's Wise Words:** The word of God helps me overcome the tempter.

# The Second Temptation of Jesus

The devil tempted Jesus a second time. This time, he took Jesus to the holy city and had him stand on the highest point of the Temple. He then told Jesus to throw himself down from that height because God had promised in his word to protect him. But Jesus knew better. Jesus said, "It is written." This is what Jesus meant by "it is written" - he was going to quote something from the word of God (the Bible).

Jesus said that it was wrong to test God. For example, just because God said he'd protect you from all harm doesn't mean you should jump from a moving truck or jump from the upper floors of a tall building on purpose and expect him to save you. That is a foolish thing to do. The devil used the word of God to tempt Jesus to do what was wrong. The word of God must not be used to tempt people or test God. Nor should you use the word of God to lie, cheat or do any bad thing. We must use the word of God to overcome sin and all wrongdoing.

## Dig Out The Answers

1. What did Jesus use to overcome the devil?
2. What's Jesus' way of using the word of God?
3. What's the devil's way of using the word of God?

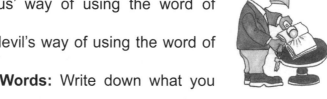

**In Your Own Words:** Write down what you learned.

**My Prayer:** God, help me know your word and keep it in my heart so I can use it to overcome wrongdoing.

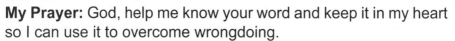

**Today's Wise Words:** Use God's word in Jesus' way to overcome temptations.

37

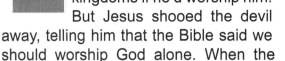

# The Third Temptation of Jesus

The devil tempted Jesus a third time. This time, the devil took Jesus to a very high mountain. From there, Jesus could see all the kingdoms of the world and its riches. The devil told Jesus he'd give him all those kingdoms if he'd worship him. But Jesus shooed the devil away, telling him that the Bible said we should worship God alone. When the devil saw that Jesus had overcome him, he went away. Jesus defeated the devil because he knew the word of God. Only God must be worshipped.

Do you know that the kingdoms of the world and the worlds to come all belong to God the Father, Son, and Holy Spirit? Sometimes the devil tricks us by offering to give us something we already have. If you have Christ in your heart, you have all good gifts from God. You don't need to do something wrong to get what you need or want. You just have to ask God.

**Dig Out The Answers**

1. Who is the only one that all men must worship?

2. What helped Jesus to overcome the devil?

**In Your Own Words:** Write down what you learned.

**My Prayer:** Lord, help me worship you alone through Jesus Christ. Let me know that I have all that I need because I have Jesus in my life. I only need to ask you in prayer, in Jesus' name. Amen.

**Today's Wise Words:** Worship the Lord your God, and serve him only.

# Jesus Begins His Ministry

**READ**
Luke
4:14-21

**Day 23**

Jesus, filled with the power of the Holy Spirit, began preaching in the region of Galilee. He taught the word of God in small meetings held in their meeting-places (which were called "synagogues"). Jesus worshipped regularly on the seventh day of the week because God commanded us to keep that day holy. One Sabbath, Jesus went to the synagogue in Nazareth, his hometown. He was asked to read the word of God, which was on a scroll. Jesus opened to a passage in Isaiah. The passage talked about someone filled with the Holy Spirit who would come and preach good news to the poor, open the eyes of the blind, and set free those who are in chains, and suffering from the hands of other people.

When Jesus had finished reading from the scroll, he told all the people he was the one that was coming to do all the good things listed in the passage he'd just read. Jesus is the Savior. He saves us from sin, heals us when we are sick, and makes us happy everyday.

**Dig Out The Answers**
1. What did Jesus do on the Sabbath day?
2. From which book did Jesus read while in the synagogue?
3. What did Jesus say after he had finished reading the scroll?
4. List some of the things that Jesus came to do for us?

**In Your Own Words:** Write down what you have learned.

**My Prayer:** Thank you, Lord, for sending Jesus to save me and heal me when I fall sick. Amen.

**Today's Wise Words:** Jesus came to save and heal us.

## READ

### Jesus' First Followers

**Matthew 4:18-22**

**Day 24**

One day, Jesus was walking beside the Sea of Galilee. He saw two fishermen, the brothers Simon and Andrew. They were fishing. Jesus called out to them, "Come, follow me." Jesus told them he would teach them how to bring men to God. Simon and Andrew were delighted. They stopped fishing and followed Jesus. Nearby, John and James were also fishing with their father, Zebedee. Jesus saw them and called them to come and follow him.

And you know what they did? They followed him immediately. How obedient! You must also follow Jesus.

### Dig Out The Answers

1. What did Jesus promise to teach Simon and Andrew?
2. Did Simon, Andrew, John and James follow Jesus when they were asked?

**In Your Own Words:** Write down what you learned.

**My Prayer:** Dear Lord Jesus, help me follow you everyday by reading the Bible and obeying it. That way I can bring others to follow you, too. I pray in your name. Amen.

**Today's Wise Words**: I must follow Jesus everyday. He will teach me how to bring others to God.

**Luke 5:27-31**

**Day 25**

One day Jesus met a tax collector called Levi. Tax collectors collected moneys from people to give to the government. But in Jesus' time the tax collectors sometimes collected more than they should. Then they kept the rest of the money for themselves. Many people in Jesus' time hated the tax collectors because they were cheats. Jesus went to the booth where Levi sat collecting taxes. Jesus told Levi to follow him. Levi was delighted. He left everything and followed Jesus. He was so happy he threw a party for Jesus at his house. But the Pharisees, and the teachers of the law, were not happy. The teachers of the law were men who knew the Bible very well in Jesus' time. People usually came to see them to solve problems they had with others. The Law of Moses is found in the first five books of the Old Testament, which are part of the Bible.

They complained about Jesus dining with a bad person like Levi. They did not understand that God loves people who do wrong things too.

**Dig Out The Answers**

1. Who did Jesus find at the tax booth?
2. What did Jesus tell him?
3. What did Levi do when Jesus told him to follow him?
4. Why were the Pharisees angry?

**In Your Own Words:** Write down what you learned.

**My Prayer:** God help me understand that you still love me even when I do wrong things, in Jesus name. Amen.

**Today's Wise Words:** Jesus loves people even though they do wrong things, and wants them to change and follow him, too.

## READ

**Jesus Calls Philip**

**READ**

John
1:43-50

**Day 26**

One day Jesus found Philip and told him to follow him. And guess what! He did. He followed Jesus and even more. He was so delighted he went looking for Nathaniel. Philip told Nathaniel he had found the man the Law and Prophets talked about. First Nathaniel couldn't believe it. If Jesus was really from a small village like Nazareth, then he couldn't be the Christ, the Savior. Nathaniel didn't believe that the Savior the prophets spoke about would come from Nazareth. But when Jesus told Nathaniel things about himself that nobody else knew he believed that Jesus was truly the Messiah (meaning God's chosen one, the Son of God, anointed like a king for a special job). Nathaniel decided to follow him. He was delighted, too. Jesus knows everything about me.

**Dig Out The Answers**
1. What did Philip do when he found Jesus?
2. Why did Nathaniel come to believe in Jesus after all?

**In Your Own Words:** Write down what you learned.

**My Prayer:** God, let me know that Jesus knows everything. Amen.

**Today's Wise Words:** Jesus knows everything about me.

42

# READ

## Jesus' First Miracle

**John 2:1-11**

**Day 27**

Jesus and his family were invited to a wedding at Cana. Jesus went with his disciples. There were so many guests. They were served food and wine. But oops! the wine was soon finished. Just imagine inviting friends to your house for a party and oops! you run out of juice or soda. It's quite embarrassing! So, Jesus' mother asked him to help.

Jesus told the servants to fill up all the stone jars with water. When they were done, he asked them to scoop a cup for the man in charge. The man in charge tasted it. It tasted better than the wine that had been served earlier. Jesus had turned the water into wine! And not only that, his wine tasted the best. Jesus doesn't just perform miracles but performs the best.

**Dig Out The Answers**
1. What got finished at the wedding banquet?
2. What did Jesus do to solve the problem?
3. Does Jesus care that your birthday party goes well?

**In Your Own Words:** Write down what you learned today.

**My Prayer:** God, help me know that Jesus performs miracles. Give me faith to trust you for a miracle in my life today, in Jesus' name. Amen.

**Today's Wise Words:** Jesus performs miracles.

43

## READ

Luke
4:38-39

**Day 28**

# Jesus Heals Simon's Mother-in-law

Jesus went to Simon and Andrews' home after worship at the synagogue. When they got home, they found Simon's mother-in-law sick in bed with a fever. Simon and Andrew asked Jesus to help. Jesus told the fever to leave Simon's mother-in-law. And immediately she became well and even served food to Jesus and the others. Everything you can think of in this world has to obey Jesus. You must be glad to have a friend like that! He is all-powerful.

**Dig Out The Answers**
1. What did Simon and Andrew do when they found Simon's mother-in-law sick?
2. What should you do when you or any of your family members fall sick?

**In Your Own Words:** Write down what you learned.

**My Prayer:** God, help me always to ask Jesus to help me when I have a need, just as Simon and Andrew did, in Jesus' name. Amen.

**Today's Wise Words:** Jesus is always ready to help me. I only have to ask him.

44

# Jesus Walks Away from Trouble

**Day 29**

One day Jesus had to go through a region in Palestine called Samaria. The people there were called Samaritans. The Samaritans were descendants of Jews who hundreds of years earlier had married people from other countries (descendants are children, great-grandchildren, great-great-grand-children and so on; the family keeps growing as the children marry; all those born later in this family become their descendants).

The Jews are descendants of Jacob (read the story of Jacob in the Genesis chapters 25 - 35 in your spare time). Jesus was a Jew. Why did Jesus decide to go back to Galilee? The Pharisees, (see Day 18) were upset with Jesus. Jesus said that the Pharisees did not want to please God, but rather people. They didn't like Jesus because he preached the truth. Jesus was also making many disciples and the Pharisees became jealous. Jesus decided to leave Judea for Galilee. Jesus was a man of peace. He didn't want a quarrel between him and the Pharisees, so he decided to leave the place where he was. Do you know it's better to walk away from persons who want to quarrel or fight with you?

**Dig Out The Answers**
1. What did Jesus do when he saw that the Pharisees were upset with him?
2. What do you do when someone wants to quarrel or fight with you?

**In Your Own Words:** Write down what you learned.
**My Prayer:** God, help me walk away from quarrels and fights just like Jesus did. Amen.

**Today's Wise Words:** Walk away from quarrels and fights.

# Jesus and the Samaritan Woman

## READ
### John 4:5-9

We are continuing yesterday's story. Jesus came to a town in Samaria called Sychar. He was tired so he sat down by Jacob's well. A well is a deep hole in the ground containing water. Before long a Samaritan woman came by, ready to draw water from the well. Jesus asked the Samaritan woman for water. Well, the Samaritan woman was very surprised because Jews did not like Samaritans. She wondered how a Jew could ask her, a Samaritan woman, for water. Jesus teaches us in this story to be humble and to ask for help when we need it.

Were you ever surprised by a kind deed from a person you thought hated you? What about showing kindness to someone that you don't particularly like? That's what Jesus wants us to do. He wants us to love and respect all people no matter where they come from or what they look like.

**Dig Out The Answers**
1. Why do you think Jesus decided to sit by the well?
2. What did Jesus ask the Samaritan woman?
3. What do you do when you need something?

**In Your Own Words**: Write down today's lesson.

**My Prayer**: God, teach me to be kind to people even though they may do things I don't like, or look different.

**Today's Wise Words:** Be kind to people no matter where they come from or what they look like.

**Day 31**

John
4:10

You remember that Jesus asked the Samaritan woman for water. She was very surprised, because Jews did not like Samaritans and they would never even ask them for help. Why would Jesus dare ask her for water? Jesus gave an answer in the passage we read today. The Samaritan woman did not know that Jesus was the Messiah, the Savior of the world. So, Jesus told her about the gift of God that he alone could give. And that *gift* is eternal life. Eternal life means you live forever in heaven with Jesus. God wants to give everyone this gift. Jesus told the Samaritan woman that if she asked him, he would give her living water.

The living water is the Holy Spirit. When you ask Jesus to forgive your sins and to become your Lord and Savior, he sends the Holy Spirit to live in you. You have eternal life if the Holy Spirit lives in you. Jesus wants everyone to ask him for living water. Jesus wants everyone to have the gift of God, which is eternal life. Jesus was eager to tell the Samaritan woman the good news. Jesus wants us to tell our friends about him, too.

**Dig Out The Answers**
1. What did Jesus promise to give the Samaritan woman?
2. What is the gift of God? Who is the living water?
3. What does Jesus want us to tell our friends?
**In Your Own Words:** Write down what you learned.

**My Prayer:** God, thank you that Jesus has offered to give me eternal life, when I come to him to save me.

**Today's Wise Words:** Jesus gives eternal life to those who turn from their bad ways and ask him.

## The Samaritan Woman Questions Jesus

**READ**

John
4:11-14

**Day 32**

We are still reading the story about Jesus and the Samaritan woman. Jesus had told the Samaritan woman that he was able to give her "living water" or "life-giving water". The Samaritan woman didn't expect that answer from a thirsty traveler! So she asked Jesus how he was going to give her that living water when he had no ropes or buckets to draw water from the well. The Samaritan woman was talking about *physical water*, but Jesus was talking about *saving her from sin*.

Just like the Samaritan woman, we all pay more attention to the physical things we need – food, water, dresses, toys, and the like. God wants us to pay more attention to *living right* with him. Why? God cannot accept us as we are, because God is holy. To be able to come to God, we must be holy as God is. God sent Jesus to die on the cross so his blood would wash away all our sins, and then we can become holy. If you have Jesus in your life, you have eternal life.

Which is wiser – to get all the things you need (toys, dresses, food, all the fun you want) and end up in hell? Or to ask Jesus to wash you from your sins so you will get to live with him forever in heaven? Heaven is going to be a very exciting place. You'll get much better things than what you are getting right here on earth and the fun will never end. Wow!

**Dig Out The Answers**
1. What kind of water did Jesus offer the Samaritan woman?
2. What is "living water"?
3. Do you have living water in you? How do you know?
**In Your Own Words:** Write down what you learned.
**My Prayer:** Thank you, Jesus, for giving me living water, so that I can live forever. Amen.

**Today's Wise Words:** Jesus gives "living water".

48

## The Samaritan Woman Asks for Living Water

**Day 33**

The Samaritan woman was wise. She asked Jesus to give her this life-giving water. Living water is the same as life-giving water. How do you become wise? You become wise by asking Jesus to give you life-giving water. As explained earlier, we receive the gift of eternal life when we ask Jesus to forgive our sins, and to become our Lord and Savior.

Probably, you have said this prayer before. You only have to say it once, and that's all – but you have to mean it! If you have said it, and you really meant it, you are now a child of God, full of the living water who is the Holy Spirit. You also have the gift of God, which is eternal life. Once you become a child of God, the Holy Spirit helps you say 'no' to sin and 'yes' to doing right. When you do the wrong thing, you ask God to forgive you. Then you ask the Holy Spirit to give you power not to do it again.

### Dig Out The Answers
1. What did the Samaritan woman ask Jesus to give her?
2. Are you full of "life-giving water"? What does that make you?

**In Your Own Words:** Write down what you learned.

**My Prayer:** God, thank you, I am your child because I have asked Jesus into my life.

**Today's Wise Words:** Living water is the Holy Spirit who comes into the hearts of those who ask Jesus to become their Lord and Savior.

49

# Samaritan Woman Asks about Worship

**READ**

John
4:19-21

**Day 34**

Jesus was still chatting with the Samaritan woman. Jesus had told the woman some things about herself that Jesus couldn't have known unless he was a prophet. Now she believed that Jesus was a prophet. What an opportunity – she was actually talking to a prophet! She had questions for Jesus. She wanted to know where God should be worshipped – on a mountain nearby, or in Jerusalem. Jesus explained to her that there was no need to go to some special place to worship God. The Holy Spirit living in you helps you worship God by teaching you more about Jesus. You can worship God wherever you are – school, home, playground or church.

### Dig Out The Answers
1. Where can you worship God?

**In Your Own Words:** Write down what you learned.

**My Prayer:** God, help me know that I can worship you anywhere. Let your Holy Spirit teach me more about Jesus who is the truth.

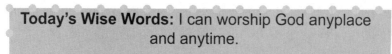

**Today's Wise Words:** I can worship God anyplace and anytime.

# Salvation Is from the Jews

**READ**

**John 4:22**

**Day 35**

We are still reading about the Samaritan woman and Jesus. Jesus was still explaining what worship was all about. The Samaritan woman had asked Jesus whether the right place to worship was only Jerusalem. The Samaritans did not go up to worship in Jerusalem, but worshipped on a mountain nearby. Jerusalem was the city where all Jews went to celebrate and worship God. God chose Jerusalem as the only place of worship at that time.

We have already talked about who the Samaritans were (Day 29). But the Samaritans who also lived in Israel disobeyed God and worshipped on a mountain nearby. The Temple was in Jerusalem where the priests taught the Jews, and showed them how to live right with God. Do you remember that Jesus and his parents went to Jerusalem to celebrate the Passover feast? Jesus' parents obeyed God. Jesus told the woman that the Samaritans did not know God. Those who know God obey him.

Do you obey God? Jesus also told the woman that God had planned to save the world by a Jew. And you know who that Jew is? That Jew is Jesus. You don't know God if you don't obey him. God is asking everyone in the world to make Jesus his Lord and Savior. Have you obeyed?

**Dig Out The Answers**
1. Those who know God _____ him.
2. What is the one thing God is asking everyone in the world to accept?
3. Those who don't accept Jesus as Lord and Savior don't _____ God.
**In Your Own Words:** Write down what you learned.
**My Prayer:** God, thank you for helping me to obey you by accepting Jesus as my Lord and Savior. Amen.

**Today's Wise Words:** Those who know God obey him.

## True Worshippers

Jesus was still explaining what worship was all about. If you remember, the Samaritan woman had asked Jesus where to worship God. Jesus explained that you could worship God anyplace or anywhere. Jesus also told the woman that "those who know God obey him". The Samaritans did not know God so they did not obey him. Jesus pointed out that God was going to save the world through the Jews. How did God do that? – He sent Jesus to die on the cross for our sins. Jesus was a Jew. In today's verse, Jesus explained to the woman that people who really wanted to worship God would do so through the help of the Holy Spirit. The Holy Spirit living in them would also teach them all about the truth. Jesus is the truth. God accepts worship only from people who have the Holy Spirit in their hearts. We worship God when we obey what we read in the Bible through the help of the Holy Spirit. God is looking for people who have the Holy Spirit living in them to worship him. If you have the Holy Spirit in you, God accepts your worship.

### Dig Out The Answers

1. God is looking for people to worship him through the help of the _____.
2. The Holy Spirit teaches us to worship God in truth. Who is the truth?

**In Your Own Words:** Write down what you learned.

**My Prayer:** God, thank you that I am able to worship you in spirit and truth because the Holy Spirit lives in me.

**Today's Wise Words:** God accepts worship from those filled with the Holy Spirit.

# True Worship

Day 37

Today, Jesus explains why we have to worship God in spirit and truth. We have to worship God in spirit and truth because God is Spirit. God is Spirit so he is everywhere you go. Also, because God is Spirit, you can only worship him in spirit, that is, through the help of the Holy Spirit. God is everywhere so you can pray to him anywhere you find yourself. Would you memorize this verse?

"God is spirit, and his worshipers must worship in spirit and truth." (NIV)

**Dig Out The Answers**

1. God is everywhere so I can worship him __.
2. God is spirit so I have to worship him in __.

**In Your Own Words:** Write down what you learned.

**My Prayer:** Tell God to help you to continue to be a good worshiper.

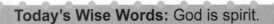
**Today's Wise Words:** God is spirit.

53

## READ

John
4:25-26

# Jesus Is the Messiah

**Day 38**

The Samaritan woman was now all excited. Both Jews and Samaritans knew that one day God was going to send the Messiah. Messiah means Christ, and Christ means the Savior, anointed like a king to do a very special job. The Samaritan woman also knew about the Messiah. "Probably, this man I'm talking to is the Messiah," the Samaritan woman might have said to herself. It was the way Jesus explained to her what worship was all about. So she asked Jesus about it. And she received the greatest news of all. She was actually talking to the Messiah, the Savior of the world. How exciting!

Have you talked to Jesus, the Savior of the world? I hope you have asked him into your life to be your Savior and Lord. Continue to talk everyday to him by reading the Bible and praying. Jesus makes life very exciting.

### Dig Out The Answers
1. Who did Jesus say he is?
2. What does Messiah mean?

**In Your Own Words:** Write down what you learned today.

**My Prayer:** God, I thank you for sending Jesus, the Messiah, and Savior of the world.

**Today's Wise Words:** Jesus is the Messiah, Christ or Savior.

54

# Come, See the Messiah

**Day 39**

The Samaritan woman was so happy she had found the Messiah, Christ the Savior. What could she do? She had to tell somebody. She decided to go back to town. She told them about Jesus, "Come, see a man who told me everything I ever did." The people came out in droves to see Jesus. Do you know Jesus knows everything you did in the past? Jesus knows what you are doing now. Jesus even knows what you will do in the future. In fact, Jesus knows everything about everybody in the world. What a great God he is! So you don't have to be afraid, you can go to Jesus, the one who knows everything about you whenever you have a problem.

**Dig Out The Answers**
1. What did the Samaritan woman do when she found Jesus?
2. What did she tell the people in her town?
3. What does Jesus know about you?

**In Your Own Words:** Write down what you learned.

**My Prayer:** Thank you, Jesus, that you know everything about me. You are God and you are my Savior. Amen.

**Today's Wise Words:** "Come, see a man who told me everything I ever did."

# READ

## Jesus Stays with the Samaritans

John 4:39-42

**Day 40**

The Samaritan woman had gone back to town to tell about Jesus, the Christ or Messiah. The people of the town believed in Jesus because of what the woman said. She had told them that Jesus was the Savior and he knew everything she ever did. They wanted to hear more of Jesus' teaching. They asked Jesus to stay for a while.

Jesus stayed in the town for two more days. He taught them. And many more in the town came to believe that Jesus was indeed the Savior of the world. Today, the Holy Spirit teaches us when we read the Bible, pointing to and increasing our faith in Jesus, the Savior of the world.

### Dig Out The Answers

1. Why did many more in the town believe that Jesus was the promised Savior of the world?
2. What did the people in the town ask Jesus to do?
3. Why did they ask Jesus to stay?

**In Your Own Words:** Write down today's lesson.

**My Prayer:** God, thank you that your Holy Spirit lives in me and teaches me more and more that Jesus really is the Savior of the world.

**Today's Wise Words:** The Bible points me to Jesus.

56

**Matthew 5:1-3**

Day 41

Jesus now had disciples (followers who learned from him). Jesus wanted to teach them about the kingdom of God. All that Jesus taught in the book of Matthew, from chapter 5 to 7, is called "The Sermon on the Mount". "Beatitudes" are the blessings, which Jesus described in verses 3 to 12 of chapter 5.

Now that you are a disciple or learner of Jesus, he wants to teach you, too. Jesus teaches us that we are happy when we know we are poor in spirit. A poor person is a needy person. Poor people sometimes don't have enough food or clothing and some have no money at all. So a person who is poor in spirit is a person who realizes he needs Jesus to provide for him. Everybody in the world has *a need to worship God*. And only Jesus can provide that need. God's Holy Spirit helps us realize how much we need Jesus everyday. When you see your need of Jesus, you go to him in prayer, read his word often and obey it. This way, you get to know Jesus better and have more of him. And the more you know Jesus, the happier you become. The word "blessed" means the happiness and favor, which God gives to those who are citizens of heaven and do the things Jesus spoke about in these verses. God will give you special attention just like you pay special attention to your favorite toy or best friend.

**Dig Out The Answers**
1. What is the one need that everybody in the world has?
2. There is only one person who can meet that need. Who is he?
3. Who helps us realize that we need more of Jesus everyday?
**In Your Own Words:** Write down what you learned.
**My Prayer:** Help me Jesus to pray, read the Bible, and obey everyday so I'll have more of you and be happy.

**Today's Wise Words:** I need more of Jesus everyday to stay happy.

57

# The Beatitudes: those who weep

Jesus continued to teach his disciples. You are also a disciple of Jesus and he wants to teach you, too. Jesus taught his disciples that sometimes they would be sad and weep, but he would comfort them. There are things that make us sad in this world. For example, sometimes people are mean to you because you do not want to follow them to do evil. Other times you do not want to share a toy or be kind to a friend. Or you are mean to your sister or brother. When we do wrong things we become sad because the Holy Spirit living in us tells us they are wrong. But when we go to God and tell him we are sorry, he forgives us and comforts us. At other times we are sad because somebody we love falls sick or dies or is hurt. In such times God wants us to pray. When we do so, the Holy Spirit who is also called "the Comforter" comes to comfort us. Remember to pray anytime you feel sad and God will send the Holy Spirit to comfort you and make you happy again.

**Dig Out The Answers**
1. Write down some of the things that make you sad.
2. What do you have to do when you are sad?

**In Your Own Words:** Write down what you learned today.
**My Prayer:** God, help me come to you in prayer when I am sad and you will comfort me.

**Today's Wise Words:** I will go to God in prayer when I am sad.

**Day 43**

# The Beatitudes: the humble

Jesus also taught his disciples that, "humble people will inherit the earth". Jesus wants us to be humble because he himself is humble. Do you know that Jesus is equal to God the Father in power and yet he obeyed his Father, left heaven and came to earth and died to pay for our sins?

A humble person does not mind doing things which nobody else wants to do and which could save others – like picking a banana peel from the hallway at school so nobody slips and falls.

Humble people *keep working* hard on good things even if they are not rewarded. They don't want to be powerful and important. *They are happy just doing what is right, no matter what, because they want to please God and love people.* Humble people ask the Holy Spirit to give them strength everyday to do even the most dirty and difficult jobs. And one day, God is going to make them rule the world. You can ask the Holy Spirit to help you to be humble at all times and that will make you happy.

**Dig Out The Answers**
1. Why are humble people happy?
2. Who gives the humble strength to do even dirty and difficult work?
3. How can you also become humble?
**In Your Own Words:** Write down what you learned today.

**My Prayer:** God, help me keep practicing being humble by doing what is right even if it makes me unpopular. Holy Spirit, give me strength to keep working hard on my chores.

**Today's Wise Words:** Humble people are happy people.

# The Beatitudes: hunger and thirst

**READ**

Matthew
5:6

**Day 44**

The disciples loved to listen to Jesus' teachings. All Christians love to listen to Jesus. Jesus taught the disciples that people who are always eager to find out more about God so they can live right by loving other people are blessed. Jesus said that such people are hungry and thirsty for righteousness.

When we really want to live right, God's Holy Spirit gives us the power to do so. We are able to love God and love our neighbors and this makes us very happy. How do you find out how to live right? We learn to live right by studying God's word daily. When we try to live right and never get tired of it, we become happy just like special guests at a great banquet – feeding on the best of all the goodies served.

**Dig Out The Answers**
1. Where do you find out how to live right?
2. What does Jesus want us to hunger for?
3. What does Jesus want us to thirst for?

**In Your Own Words:** Write down what you learned today.

**My Prayer:** Jesus, help me do what is right at all times. Amen.

**Today's Wise Words:** Be eager to do the right at all times.

**Matthew 5:7**

**Day 45**

Jesus taught about being merciful. God's *mercy* is his kindness to all people. That is why God is always kind to us, even when we let him down. He gives us parents to take care of us, friends to play with, snow to build castles with tunnels, or snow angels and snowmen, rain to provide water for plants and animals; and the sun rises every morning. Above all, he sent Jesus to come and save us from our sins. And because of this great kindness we have received from God, God expects us to show the same kindness to other people.

Sometimes it is hard to be kind to someone who is always mean to you. But when we remember that God is always kind to us, it becomes easy to be kind to others, too. People who remember to be kind to others because of the kindness they have received from God are happy people. They are happy because they know that God's mercy is always on them.

## Dig Out The Answers

1. What does mercy mean?
2. Who first showed us mercy?
3. Why do we have to show mercy or kindness?

**In Your Own Words:** Write down today's lesson.

**My Prayer:** God, teach me to be kind to others always, in Jesus' name. Amen.

**Today's Wise Words:** Show mercy to other people.

# READ

## The Beatitudes: the pure in heart

**Matthew 5:8**

**Day 46**

Are you enjoying listening to Jesus? The disciples did and I hope you are too! Jesus taught that only those with a pure heart would see God. A pure heart is a heart without sin or any wrongdoing. Do you think there's such a heart? Well, there is! When you ask Jesus to forgive your sins and invite him to be your Lord and Savior, your heart becomes pure. Right! The blood of Jesus washes away all your sins of the past, the sins you are committing now and the sins you'll commit in the future. How marvelous! And only those with pure hearts can see God. And now that you have a pure heart, you can see God.

But how do we see God? Because we have been washed and made clean, we are able to understand God's word, obey it and know how God works in our lives and other people's lives. A pure heart is a heart full of God's love. When we have a pure heart we see God's love all around us.

**Dig Out The Answers**
1. What is a pure heart?
2. How do you get a pure heart?
3. What do you find in a pure heart?

**In Your Own Words:** Write down what you learned today.

**My Prayer:** God, thank you that the blood of Jesus Christ has washed away my sins. Let my heart, and life, continue to flow with your love and help me see your love all around me. Amen

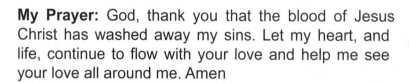

**Today's Wise Words:** I can see God's love everywhere when my heart is pure.

62

# The Beatitudes: the peacemakers

**READ**

Matthew 5:9

**Day 47**

As Jesus went on explaining all these things you may think the disciples were stretching their legs. I am sure they did, but they soon settled down again to listen to Jesus.

Jesus teaches that people who bring peace to others are sons of God. Do you know that Jesus is the greatest peacemaker in the world? Yes, it's true. Only Jesus can give us real peace. Millions of people in the world are against God and his ways. They have no peace, because they can't and won't obey him. But Jesus' blood paid for their sins as well as ours, and made it possible for anyone to have peace with God.

Every child of God should become a peacemaker. Peacemakers tell their friends and relatives how to get the peace of God. They tell their friends to come to Jesus to find peace. Only Jesus gives true peace. Jesus said that peacemakers are happy people. So go and be a peacemaker, today.

### Dig Out The Answers

1. Who is the greatest of all peacemakers?
2. How do we become peacemakers?
3. What do peacemakers tell their relatives and friends?

**In Your Own Words:** Write down what you learned.

**My Prayer:** God, make me a peacemaker. Let me tell others to receive Jesus into their lives, Amen.

**Today's Wise Words:** Jesus has made me a peacemaker.

63

# The Beatitudes: are you persecuted?

**READ**

**Matthew 5:10-12**

**Day 48**

The disciples loved what they were hearing. They listened with great intent, and I hope you do too. Jesus taught that you are blessed when you are treated badly for believing in him and obeying him. Do you know that many Christian children like you in so many countries are treated badly because they believe in Jesus and obey him? Jesus wants us to stand firm and never to give up believing in his name and obeying his word. You know why? Because one day, you are going to reign like a prince with him in heaven! You will not end up in hell like those who refuse to believe in Jesus.

Sometimes, people may laugh at you for talking about Jesus, or when you try to be good or do what is right. When that happens Jesus says, "be happy" because heaven is already your home. And heaven is going to be lots of fun. You can't imagine it just yet!

**Dig Out The Answers**

1. Did somebody ever make fun of you because you talked about Jesus?
2. What did you do?
3. What does Jesus want you to do?

**In Your Own Words:** Write down today's lesson.

**My Prayer:** God, let your Holy Spirit make me strong inside so I will always stand up for Jesus and obey him even if I'm teased and laughed at, in Jesus' name, Amen.

**Today's Wise Words:** I am a citizen of heaven if Jesus lives in me.

**READ**

**Day 49**

Jesus said, "You are the salt of the earth". You are wondering what that means. You know we put a little salt in food for *flavor*. Food with flavor tastes good. Salt is also added to meat to keep it from *spoiling*. Every Christian has salt. The salt in us is Truth and Love. Jesus is the Truth and Jesus is Love. When Jesus lives in our hearts, it means we live by the truth and are filled with love.

The world is full of sin, and sin is like very rotten food. You'll fall sick or even die if you eat rotten food. Sin makes people sick and kills them just like rotten food. When you have Jesus in you, the Holy Spirit keeps you from being destroyed by sin. Jesus gives you power to overcome sin because he lives in you and he is the salt. Anytime we obey God, we are behaving like salt in the world. We keep sin from spreading too fast and destroying people's lives. We also brighten up people's lives when we obey Jesus. For example, being a friend to a new child in your school/class, sharing a toy with a mean person, or giving up your pocket money or allowance to help a missionary spread God's word in other countries – all these things make them glad. It means you are adding flavor to their lives just like salt in food. You are also pointing them to Jesus, the Savior.

**Dig Out The Answers**
1. Who is the salt in your life?
2. What are the two things salt does to food?
3. What do you do to be the salt of the earth?
**In Your Own Words:** Write down what you learned today.
**My Prayer:** Dear God, help me live by the truth in your word and to love like Jesus so I will continue to be the salt of the earth, in Jesus name, Amen.

**Today's Wise Words:** Jesus has made me the salt of the earth.

65

**Day 50**

# Light of the World

God has saved us through Jesus to be a blessing to the world. One of the blessings we discussed yesterday was that we are the "salt of the earth". Jesus also taught that we are the "light of the world". What does that mean? When you walk into a dark room you switch on the light. Why? Because light helps you see! Good. Did you ever visit a dark cave? Or did you ever walk into a dark room with only a spark of light? What did you fix your eyes on – the darkness or the light? The Light. Of course! A small spark of light in a dark place is easily seen. That's how powerful light is. Jesus is the Light. Jesus helps us see God as he is. When we have the light of Jesus in us, we see clearly what is right and what is wrong and are able to do what is right. As we walk with Jesus we become happy and enjoy peace. Then people begin to take notice. They look up to us just as we look at the spark of light in the darkness. And by our lives we may lead them to Jesus – the Savior.

**Dig Out The Answers**
1. Who is the light of the world?
2. How do you become the light of the world?
3. What do you do as the light of the world?

**In Your Own Words:** Write down what you learned today.

**My Prayer:** Jesus, help me walk in your light so I can lead others to you. Amen.

**Today's Wise Words:** Jesus has made Christians the light of the world.

# Jesus Fulfilled the Law

**Day 51**

God has set rules or laws for everyone to obey. God does not change and God's word does not change. Ever! God's law is also God's word. Have you ever read the Ten Commandments? Probably you have. Do you think you can keep them all without ever breaking one? Of course not! Nobody in the world has ever been able to keep the commandments because we don't have the power to keep them all without breaking one. God knows that because we are sinners, it will be impossible for us to keep the law. And all those who disobey God will end up in hell after they die. But wait!

God is good. He let Jesus Christ, his only Son, come down to earth to die for our sins. While Jesus was on earth, he obeyed the whole law without breaking one. Yes, Jesus was the only one who kept the whole law. He never sinned. When you accept Jesus as your Lord and Savior, God sees Jesus in you. He sees you as perfect, just like Jesus who really obeyed the law perfectly. Now that you have Jesus in your heart you are not a lawbreaker.

**Dig Out The Answers**
1. Who never sinned and obeyed God's law perfectly?
2. What happens to those who break God's law?
3. What has to happen before God sees you as somebody who obeys the law perfectly?

**In Your Own Words:** Write down what you learned.

**My Prayer:** Thank you, God, that I have Jesus in my life, so you see me as an obedient child, and I am on my way to heaven to enjoy eternal life. Amen.

**Today's Wise Words:** Because Christ obeyed the law perfectly; all who believe in him will not be condemned for not keeping the law.

# Wicked Words and Anger

Day 52

Jesus made it clear that it is impossible for anyone to obey the law. And he also added that if anyone wished to enter heaven, that person would have to obey the Law better than the Pharisees. What did he mean?

The Pharisees (see Day 18) tried hard to obey the law. The law said that we should not kill our fellow man. Jesus, who is God, understood the true meaning of all God's laws. So Jesus explained the law better than the Pharisees. Jesus teaches that even if you are angry with somebody without any reason, God sees you as a killer (murderer). Also, when you call somebody "a fool" out of anger, God sees you as a killer. Wicked thoughts kill people secretly and wicked words kill people slowly. Then how can anybody get to heaven since we all sometimes get angry and think, say and do bad things? Only through Jesus Christ! God's law is so right and good that only Christ could keep it because he himself is God. When we accept him as Lord and Savior, God sees us the same way he sees Jesus – perfect and obedient children. This is God's mercy.

**Dig Out The Answers**

1. When you are angry with somebody without a reason what does God call you?
2. Why will God stop seeing you as a killer when you get angry sometimes?

**In Your Own Words:** Write down what you learned today.

**My Prayer:** Thank you God that you don't see me as a killer when I get angry sometimes, because Jesus Christ lives in my heart. Amen

**Today's Wise Words:** God's law is very good and righteous.

# Make Up with Those You Offend

Jesus wants us to love our neighbors and to be at peace with everyone. We worship God when we live at peace with our neighbors. We also worship God by the offerings we give at church.

A good worshipper of God must learn to love other people - being kind to them, forgiving when they are wronged, and asking for forgiveness when they wrong others. When we sin by doing wrong things, we are not able to see God clearly, and so we are not able to enjoy our worship at church too. When we love others, we enjoy time spent with God – praying, reading the word and going to church services. How we live with others is so important to God that he would rather have us solve problems we have with others before coming to worship him. That's what is meant by "leave your gift at the altar and go make up with your brother, then come and offer your gift." Loving others is part of worship.

## Dig Out The Answers

1. Why is it important to love your neighbor and live at peace with everyone?
2. What do you do when you hurt someone?
3. What do you do when somebody hurts you?

**In Your Own Words:** Write down what you learned.

**My Prayer:** God, please make me a good worshipper by teaching me to forgive those who wrong me and make up with those I wrong, in Jesus' name. Amen.

**Today's Wise Words:** Good worshippers of God make up quickly with those they wrong.

# READ

## Are You Trustworthy?

**Matthew 5:33-37**

**Day 54**

Jesus also teaches us to be the kind of people who can be trusted. As children of God, Jesus wants us to be so trustworthy that others believe all we tell them. That is trust. There are people who always have to mention God's name for every promise they make. That is taking God's name in vain. It means you show no respect for the holy name of God. God doesn't want his children to be like that. God doesn't want us to make promises to people by using his name, or heaven, or earth or even the hairs on our heads to make people believe us. God doesn't want us to mention his name for every little promise we make because we are the kind of people that speak the truth always.

So for example if you forget to take the trash out and your parents ask about it, just say "yes, I forgot to take it out, but I'm going to do it, now". Jesus wants us to learn how to answer with a simple "yes" or "no" because we are trustworthy.

## Dig Out The Answers

1. What are you doing when you always mention God's name in your promises to others?
2. How do you become the kind of person that people trust or believe?
3. How does Jesus want us to answer questions?

**In Your Own Words:** Write down what you learned today.

**My Prayer:** God, teach me to speak the truth always, so others will always believe what I tell them, in Jesus' name. Amen.

**Today's Wise Words:** Simply say "Yes" to a "Yes" question or "No" to a "No" question.

70

# Tit for Tat – Oh No!

I hope you are enjoying all that Jesus has been teaching so far. Great! What Jesus means by turning the other cheek when someone strikes you is to forgive the person. We are not supposed to do tit for tat, butter for bread. That's what is meant by, "an eye for eye and a tooth for a tooth". You remember the lesson on Christians as salt of the earth? Good! For example, if someone hits you with a hockey stick and you hit back, what do you think is going to happen? You will probably have a big fight. So to prevent wrongdoing from spreading, Jesus wants us to forgive. Sometimes you have to report certain incidents on the school field or park to your supervisor or parents. They are able to solve such problems. But you must not think evil things in your heart against the person who hurt you. You must be willing to be kind to him even after what happened. The Holy Spirit living in you helps you love at all times.

## Dig Out The Answers

1. What does it mean to turn the other cheek?
2. When somebody hurts you while on the playground what do you do?
3. Are you supposed to continue to love that person anyway?
4. Who helps you forgive and love those who are mean to you?

**In Your Own Words:** Write down what you learned.

**My Prayer:** God, help me forgive those who hurt me, and give me power to be kind to them, in Jesus' name. Amen.

**Today's Wise Words:** Turn the other cheek.

# Be Good in an Unfair World

**READ**
Matthew
5:40

Day 56

You know, at times people don't play fair. Jesus wants us to know that the world doesn't play fair but God is always good. So we can also be good in this unfair world. That's what Jesus meant by "if someone sues you for your shirt, give up your coat as well". Jesus' life on earth tells how we should be good even though we live in an unfair world.

You know that Jesus came to earth to die for us so we'd be set free from our sins and the power of evil. Right. But when he came people said he was a bad person and called him names. Was Jesus angry with them? No. Jesus was even willing to die for all the people who called him bad names and wanted to have him killed. But he rose again from the dead and he lives forever. And one day, you will also live forever in a splendid kingdom as you continue to be good to people even though they don't play fair.

**Dig Out The Answers**

1. What did Jesus do to show us how to be good in an unfair world?

2. So from today, how are you going to live even though others may not play fair?

**In Your Own Words:** Write down what you learned today.

**My Prayer:** God grant me power to be good to others who don't play fair, in Jesus' name. Amen.

**Today's Wise Words:**
Be good to children who don't play fair.

# Be Kind When Others Try Your Patience

**READ**

Matthew
5:41

Day 57

Jesus wants us to be kind to people who push us around. Why? - because it helps us grow more patient and humble, and Jesus wants us to do it cheerfully. That's what Jesus meant by "if someone forces you to go one mile, go with him two miles". If one of the children in your class drops a pencil and you pick it up, but then drops a whole pack of crayons later on, on purpose, what do you do? You should still try to pick them up, although the person may be trying to take advantage of you. It sounds very hard but the Holy Spirit living in us gives us power to be patient and humble. Your patience and humility may lead the person to Christ. And you are being a *light* in the world.

**Dig Out The Answers**

1. Have there been times that somebody tried to force you to do extra work?
2. What did you do?
3. What does Jesus teach us to do?

**In Your Own Words:** Write down what you learned today.

**My Prayer:** God, give me patience and humility when people try to take advantage of me, in Jesus' name. Amen.

**Today's Wise Words:** Be patient with people who push you around.

73

# Give to Those Who Ask You

Jesus also expects us to give to those who ask us. Have you ever given to a friend who was in need? Perhaps he needed someone to play with. Or he was afraid and needed someone to go along. Or he forgot his lunch and you shared yours? Did you feel happy that you were able to help out? Yes. Jesus expects us to give to those who wish to borrow stuff from us – maybe your toys, skates because they can't afford them. Maybe they want to play on your swings or in your yard, or to ride your bike. When we give to those who need and share the things we have and cherish, we are actually learning to be like Jesus. Those receiving our kindness see the love of God around them and may decide to give their lives to Christ. And we also continue to feel happy and blessed.

**Dig Out The Answers**

1. Jesus expects you to _____ to those who ask you.

2. What do you do when someone wants to borrow your bike or toys?

3. When we obey Jesus, what good things follow?

**In Your Own Words:** Write down what you learned today.

**My Prayer:** Jesus, help me obey by giving to those in need. Amen

**Today's Wise Words:** Share with those in need.

74

## READ
**Matthew 5:43-44**

# Love Your Enemies

There are four important things Jesus wants us to know in these verses. As Christians Jesus expects us to *love our enemies, bless them that curse us, do good to those that hate us, and pray for those who persecute us.* What does it mean to love your enemy? Jesus wants you to have mercy on them just like he had mercy on you and saved you from your sin. You must not wish something evil for that bully or mean child in your school. You must pray that he/she comes to know Jesus as Lord and Savior

Jesus also wants us to be friendly and speak kind words to children who use lots of swear words and wish us evil. That way, we stop evil behavior from spreading. We must also learn to be kind to those who are continually mean to us. And you also know about children who play all kinds of tricks and jokes on you because you are a Christian. Jesus says to pray for them. We can do all the above because the Holy Spirit lives in us, and gives us power to love, bless, do good and pray even for our enemies. We also know that Jesus loves us no matter what. And we want to share Jesus' love with them.

**Dig Out The Answers**
1. List the four things that Jesus expects us to do?
2. Who gives us power to do these four things?
3. What happens to the world when we do these four things?
**In Your Own Words:** Write down what you learned today.
**My Prayer:** Holy Spirit, please keep giving me power to love, bless, do good and pray for those who treat me badly, in Jesus' name. Amen.

**Today's Wise Words:** With the Holy Spirit's help I will love, bless, be kind, and pray for my enemies.

# Be Perfect

Yesterday we learned four important things Jesus expects of us. With the help of the Holy Spirit, we are to *love our enemies*, *bless those who curse us*, *do good to those who hate us,* and *pray for those who persecute us.* Jesus is saying that when we love, bless, do good, and pray for our enemies, we show the world that we are indeed the children of God. We are loving people just the way God loves.

God loves both good and evil people because he provides rain to make plants grow to give all food. God also makes the sun rise every morning. You know, plants also need sunlight to grow. God doesn't say that because these people are bad, there's not going to be any sunlight for them today. No! Everybody in the world, good or bad, enjoys both sunlight and rain. The God we serve is good. Remember, the good things we do tell the world that Jesus lives in us and can make us perfect. How wonderful!

**Dig Out The Answers**
1. Who makes us perfect?
2. Who gives us power to love those who hate us?
3. What does Jesus want us to do to be perfect?
**In Your Own Words:** Write down what you learned.
**My Prayer:** Thank you, God, that when Jesus lives in my heart and I let him control me, I can be perfect. Help me stay perfect by loving those who hate me, in Jesus' name. Amen.

**Today's Wise Words:** Be perfect as your Heavenly Father is perfect.

# Give with a Good Heart

**Matthew 6:1-4**

**Day 61**

Jesus wants us to give to the poor, but he wants us to do this with a good heart. Jesus says that people who give to the poor because they want to show off are hypocrites. Hypocrites want others to praise them for giving to the poor, so they choose to give at places where everyone will take notice of them. It doesn't mean you should refuse to drop money to the poor person sitting by the roadside. No. Give to the poor because you have compassion on them, not because you want to show off or because you want others to praise you, or because it makes you feel good. So from today, set money aside to give to the poor because Jesus wants you to do so. And do it because you want to show God's love to that poor person. Then God will bless you for your kindness.

**Dig Out The Answers**
1. What do hypocrites do?
2. Why do we have to give to the poor?
3. What does God do for us when we give to the poor for the right reasons?

**In Your Own Words:** Write down what you learned today.

**My Prayer:** God, help me give to the poor because I have compassion on them, in Jesus' name. Amen.

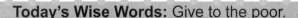

**Today's Wise Words:** Give to the poor.

# Pray In Secret

Jesus expects us to pray always. Prayer is talking and listening to God. Jesus wants us to pray because we love him and want to know him more. Jesus warns us not to pray like hypocrites. Hypocrites love to pray at places where people will take notice of them. Hypocrites pray because they want others to see them. And people of course do take notice of them, and that is the reward they get. Wouldn't you rather have your prayers answered than wanting others to see how well you pray?

We should not pray because we want to impress others. God will not answer such prayers. God will hear your prayer and reward you because you sincerely want to know him and live for him. You must learn to talk to God in prayer by yourself. The prayer is between you and God and it is not important for others to hear unless you want to show off. This is different from being called upon to pray at church or family devotion where you have to speak out for all to hear. Let's learn to talk to God in prayer alone because we love him and want to live for him.

**Dig Out The Answers**
1. Why do hypocrites pray where there are lots of people?
2. Does God hear the prayer of the hypocrite?
3. Why should you pray?
4. Where should you pray?

**In Your Own Words:** Write down what you learned today.

**My Prayer:** God, help me pray because I love you and want to know you more, in Jesus' Name. Amen

**Today's Wise Words:** I will pray because I love Jesus and want to live for him.

# Pray with Your Heart

Jesus teaches another important lesson about praying. Jesus doesn't want us making long prayers, thinking that God will hear because they are long. When we say prayers, which we know by rote, we may not pay attention to the words. We may just keep repeating them day after day. It's just like a baby babbling words that no one understands. Jesus wants us to pay attention to what we say to God in prayer, because we need him and love to talk to him.

Jesus also wants us to know that God doesn't answer our prayers because they are long. It's not how long or short your prayers are but whether you trust God to answer them. We must remember that God knows all that we are about to ask him in prayer before we do. God knows everything because he created everything. Remember that there may be times that you may talk to God for a long time because you are very sad or in trouble, which is okay. Just be sure that you mean all that you tell God about your problem.

## Dig Out The Answers

1. Why do some people make long prayers?
2. What does God know before we go to him in prayer?

**In Your Own Words:** Write down what you learned today.

**My Prayer:** Father God, teach me to pray about my needs believing that you already know about them and will answer, in Jesus' name. Amen.

**Today's Wise Words:** Don't just *say* your prayers – *pray* them.

79

# The Lord's Prayer: Our Father

**Day 64**

Jesus now teaches us how to pray. The Lord's Prayer is a message from us here on earth to God in heaven. The passage you read today tells you whom to talk to when you go to pray, and that person is God, *Our Father*.

Jesus tells us to pray only to God. We are never to pray to angels or saints or anyone else. We can call God "Our Father" because Jesus' blood washed away our sins when we asked him to come and live in our hearts. "Our Father" also means that God has many children – all those who have Jesus in their hearts. And that means you and I belong to the family of God. The Lord's Prayer also tells us where God lives – God lives *in heaven*. That means God is above everything in the universe and rules over everything. And because of this you can be sure he is able to do all you ask him in prayer.

"Hallowed be thy name" means we should make God's name holy. We make God's name holy by praising him for being perfect and pure. By praising him we are telling him that we are sure he'll answer us so others may see how great he is. We also make his name holy by obeying him everyday. So remember how great God is when you go to pray.

**Dig Out The Answers**

1. We are supposed to pray only to _____, and not to_____.
2. Where does God live?
3. How did God become your Father?
4. How do you make God's name Holy?

**In Your Own Words:** Write down what you learned today.

**My Prayer:** God, help me know you are my father in heaven and you are holy.

**Today's Wise Words:** 'Our father which art in heaven, hallowed be thy name.'

# The Lord's Prayer: thy kingdom come

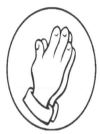

Now we know whom to call on when we go to pray, God, our Father. We also know that God lives in heaven and we should make his name holy. Jesus now teaches us to pray "Thy kingdom come". Do you remember what John the Baptist was preaching – "repent, for the kingdom of heaven is near"? Do you remember that Jesus also preached the same thing? Jesus wants us to look forward to the day when He will return to earth and rule as the King of Kings. That's why we need to tell our family and friends to give their lives to Jesus. Jesus wants us to remember that our true home is in heaven.

"Thy will be done" means that we are willing to let God lead us in everything we do because God is perfect and never makes mistakes. Heaven is a perfect place, full of rest and great happiness because only God's will is done there. When you as a child of God obey him, you bring a piece of heaven into the world. Jesus wants us to remember to ask these two things when we pray: "thy kingdom come" and "thy will be done on earth as it is in heaven". Remember, God's *will* is what God *wants* or that which *pleases* God.

**Dig Out The Answers**

1. Why should you remember to ask God "thy kingdom come" in your prayers?

2. Heaven is perfect because God's will is done there. How can you bring a piece of heaven to earth?

**In Your Own Words:** Write down what you learned.

**My Prayer:** Lord God, help me look forward to Jesus' coming and help me do your will in Jesus name. Amen.

**Today's Wise Words:** "Thy kingdom come. Thy will be done on earth as it in heaven."

81

# The Lord's Prayer: give us our daily bread

**Day 66**

The Lord's Prayer started with God our Father, who is holy. We also talked about how we should look forward to Jesus' coming back to rule on earth. We are also asked to pray that God's will be done on earth. We call these things "spiritual needs". Spiritual needs are what we need to know about God and what

we need to do to stay happy as his children. Now the Lord's Prayer moves on to what our bodies need. Those are "physical needs". God knows that we need food to live, so he wants us to ask him for that. Daily bread also means we can ask for other things we need in this life – clothing, friends, toys, books etc.

We are also to remember not just to ask for ourselves but for others as well. That's why Jesus tells us to pray "give Us" and not "give Me".

God doesn't want us to worry about tomorrow. That's why the verse says "give us *today* our daily bread" and not *tomorrow*. Remember that God loves you very much and wants to give you all that you ask for in prayer.

## Dig Out The Answers
1. Why does the passage say "give Us" and not "give Me"?
2. What things make up "our daily bread" apart from food?
3. Does God want us to ask for the things we need?

**In Your Own Words:** Write down what you learned.

**My Prayer:** Tell God what you need in prayer.

**Today's Wise Words:** "Give us today our daily bread."

**READ**

Matthew
6:12

Day 67

Just as we ask God to give us the things we need daily, we must also ask him to forgive us daily. "Forgive us our debts," – what does it mean?

*Debt* is something you owe somebody. For example, if you borrow money from a friend, then you owe that friend. You have to pay that friend back the money you borrowed. In the same way we also owe God for breaking his laws, that is, for doing wrong things everyday. Our *sins* are our debts. But remember that Jesus paid our debts on the cross. The blood of Jesus washed you from all your sins when you asked Jesus into your heart.

We are Christians but we still do the wrong things sometimes. When we do, God tells us to ask Him for forgiveness. The *blood of Jesus washes us clean* every time we ask for forgiveness. When we ask for forgiveness, we are also telling God that we need his Spirit to help us stop doing wrong things. And that's what happens. God gives us *power* to overcome that sin.

Whenever we ask for forgiveness, the words of this prayer remind us to forgive those who wrong us. That's what is meant by "as we also forgive our debtors." Other Bible versions read *trespasses* instead of *debts*. They mean the same thing.

**Dig Out The Answers**
1. What do we enjoy when we know that our sins are forgiven?
2. What three things happen when we ask God for forgiveness?
3. Why do we have to forgive others?
**In Your Own Words:** Write down what you learned.
**My Prayer:** God, teach me to ask for forgiveness when I do wrong things. Also, help me forgive those who wrong me, because you keep forgiving me.

**Today's Wise Words:** "Forgive us our debts as we also forgive our debtors.

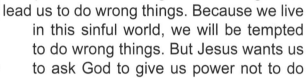

# The Lord's Prayer: lead us not into temptation

**Day 68**

Temptations are thoughts or feelings that lead us to do wrong things. Because we live in this sinful world, we will be tempted to do wrong things. But Jesus wants us to ask God to give us power not to do wrong things when we are tempted. For example, when you are tempted to tell a lie, remember the word of God that says we should speak the truth to one another, and then you will not sin.

Knowing the word of God is one way of getting out of temptation. The Bible tells what God expects of us, and the Holy Spirit gives us power to obey. Jesus also tells us to pray that God will deliver us from evil. The devil is "the evil one" – he is behind all the evil in the world. We cannot overcome the devil by our own strength. So Jesus tells us to ask God not to allow the devil to strike or hurt us. Only God through Jesus can keep the devil away from us.

**Dig Out The Answers**

1. What do you need to know so you'll overcome temptations?

2. Who gives you power to overcome temptations?

3. Who protects you from evil and the evil one?

**In Your Own Words:** Write down what you learned.

**My Prayer:** God, please help me out when I am tempted, and protect me from the devil in Jesus' name. Amen.

**Today's Wise Words:** God helps me out when I'm tempted. God protects me from evil.

# Forgive

Does it mean that, if you don't forgive your sister or brother or friend for wrongs done to you, God will not forgive the wrong things you have done to others? Does it then mean that I am going to hell? No. The day you asked Jesus to forgive all your sins and come into your heart, he did. Right. And he also forgave every sin you did in the past and even the ones you haven't done yet. Isn't that wonderful?

But when we come to God in prayer to ask for forgiveness, we are bound to forgive those who have wronged us. That way we are being sincere and honest. When you find it hard to forgive, be honest to God and ask him for strength to help you forgive.

God doesn't want us to come to him in anger. We remain angry with people we don't want to forgive. And we take the same angry attitude into prayer. Do you think you can make good conversation with a friend who is always angry? No. Prayer is a conversation with God. You will enjoy your time in prayer and receive answers if you learn to forgive those who wrong you. Those who forgive are those who know how much God loves them. So they love others by forgiving them, too.

## Dig Out The Answers
1. What is prayer?
2. What do you have to do to make you enjoy praying to God?
3. Those who forgive wrongs done to them know how much ___.
**In Your Own Words:** Write down what you learned.
**My Prayer:** God, help me to forgive wrongs done to me, so I can enjoy praying to you, in Jesus' name. Amen.

**Today's Wise Words:** Forgive so that you'll be forgiven.

85

# Fasting – what it is!

**READ**
Matthew
6:16-18

Fasting means going without food till sunset. When fasting, people spend much time reading the Bible and praying. Jesus expects Christians to fast because it helps our faith grow stronger. Fasting also makes us humble, teaching us to depend on God more and more. You may not be able to fast now because you are a child. Be sure to ask your parents or guardians about the right age for you to learn how to fast.

Fasting is just like prayer. Jesus wants us to fast because we love him, and want to know him better, not because we want people to praise us. When we decide to fast, we must look cheerful and be careful not to let others know what we are doing. It is between you and God. When we fast sincerely God answers our prayers (even if not always in the way we expected). People fast for various reasons; sometimes a dear one is sick and needs healing. Others fast because they need wisdom and strength.

**Dig Out The Answers**
1. What is fasting?
2. How should we look when we fast?
3. What kind of fasting does God reward?

**In Your Own Words:** Write down what you learned.

**My Prayer:** God, when I am ready to fast, help me do it the right way, in Jesus' name. Amen

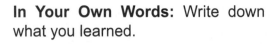

**Today's Wise Words:** God rewards those who fast in secret.

# Treasures in Heaven

Jesus wants us to use the things we cherish most to serve him. The things we cherish most are our treasures. Probably it is your favorite toy. Whenever you share that toy with a friend you are serving Christ. Maybe it's your weekly allowance. You may be proud of yourself because you save like Scrooge. But when you give part of your allowance to missions and charity you are serving Christ. Anytime you give up something you cherish to help the work of God on earth, you add to your treasures in heaven.

Treasures in heaven are safe because heaven is a perfect place. It is wise to use the things we cherish to serve Christ here on earth. Keeping your treasures to yourself here on earth is a foolish thing to do. Everything in this world wears with time or rusts or gets stolen. So it's better to save up your treasures in heaven where they'll always be safe and never spoil. We usually think a lot about the things we cherish. In the same way you'll always think of heaven because your treasures are there. Jesus wants us to think of heaven, always. The more we think of our treasures in heaven, the more we look forward to Jesus' second coming, and the more we obey.

**Dig Out The Answers**
1. Name one thing you cherish a lot.
2. What does Jesus expect you to do with it?
3. How do you add to your treasures in heaven?

**In Your Own Words:** Write down what you learned.

**My Prayer:** God, help me give all that I treasure to serve you, in Jesus' name. Amen.

**Today's Wise Words:** "Store up for yourselves treasures in heaven".

87

## READ
**Matthew 6:22-23**

**Day 72**

# Eyes Full of Light

Do you remember that Jesus is the light of the world? Right. You also know your eyes help you see around. Without your eyes you won't know what you look like or what the world around you looks like. Jesus is saying that we need eyes that are filled with his light.

The light of Jesus in our eyes helps us see God's love all around us. The light of Jesus in our eyes helps us see right from wrong. When we have the light of Jesus in our eyes, we see, know, and do what is right with our bodies. Without the light of Christ, our eyes are bad. Bad eyes see badly and are unable to lead the body to do what is right. Thank Jesus for giving light to your eyes to see the love of God all around.

### Dig Out The Answers

1. Who gives light to your eyes?
2. What does the light of Jesus do for your eyes?
3. What do good eyes see?

**In Your Own Words:** Write down what you learned.

**My Prayer:** Thank God that Jesus gives light to your eyes to see right from wrong.

**Today's Wise Words:** Your eye is the lamp of your body.

## READ

You Can't Have Two Masters

**Matthew 6:24**

Day 73

Who is your master? A master is your boss, someone that you have to obey at all times. The one you obey is your master. Jesus is saying in this passage that we cannot serve two masters. What Jesus means is this: you cannot obey God and obey the world at the same time. "Money" in this verse stands for things in the world. What do you  think about, most of the time? How do you use the time you have? What are the things you cherish most?

Jesus wants us to fix our thoughts, and use our time and the things we have, for God. If we are always thinking about money and how to get more, then money is our master. When we think about something a lot, it means that thing means a lot to us. In the same way when we think a lot about God, that means we love God a lot, and he is truly our master. So from today make up your mind to think about Jesus a lot, spend time with Jesus a lot, and use the things you own to serve Jesus, too. That way you show that Jesus is truly your master.

**Dig Out The Answers**
How do you show that Jesus is your master?
**In Your Own Words:** Write down what you learned today.

**My Prayer:** God, please help me show that you are my master. I want you to be my master because you know everything and you never go wrong. As my master you'll always give me the best because you are the best ever.

**Today's Wise Words:** Jesus is my only master.

# READ

**Day 74**

## Don't Worry

Jesus doesn't want us to worry. Sometimes we do worry about things we need. Jesus says not to worry. When we worry about the things we need – food, clothes, drink – do you know what we are doing? We are fixing our thoughts on the world. Worrying makes us sad, and takes away our faith in the power of God. When we worry, we are also telling God that he is not wise. But God, the *all-wise,* and owner of the whole universe, knows all things. God knows exactly when to give us what we need. He knows exactly what to give us. He also knows exactly how much to give us. That's why God tells us not to worry.

As we learned earlier, we must fix our thoughts on God and not on the things in the world. Only God can provide all the things we need. It doesn't mean that if you need something you shouldn't ask your parents. By all means ask. God gave you parents and guardians to take care of you. If they say they don't have what you want, then pray to God and accept whatever answer he gives. God is a good God and is always ready to give us the things that are best for us.

**Dig Out The Answers**

1. When we worry, what are we actually doing?
2. Why is God *all-wise*?
3. Write two things that happen to us when we worry.

**In Your Own Words:** Write down what you learned.

**My Prayer:** God, help me to trust you and not to worry about anything, in Jesus' name. Amen.

**Today's Wise Words:** Don't worry

# Seek First The Kingdom

Jesus wants us to look at the beautiful world around us when we are about to worry. God wants us to look at the birds of the air – or at beautiful wild flowers like lilies. He even wants us to look at the green grass. You'll see that all these are truly beautiful things God made. Jesus is saying that we are more important than all these beautiful things in the world. If we are more important than these things that God takes care of (flowers, birds, grass) then we must be sure that God will take care of us. We are more important, and so we should not worry. What does Jesus want us to do? He wants us use our energies to serve God, living and obeying him.

And do you know what God promised? He will give us all the things we need. As God's children, Jesus wants us to trust God at all times. We must trust him to take care of us so much that we don't even think about what could happen next.

**Dig Out The Answers**

1. When you are about to worry, Jesus says to look at _____.

2. What did God promise to do for us if we seek and serve him?

3. Who are the most important things God created?

**In Your Own Words:** Write down what you learned.

**My Prayer:** Father God, let me seek and serve you first, and you will always take care of me, in Jesus' name. Amen.

**Today's Wise Words:** Seek first the kingdom of God and his righteousness.

# READ

Matthew 7:1-2

## Stop Finding Fault

Jesus is telling us not to judge others. What does it mean to judge, in this passage? Jesus is saying that we should not make a habit of finding fault with others. When we do that, others will also find fault with us. God is the only one who judges all people, because he is holy. Why shouldn't we judge others? Because we do not know the reasons why people do what they do. You can't go into people's minds and find the reasons. Only God knows what goes on in everyone's mind.

Do you think it would be fun if others find fault with everything you do? I bet you'd be the saddest person on earth. We need to be careful not to find fault with others, because we also have many faults and yet Jesus loves us just the same. Instead of finding fault, pray for the person.

### Dig Out The Answers
1. What does it mean to judge others?
2. Who is the only true Judge? Why is that?
3. Instead of finding fault what should we do?

**In Your Own Words:** Write down what you learned.

**My Prayer:** God, help me not to make a habit of finding fault with others. Rather, help me pray for them in Jesus' name, Amen.

**Today's Wise Words:** Judge not and you will not be judged.

# READ
## Matthew 7:3-5

# Check Your Eyes Out

A "speck" is something very small like a little piece of sawdust. A "plank" is like a big log. Sometimes we are eager to point out the faults in our friends. But we forget to take notice of our own faults. That's what Jesus means by "speck in your brother's eye" and "plank in your own eye". Jesus is not saying that you shouldn't point out what your friend is doing wrong if it will help. But it is good to know your own faults and ask God to help you too.

When you are willing to change your bad attitudes, your friend will be willing to listen to you when you point out his faults, too. Faults are bad attitudes, bad habits, and wrong actions. When we know our own faults, it helps us treat others gently who have the same faults. We learn to be patient with one another and help each other change for good.

**Dig Out The Answers**
1. What do you need to do before pointing out a friend's fault?
2. When we know about our own faults it helps us _____.
3. What should we do about our faults?
**In Your Own Words:** Write down what you learned.

**My Prayer:** God, please let me know my faults and help me change even as I help my friends out of their faults too, in Jesus' name. Amen.

**Today's Wise Words:** Take out the plank in your own eye.

# Don't Throw Pearls to Pigs

**Day 78**

Do you think if you gave a pig a very costly gold necklace, it'd be happy? No! A pig wouldn't notice the difference. Sometimes we may point out what a friend is doing wrong, but he may not listen. Why? He wasn't ready to listen yet. Or maybe, he was not in a good mood. Or yet still, you said it in front of other people, which made him angry.

When we give advice to people who won't accept it, it is like "throwing pearls to pigs". Pray to God to help you know the right time to talk to somebody about something he is doing wrong. That way, the person will listen to you and you may not have wasted your time or destroyed your friendship. Sometimes God doesn't want us to talk to people about their faults. He just wants us to pray for them. That's all. So make sure God leads you in everything you do.

**Dig Out The Answers**

1. Why is it important to pray before you talk to a friend about his faults?
2. Why would a friend not listen to your advice about his faults?
3. Does God always want us to talk to our friends about what they do wrong?

**In Your Own Words:** Write down what you learned.

**My Prayer:** God, please help me pray before advising a friend about his faults, in Jesus' name.

**Today's Wise Words:** Do not throw your pearls to pigs.

## Ask, Seek, Knock

We have been talking about finding fault with people. We have learned that it is not always wise to talk to others about what they are doing wrong. Sometimes we just have to pray for them. Jesus says in this passage that we need to "ask" God in prayer how to live with others. We also have to "seek'" God in prayer as the most cherished friend in the whole wide world. When we come to God in prayer, we must understand that we are coming into our Father's house and he will always open the door for us when we "knock".

Jesus wants us to understand that prayer is very important. Asking is praying. You *ask* with your *voice*. You use *words* to express your prayer. Seeking is more praying where you *sincerely desire* the things you ask for in prayer. Knocking is much more praying when you obey by *using your own hands and efforts* to help bring about what God wants in your life.

Jesus wants us to grow in prayer. Through prayer, God teaches us how to treat people we meet for the first time or those we know already. The more we "seek" God in prayer, the more we know him. And the more we know him, the more we will continue to "knock" at the door of prayer. Why? – because we know that he always answers prayers. God promised to answer and he always does.

**Dig Out The Answer:** Read verse 8. It is a promise. What does God promise there?
**In Your Own Words:** Write down what you learned.
**My Prayer:** Holy Spirit, teach me to talk and listen to you in prayer. Help me know that the Father will always answer my prayers in Jesus' name.

**Today's Wise Words:** "Ask and it will be given, seek and you will find, knock and the door will be opened".

# God Gives Good Gifts

Jesus wants you to know that God is your Father if you have Jesus in your life. Just as you go to your parents when you need something, God wants you to come to him when you have a need.

Do you ever think your parents will refuse to give you food to eat or water to drink if you ask? No, of course not. And that is right.

Parents always try to give their children what they need. Jesus wants us to know that God's love, kindness and goodness is much greater than our parents'. God knows much more about what we need than our parents do. Thank God, you have good parents, but God is even better. And that should make us always want to come to God in prayer when we have a need. God knows how to give good gifts better than anyone else in the world.

**Dig Out The Answers**

1. Why is God the best Father or Parent?
2. Because God is a better Father, we can go to him when we _____.
3. Who gives us good gifts?

**In Your Own Words:** Write down what you learned.

**My Prayer:** Father, you are the best parent I have, so you'll always provide for me, in Jesus name, Amen.

**Today's Wise Words**: Your Father in heaven gives good gifts to those who ask him.

# The Golden Rule

Yesterday we learned that prayer is very important. Through prayer God teaches us how to treat others. When we pray, God makes us strong and bold so we can do what is right. We don't have that kind of strength in ourselves.

In today's verse Jesus is telling us to treat others well, just the way we'd like to be treated. Today's verse is known all over the world as "The Golden Rule". It is something that we all find difficult to do. It is our nature to get even. It is our nature to pay back evil for evil and good for good. Our nature is a very bad nature. That is why Jesus encourages us to ask, seek, and knock in prayer.

How do we know how to treat people well? By reading the word of God. When we pray the Holy Spirit reminds us of what we have read in the Bible, and makes us willing to treat others well. The Holy Spirit lives in all who have accepted Jesus as Lord and Savior. Can you remember a time that the Holy Spirit helped you to show kindness to someone who was bad to you?

**Dig Out The Answers**
1. What is today's verse called all over the world?
2. How are we supposed to treat other people?
3. Where do we learn to treat others well?
4. Who reminds us and gives us power to treat others nicely?

**In Your Own Words:** Write down what you learned.

**My Prayer:** God, please help me treat others well, in Jesus' name. Amen.

**Today's Wise Words:** Do to others what you would have them do to you.

97

# The Narrow Gate

Jesus wants us to understand that there are only two ways that we can choose to go. There is the way of sin or the way of holiness. The way of sin is the bad and wrong way that leads to hell. The way of holiness, the good way, is the way to heaven. You can't be on both ways. You are either on the way to heaven or on the way to hell. All those who have asked Jesus to forgive their sins, and accepted him as Lord and Savior are on their way to heaven. Are you on that way?

Jesus is the 'gate' that leads to heaven. Jesus is the narrow way that leads to heaven. Why is the gate small? The gate is small because it is hard to get in when you are proud and feel big. At Jesus' gate you must be willing to feel small by accepting that there's nothing good in you. You are full of sin and need the blood of Jesus to wash away your sin. Those who feel big cannot enter through the small gate because they feel they are so good they don't need God. The way is narrow, because on that way the Holy Spirit helps us do what is right and most of the time it is difficult for us because we are used to doing wrong things. But, remember there are lots of fun and adventure on this narrow road. Don't miss it for anything in the world!

**Dig Out The Answers**
1. What are the two ways Jesus spoke of?
2. Why is the gate to life or heaven small?
3. What do you need to do to get onto the road that leads to life?
4. Why can't some people get into the small gate?
**In Your Own Words:** Write down what you learned.
**My Prayer:** God, I thank you that I am on my way to heaven because Jesus lives in me.

**Today's Wise Words:** Small is the gate and narrow the road that leads to life.

# READ

## Wolves in Sheep's Clothing!

**Matthew 7:15-16**

**Day 83**

The prophets of the Old Testament were teachers of God's word. God sometimes showed them things in the future before they happened. The prophets in your church then, are the teachers who help you understand God's word. This could be your pastor, your Sunday school teacher or your parents.

Jesus in this passage tells us not to believe everybody who claims to be a teacher of God's word. Why? Not everyone who teaches the word of God is actually a Christian. Some people actually pretend to be Christians when they are not. They are false prophets, which means they are phony. Jesus describes them as "wolves in sheep's clothing". Wolves attack and harm you, but sheep are gentle and calm. These phony teachers pretend to be calm and gentle as sheep, but inside they are harmful like wolves. You'll never suspect that they are phony because they appear to be good people. They mix with Christians to bring confusion, fights, quarrels, and even stop people from believing in God. Even though you are a child, Jesus wants you to be careful and avoid phony teachers who claim to teach God's word.

**Dig Out The Answers**
1. Who are the prophets in your church?
2. How does Jesus describe phony teachers of God's word?
3. What does Jesus want us to do about phony teachers?

**In Your Own Words:** Write down what you learned.

**My Prayer:** God, please deliver me from phony teachers who claim to teach your word.

**Today's Wise Words:** Watch out for false prophets.

# READ

**Matthew 7:17-18**

**Day 84**

## Good Trees and Bad Trees

Today, Jesus is going to show you how to recognize a false teacher or prophet when you see one. He does this by using trees and the fruit they bear as an example. Every good tree bears good fruit. A bad tree bears bad fruit. You can tell a good tree from a bad tree just by looking at the fruits they bear. Good fruits are good works and bad fruits are evil/bad works

Sometimes a bad person may do a good deed, or drop a good truth or teaching. This does not mean that the bad person is bearing fruit. It is just like a bunch of grapes hanging over thorn bushes. Would you say that thorn bushes bear grapes? No! Watch how those who teach God's word live; how they talk, how they act toward others. Are they proud and full of themselves? Or are they bearing good fruit, that is, good works? Do they do what they teach? Those who have the Spirit of God living in them are sure to bear good fruit. Phony teachers will always bear bad fruit, and you are sure to find them out!

### Dig Out The Answers
1. What is good fruit? What is bad fruit?
2. Can an evil person bear good fruit? Why?
3. How do you tell good teachers from phony ones?

**In Your Own Words:** Write down what you learned.

**My Prayer:** God, help me bear good fruit and help me watch out for phony teachers, in Jesus' name.

**Today's Wise Words:** Every good tree bears good fruit but a bad tree bears bad fruit.

## Good Fruit Comes from Good Trees

**READ**

Matthew
7:19-20

Day 85

Jesus gives a warning to false teachers. If they don't have a change of heart and sincerely give their lives to Christ, God will cast them into hell's fire. God is very hard on phony teachers who bring sorrow and suffering to his true children. And yet still, God wants such phony teachers to change because he loves them, too. That's why Jesus warns them of what will happen to them in future if they don't change. Jesus warns us not to have anything to do with phony teachers, but you can still pray for them to become true followers. This is also a warning to all of us. We must be sincere followers of Christ; otherwise on judgment day, God will cast us into hell. Follow Christ with all your heart. You know you are following Christ with all your heart when you learn to obey him and bear good fruit.

**Dig Out The Answers**
1. What happens to phony teachers who refuse to change?
2. How can you tell whether you are a sincere follower of Christ?

**In Your Own Words:** Write down what you learned.

**My Prayer:** God, please help me follow Jesus Christ with all my heart by obeying him and bearing good fruit, in Jesus name, Amen.

**Today's Wise Words:** Every tree that does not bear fruit is cut down and thrown into the fire.

# Away with False Teachers!

Jesus wants us to follow God sincerely. God is very patient with his children when they are tempted and fail. When we confess, he forgives us and gives us power to overcome. But, there are some who preach the word of God, who seem able to tell what is going to happen before it does, and who perform miracles, yet they are not Christians.

Did you ever read about king Saul? He prophesied but didn't obey God. Do you know that Judas Iscariot, the disciple who betrayed Jesus, also cast out demons when Jesus sent them out to preach the good news? And yet he didn't follow Jesus with all his heart. We can fool people, but no one can fool God. Judas Iscariot couldn't fool Jesus. Jesus knew all about the wickedness in his heart.

Don't just trust everybody who claims to perform miracles, prophesy or cast out demons in the name of Jesus. On judgment day, God will cast some people into hell because they never obeyed him even though they'd talk about all the wonderful things they did in God's name. Those who love God sincerely obey the Bible daily and one day they'll enter heaven. God's will is what we read in the Bible.

### Dig Out The Answers
1. Who will enter the kingdom of heaven?
2. Who will be cast into hell?
3. Where do we find the will of God to obey?
**In Your Own Words:** Write down what you learned.

**My Prayer:** God, please help me do your will at all times, in Jesus' name, Amen.

**Today's Wise Words:** Those who do the will of God will enter heaven.

# The House on the Rock

Jesus is God, so we believe that everything Jesus says is true. Because we believe him we act on what he says, and we obey him. Jesus calls those who hear his words and obey them "wise".

Take a human example. If your mother asks you to get ice cream from the freezer for a snack, you'll surely rush out, open it, grab it and eat it. You went for the ice cream because you believed what your mother said, and so you obeyed. It is the same with following Jesus.

When we believe the words of Jesus to be true, we follow them or obey them. Jesus compares the *life* of a wise man to a *house* built on a solid rock foundation. Every well-built house needs a strong foundation and so does every good life, otherwise, it will fall into pieces when there is a storm. Jesus becomes the foundation of your life when you accept him as your Lord and Savior. Then you start building your life on Jesus who never fails. You build your life on Jesus by obeying what you read in the Bible. We form good habits when we obey Jesus.

Sometimes, though, obeying Jesus can get us into trouble, but Jesus has promised to help us out. Others might not want to be your friend because you like to speak the truth. In that case, remember that Jesus is able to give you not just another friend but a very good one, too. So, trust and obey Jesus everyday.

**Dig Out The Answers**
1. Who is the foundation for a good life?
2. How does Jesus become the foundation of your life?
3. What do you do to build your life on Jesus?
**In Your Own Words:** Write down what you learned today.
**My Prayer:** God, help me build my life on Jesus by obeying your word. Amen

**Today's Wise Words:** The wise man built his house upon the rock.

# The House on Sand

Jesus calls those who hear his words and refuse to obey them "foolish". Jesus compares the *life* of the foolish man to a *house* that is built on *sand*. Sand does not make for a good foundation.

It easily gives way in a storm or in strong winds. Likewise a life without Jesus will fall into pieces when there is trouble, because it doesn't have a good foundation.

When Jesus is the foundation of your life, you can turn to him in time of trouble and he'll always help you out. Also, when Jesus appears for the second time, you are sure to go to heaven with him. I hope by now you have invited Jesus into your life as Lord and Savior, so he is the foundation of your life.

## Dig Out The Answers

1. What did Jesus call those who do not obey his words?

2. What will happen to the life of the foolish when Jesus returns to earth again?
3. Who makes the best foundation for us to build our lives on?

**In Your Own Words:** Write down what you learned today.

**My Prayer:** God, please help those who are foolish to come to know Jesus.

**Today's Wise Words:** The house on sand fell with a great crash.

# READ

**Matthew 7:28-29**

**Day 89**

## The Crowds Are Amazed

We have come to the end of the 'Sermon on the Mount'. The crowds who listened to Jesus were amazed. Jesus taught with power, unlike any teacher they had heard before. They did not know that Jesus was the Son of God. Jesus is still teaching with power today. You may ask, how? He teaches us through the Holy Spirit who lives in us. Sometimes you may read something from the Bible and you are amazed how you are able to understand it so well. This is the work of the Holy Spirit. At times, too, the Holy Spirit reminds you of a verse you had read in the past that could help build your faith when you are down, or make you happy or thankful when you are sad. No man in the world ever taught like Jesus. Always remember that. And it's only when you obey the words of this powerful Jesus that you also have power to live wisely.

### Dig Out The Answers

1. Why were the crowds amazed?
2. Is Jesus still teaching us today? Who is doing that work in us?
3. How do you live wisely?

**In Your Own Words:** Write down what you learned today.

**My Prayer:** God, help me listen to the Holy Spirit as he teaches me your word. Amen.

**Today's Wise Words:** Jesus taught with authority (power).

# When Was Jesus Poor in Spirit?

**READ**

(See Day 41)

Matthew
3:13-15

Day 90

Did Jesus Live the Beatitudes and all he preached in the Sermon on the Mount?

*Days 90 to 119 dwell on passages in the Bible, which show that Jesus practiced all that he taught in the 'Sermon on The Mount', which includes the 'Beatitudes'. He set a good example for all who choose to follow him. Let's join Jesus on this adventure.*

Jesus showed he was "poor in spirit" by choosing to *identify with us* sinners when he came to John to baptize him. To *identify with us* means Jesus stood side by side with us sinners without looking down on us, although he never sinned and so wasn't really *poor in spirit*. For example, when you identify with your school, it means you cheer for your school, no matter what. Jesus who was God, and never did any wrong thing, asked to be baptized because that's what the sinners he came to save had to do. He was willing to stand with us and champion our salvation. He only asked to be baptized as an example to all who'll choose to follow him. Those who see that they need God and turn to him must be baptized just like Jesus. Why do people get baptized? People get baptized to show that they are beginning a new life with God. Before they are baptized, they ask God to forgive their sins, and ask Jesus to be their Lord and Savior, and start obeying the Holy Spirit. Jesus asked John to baptize him to show us, sinners, that we need to turn to God so we can be part of God's kingdom. Jesus practiced what he preached.

**Dig Out The Answers**
1. What did Jesus do to show he was poor in spirit?
2. Why did Jesus ask to be baptized if he never sinned?
**In Your Own Words:** Write down what you learned.
**My Prayer:** God, I thank you for showing me that I need to be baptized to tell all that I am now a Christian, in Jesus name.

**Today's Wise Words:** I must Be Baptized when I accept Jesus into my heart.

# Jesus Looks for Comfort

(See Day 42)

**READ**
Mark
14:32-36

**Day 91**

Did Jesus look to God for comfort because he was sorrowful? Yes. Jesus went to Gethsemane with three of his disciples to pray when he was about to be crucified. Jesus was very lonely and sorrowful. Jesus looked to God for comfort by praying. Jesus showed us whom to turn to when we are sorrowful or sad. We need to go to God, the Father, in prayer. God is able to make us strong and happy again. Sometimes you may feel sad because you did not do well in a class test, or you lost your pet, or your friend wouldn't play with you, or you lost a dear grandma or grandpa. Jesus says to talk to God about it, and you will feel all right again.

## Dig Out The Answers

1. What did Jesus do when he was sorrowful?

2. You talk to ___ when you are sad.

**In Your Own Words:** Write down what you learned.

**My Prayer:** God, help me talk to you in prayer when I am sad and filled with sorrow, Amen.

**Today's Wise Words:** Jesus talked to God when he was sad and so should I.

## READ

**Luke 22:39-43**

**Day 92**

Today's passage tells the same story we read about yesterday, only it goes a little further. It talks about what happens when we turn to God to comfort us. Jesus was in a garden on the Mount of Olives, praying. He went along with his disciples. Jesus was praying to God because he was very sorrowful. Jesus was sorrowful because he knew he was going to suffer and die on the

cross. Wouldn't you be very sad if you knew you were going to be captured, beaten and killed? Now, you know why Jesus was sorrowful.

After Jesus had prayed, an angel from heaven came and strengthened him. How wonderful! It is good to talk to God when you are sad. He may send an angel to help you, though you may not even know it's an angel. But most important of all, God lets the Holy Spirit comfort us, by helping us remember who God is. Sometimes the Holy Spirit may use a parent, a sister or brother, or a friend to say things that will comfort you.

**Dig Out The Answers**
1. What happened when Jesus talked to God about his sorrow?
2. Who comforts us when we are sad and sorrowful?
3. The Holy Spirit may use _____ to comfort us, too.

**In Your Own Words:** Write down what you learned.
**My Prayer:** God, help me know you always send your Holy Spirit to comfort me when I am sad, in Jesus' name.

**Today's Wise Words:** The Holy Spirit may use a brother, sister, parent or friend to comfort me when I am sad.

# What Not to Do When Sad

(See Day 42)

**READ**

Luke
22:44-46

Day 93

We are continuing the story from where we left off yesterday. Remember that God sent an angel to help Jesus as he prayed! Jesus now had strength and he continued to pray more and more. He prayed with all his heart, so much that he was sweating heavily. Remember, Jesus had brought the disciples to pray along with him? But, when Jesus went over to them, they were all asleep. They were asleep because they were tired and very, very sad.

What do you think they should have been doing when they were sad? They should have been praying to God, just like Jesus. When Jesus prayed, an angel was sent to help him. The disciples gave up praying, so they became weak and only slept.

Instead of sleeping when sad, why not talk to God? God will make you strong so your sadness does not make you weak or sick. When you are sad for a long time you can fall sick. God made Jesus strong to die for us. God also makes us strong so we can bless others by doing good things. Thank Jesus that he did not sleep when he was very sorrowful but prayed to God, and so he was given strength to die for our sins. Jesus blessed us by dying on the cross to save us.

## Dig Out The Answers
1. What did the disciples do when they were sad?
2. Was that the right thing to do?
3. Who made Jesus strong so he could die for our sins?
4. Why does God make us strong when we tell him we are sad?

**In Your Own Words:** Write down what you learned.

**My Prayer:** Thank Jesus he did not sleep when sorrowful, but prayed to his Father God. Thank Jesus that he was given strength to die for us on the cross.

**Today's Wise Words:** God makes me strong to bless others.

# When Was Jesus Lowly and Patient, Hoping in God?

**READ**

John 13:1-5

**(See Day 43)**

Jesus was celebrating the Passover feast with his disciples for the last time. Jesus knew that, but his disciples didn't know it was the last Passover feast they'd ever celebrate with Jesus.

Jesus, the Teacher, got up, wrapped a towel around his waist and began washing the disciples' feet. Even though Jesus was the boss of the disciples, he didn't feel big in his shoes. That was a very humble thing Jesus did for the disciples. By washing the feet of the disciples, Jesus teaches a very important lesson. We all need to serve others even if they don't look like us, dress like we do, or stay in beautiful homes. Jesus doesn't want us to think we are more important than any other person.

Because we have the Holy Spirit living in us, we have power to even do hard and dirty jobs to help others. You can give change to the homeless on the streets. You may help in a soup chicken around the corner. Remember to ask for permission from your parents or guardians. You may pick up garbage strewn on the school corridor even though you were not the one who created the mess. Jesus practiced what he preached.

**Dig Out The Answer**

What did Jesus do in the story to show that he was humble?

**In Your Own Words:** Write down what you learned today.

**My Prayer:** God, teach me to be humble like Jesus. Amen.

**Today's Wise Words:** Jesus was humble while here on earth.

110

# Jesus Was Humble

(See Day 43)

**READ**
John
13:12-17

**Day 95**

We are continuing the story from yesterday. When Jesus finished washing the disciples' feet, he asked them whether they understood what he just did for them. Jesus explained that even though he was their boss, he was willing to humble himself and wash their dirty feet. Jesus expected them to wash each other's dirty feet. Apart from helping the poor and needy, there is another thing we do to wash each other's feet.

When a friend wrongs you, it is good to go to the friend and talk it over. When you go to other friends and say bad things about that friend, it means you are not washing your friend's dirty feet, you are rather making it more dirty. When we talk behind other's backs, we are not washing their dirty feet. We wash each other's feet by being kind and forgiving. Do you forgive your friends? Do you say bad things behind their backs?

## Dig Out The Answer

What do we do for friends to show we are washing their feet?

**In Your Own Words:** Write down what you learned.

**My Prayer:** Pray to God to help you wash other people's feet.

**Today's Wise Words:** I can wash my friends' feet by talking things over.

111

# Jesus Doesn't Want to Be King Yet (See Day 43)

(See Day 43)

**READ**
John
6:14-15

Today's story shows us that Jesus practiced being humble. After Jesus had fed the five thousand men, plus women and children, they got very excited. If Jesus could feed this many people with five loaves of bread and two fish, the crowd figured he must be the prophet that was to come. The crowd wanted to make Jesus king. Jesus knew what they wanted to do, so he escaped to the mountain. Jesus didn't want to be king and boss over people. That's not why he came to earth. Jesus came to earth to die for our sins so we can be God's friends again, and live with him in heaven forever. We must follow the example of Jesus and be humble.

Humble people do what is right and don't want to get noticed. Jesus saved us so that we'd spread the good news, so others may come to know him, too. Jesus did not save us to make us feel big in our shoes, and to be proud as peacocks here on earth. Why? The earth is going to be destroyed one day. God is going to create a new earth and a new heaven and those who know Jesus will reign with him there. There all Christians will be princes and princesses.

## Dig Out the Answers

1. Why did Jesus come to earth?
2. Why did the people believe Jesus to be a prophet?
3. Humble people do what is right all the time and don't want to get _____.

**In Your Own Words:** Write down what you learned today.

**My Prayer:** Tell God to teach you to be a servant like Jesus.

**Today's Wise Words:** Jesus was humble and so must I.

# Jesus Rides on a Donkey

(See Day 43)

**READ**

Matthew
21:1-10

Jesus was with his Father in heaven before he came to earth, to be born as a baby. Jesus was king of everything before he came to earth, and he continues to reign as king from heaven today. But, Jesus came to earth to die to save us from our sins, not to reign as king. Jesus' kingdom is much greater and more glorious than the kingdoms of this earth. Jesus owns this earth and all of its kingdoms.

Jesus was now entering Jerusalem as we read from today's story. Jesus had told his disciples to go into a village and untie a donkey and her colt for him to ride on. The disciples found them exactly as Jesus had said. Jesus rode on the donkey as the crowd shouted "Hosanna" to him. Jesus, who owns everything, sat only on a donkey. He didn't come in chariots, with large armies or even with angels to show off. Jesus lived a very humble life here on earth even though he has always been one with God. Jesus set an example for us, to be humble and not to show off. Jesus is coming back to earth one day. And all those who live humble lives will rule the world with him. Won't that be cool?

**Dig Out The Answers**
1. While here on earth Jesus wants us to be _____.
2. When Jesus returns to earth one day the humble will _____ the world with him.
**In Your Own Words:** Write down what you learned.
**My Prayer:** Dear God, teach me to be humble and never show off so that when Jesus returns to earth I will help him rule the world.

**Today's Wise Words:** Jesus never showed off.

113

# Jesus Thirsts For Holiness (See Day 44)

**Luke 4:42-44**

*When did Jesus Hunger and Thirst for Holiness, Loving Others When It Was Difficult?*

**Day 98**

Jesus obeyed God at all times. Jesus tried to do what is right even when it was difficult. Jesus did the right thing in today's story. Jesus left to go to a place all by himself after he had healed so many people. But the crowd wouldn't leave him alone. They went looking for him and they found him. They wanted Jesus to stay in their town a little longer, but Jesus did not listen to them. Jesus told them he had to go to other places to tell them the good news of God's love.

Jesus did not listen to people; he listened to his Father God and obeyed him. We should also listen to God and obey him alone. We listen to God by reading the Bible and obeying it. We should listen to what God says to us rather than what other people say – especially those who don't know Jesus. To hunger and thirst after righteousness means obeying God at all times.

**Dig Out The Answers**

1. Why did Jesus leave the people?
2. What did Jesus do to show that he obeyed God rather than people?

**In Your Own Words:** Write down what you learned.

**My Prayer:** Tell God to make you an obedient child.

**Today's Wise Words:** Jesus obeyed God at all times and so should I.

# Jesus Loved Others When It Was Difficult (See Day 44)

**Matthew 4:23-25**

**Day 99**

We are still talking about Jesus obeying God all the time. Jesus hungered and thirsted after righteousness. Everywhere Jesus went large crowds followed him. Imagine how hard Jesus had to work. Jesus would preach the good news to the people. Afterwards he'd heal all the sick people brought as well. Can you imagine the long lines? Everybody wanted Jesus to touch the sick people they brought. Jesus healed all kinds of diseases. Jesus drove evil spirits out of people. At the end of the day, Jesus was a tired man, but he never complained. Jesus was happy that he was doing what God wanted him to do. Jesus obeyed God. Sometimes, you may also have to do lots of work to help others come to know Jesus. You may help clean up the grounds for a crusade, or serve in the kitchen, or pray with others. Jesus wants you to do all these cheerfully. You will be happy because you are obeying God. Jesus practiced what he preached.

**Dig Out The Answers**

1. Make a list of the work Jesus did in today's story.
2. Did Jesus ever complain that he was so tired he couldn't obey his Father anymore?
**In Your Own Words:** Write down what you learned.

**My Prayer:** Ask God to help you obey at all times without complaining.

**Today's Wise Words:** Jesus worked very hard without complaining.

# Jesus Loved to the End

**(See Day 44)**

## READ

Luke
9:51-53

**Day 100**

Jesus knew it was getting closer to the time of his death and resurrection. He had always known this would happen, because that's why he came to earth. Jesus knew that if he went to Jerusalem, the Pharisees and the Jews would treat him badly and kill him after. But he was willing to go to Jerusalem to die. Jesus was more interested in obeying God. He thirsted after righteousness.

Do you know that sometimes we will also suffer when we decide to do what God wants us to do? There are many Christians in many countries suffering because they obey God. They are beaten, their houses are destroyed, their children are taken as slaves, and some are put in prison. But these Christians do not stop obeying God, because they know that a better place awaits them in heaven. Jesus knew that his death would save many people so he obeyed God. When you also obey God, others may come to know Jesus because of that. They will be saved. Wouldn't you rather have others come to know Jesus because you obeyed? Jesus obeyed even when it was difficult.

### Dig Out The Answers

1. What would happen to Jesus if he went to Jerusalem?
2. Even though Jesus knew he'd be treated badly in Jerusalem, he still went. Why?

**In Your Own Words:** Write down what you learned.

**My Prayer:** God, please give me power to obey you even if I have to suffer for it.

**Today's Wise Words:** Jesus always made up his mind to obey the Father.

116

# Jesus Teaches Lovingly

(See Day 44)

**READ**
Mark
1:35-39

Day 101

Early in the morning people were already looking for Jesus. They needed Jesus in those days, and people still need Jesus today. Did Jesus say, "I can't help the people today?" No. Jesus rather went around the villages and preached the good news to the people. Jesus also traveled around a lot, preaching and driving out evil spirits from people. Do you know that Jesus also preached in churches? The churches were called synagogues.

Jesus showed us by his life how important it is to obey God. Just imagine: if Jesus had not obeyed the Father, all these sick people would not have been cured. They'd still be sick, suffering and sad. Nobody would have heard the good news that God loves everyone and wants to save one and all. Because Jesus obeyed, today many people are blessed. When you obey God, you are blessed and so are others around you.

### Dig Out The Answer

What did Jesus do here to show that he obeyed his Father?

**In Your Own Words:** Write down what you learned.

**My Prayer:** Ask God to help you obey so others will be blessed too.

**Today's Wise Words:** Jesus' obedience blessed many people.

# Jesus Responds to a Need

(See Day 45)

**READ**
Mark
6:34

Day 102

Did Jesus show mercy? That's what we are about to find out in today's verse. Showing mercy also means not waiting for the person to ask for your help before giving it. Jesus saw the crowds. He had mercy on them. Jesus realized they *needed* someone to teach them about the love of God and the ways of God. They were hungry to know more about God. Jesus began to teach them about God.

When you know an answer to a question, answer it, instead of bluffing. When you see a relative or friend in need, try to help even though they may not have asked. Sometimes, people may refuse to accept your help, but don't worry about it. Just stay out and pray till the person is ready to accept your help. When we remember how God has showed us mercy by forgiving all of our sins, it should encourage us to show mercy to others too. Jesus showed mercy.

**Dig Out The Answer**
What did Jesus do for the crowds to show that he was merciful?

**In Your Own Words:** Write down what you learned.

**My Prayer:** God, help me show mercy to others, in Jesus' name. Amen.

**Today's Wise Words:** Jesus showed mercy by teaching the people about God.

# Jesus Feeds the Hungry
## (See Day 45)

(See Day 45)

**READ**

Mark
8:1-3

Day 103

Again, Jesus had compassion on the crowd. The crowd had been with Jesus for three days. The crowd loved to listen to Jesus teach. Jesus knew that they were hungry. If they had food, probably, it was all gone by the third day. Jesus also knew that they had traveled long distances to come and listen to him. Some might collapse on the way if they were sent away hungry. You see how thoughtful Jesus was! Jesus showed mercy. What do

you do when a friend comes to play over at your house for long hours; would you think of giving him lunch or supper? That would be the right thing to do. What do you do when a child in your class forgets his lunch money or lunch bag at home? What if that child was always mean to you, would you be willing to share your lunch? That would be a very merciful thing to do. Now think about things you can do to show mercy to others.

## Dig Out The Answers
1. What do you think Jesus was going to do for the hungry crowd?
2. Write some things that you intend to do to show that you are merciful.
**In Your Own Words:** Write down what you learned.

**My Prayer:** Tell God to help you to be merciful even to those who are mean to you.

**Today's Wise Words:** Jesus was mindful of others.

# Jesus Forgives
## (See Day 45)

Jesus was going to be crucified. Was Jesus angry with the Jews who handed him over to be crucified? No. Jesus did not rain down curses on them, even though they had treated him badly. Instead Jesus asked the Father to forgive them. When people treat us badly, we show mercy by forgiving them. What about that kid that made fun of you yesterday, but today asks to ride your bike or borrow your skates? Jesus said to be merciful.

We should not pay back others for the wrong things they do to us. It's not that easy but the Holy Spirit lives in us to give us power to be kind even when it's hard. Jesus had mercy on those who showed him no mercy. He asked God to forgive them.

## Dig Out The Answer
What did Jesus do in today's story to show that he was merciful?

**In Your Own Words:** Write down what you learned.

**My Prayer:** God, help me to show mercy to those who are not even nice to me, in Jesus' name. Amen.

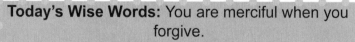

**Today's Wise Words:** You are merciful when you forgive.

# Jesus Shows Mercy to a Criminal (See Day 45)

**Day 105**

Luke 23:39-43

Remember that two thieves were crucified along with Jesus? One of the thieves insulted Jesus, saying very bad things to him. He made fun of Jesus, just like the soldiers who nailed him to the cross. But the other thief was different. He knew that he was being crucified because he did very bad things. He wanted forgiveness for the bad things he'd done. This second thief realized that Jesus hadn't done anything bad for him to be crucified. He realized that Jesus was a king, indeed. He asked Jesus to forgive him. Jesus promised the thief that he was going to be with him in heaven. Even when Jesus hung on the cross dying, he was still showing mercy, forgiving the thief. It is never too late for God to save those who turn to him. Jesus is very merciful and able to save us. It doesn't matter what you do wrong, Jesus is always willing to forgive you. Jesus still shows us mercy everyday.

## Dig Out The Answers

1. What did Jesus do in today's story to show that he was merciful?
2. What do you also have to do to show you are merciful?

**In Your Own Words:** Write down what you learned today.

**My Prayer:** God, teach me to forgive others because you also always forgive me, and show me how to be merciful at all times, in Jesus' name. Amen.

**Today's Wise Words:** Jesus showed mercy by forgiving the criminal his sins.

## The Pure in Heart Point Others to Jesus (See Day 46)

**READ**
Mark
10:17-18

**Day 106**

A pure heart is a heart without sin. Jesus never sinned even though he once lived here on earth. A pure heart sees God and loves God. In today's story, a certain man came to see Jesus. He wanted to know what he could do to get eternal life. He called Jesus, "Good Teacher". Jesus asked him, "Why do you call me good?" Jesus added that "only God is good". (Of course, Jesus himself is God!)

Jesus already knew the thinking of the young man. The young man thought that anyone who did enough good things could make it to heaven. Jesus points out to him and all of us that no one is good enough to make it to heaven. Only God - Father, Son, and Holy Spirit, is good. Jesus pointed the man to God.

When you have a pure heart, you point people to God. You tell them that only the blood of Jesus can cleanse them and make them good. Because Jesus had a pure heart he always told people to look to God to save them. Jesus has also given you a pure heart. He wants you to tell others that he alone can save them from their sins. Their good deeds cannot save them.

**Dig Out The Answers**
1. Can your good works take you to heaven?
2. Jesus pointed the young man to _____.
3. You must point others to _____ because he alone can save them from their sins.

**In Your Own Words:** Write down what you learned today.
**My Prayer:** God, help me point others to Jesus as the one who alone can save them from their sins, in Jesus name, Amen.

**Today's Wise Words:** A pure heart points others to Jesus as their Savior.

122

# The Pure in Heart Work Hard
### (See Day 46)

**READ**

Luke
21:37-38

**Day 107**

Jesus' actions showed that he had a pure heart while here on earth. What did he do in today's passage to show that he had a pure heart? Jesus worked very hard on the work God gave him. What did Jesus do during the day? He taught in the Temple. People came every morning to listen to him.

Is there a particular work you do everyday? When we work hard on the work God has given us, we see how great God is. The greatest thing that could happen to anyone is to come to know God through Jesus. You go to school everyday, don't you? Jesus wants you to work very hard when you go to school. Apart from class work, God also wants you to work hard at school on being a friend to others. When others see the good things you do, they may also want to come and know Jesus. Others will praise God for your kindness, too. When you work hard, you make God happy.

**Dig Out The Answers**

1. Jesus had a pure heart so he _____ on the work God gave him.
2. When you work hard on your schoolwork and friendships people _____ God.

**In Your Own Words:** Write down what you learned today.

**My Prayer:** God, I thank you that because I have a pure heart you will continue to help me to work hard at school and home, as well as becoming a better friend to others, in Jesus name. Amen.

**Today's Wise Words:** Jesus had a pure heart so he worked very hard.

123

# The Pure in Heart Talk to God
### (See Day 46)

## READ

**Luke 21:37**

We are reading the same verse we read yesterday. Yesterday, we learned that because Jesus had a pure heart, he worked very hard on the work his Father gave him. A pure heart seeks to please God at all times. Everyday, Jesus taught at the Temple. And every evening he went up the Mount of Olives. What do you think he went up that hill to do? Jesus talked to God about how the day went. He also thanked God for all that he'd helped him do throughout the day.

A pure heart always seeks to talk to God. Because Jesus had a pure heart he always talked to God, each day after work. Jesus has made your heart pure too. It is good to talk to him after school everyday. Jesus would love to hear from you all that happened at school. We must seek to make God our friend by telling him all that is on our minds. The more we talk to God the more we know him. The more we know him, the more we see the good things he's doing in our lives and others. God cares.

**Dig Out The Answers**

1. Jesus had a pure heart, so he always _____ to the Father up on the hill.
2. What could you do after school each day to show that you have a pure heart?
3. How do you continue to make God your friend?

**In Your Own Words:** Write down what you learned today.

**My Prayer:** God, I thank you for giving me a pure heart because I have Jesus. Help me tell you all that's on my mind, because you are a good listener, in Jesus' name. Amen.

**Today's Wise Words:** A pure heart often talks to God.

Day 108

## READ

**The Pure in Heart Bring Glory to God** (See Day 46)

**John 12:27-30**

**Day 109**

In today's passage, Jesus was praying. How did he show that he had a pure heart while here on earth? Jesus asked the Father to glorify his name. What does "glorify your name" mean? Jesus wanted only what God wanted. What did God want? God wanted Jesus to die to save us from our sins. Jesus talked to God to help him go through the suffering of dying on the cross. Jesus was about to be arrested and killed. He asked God for help. When we want only what God wants, we bring glory to his name. We make God famous when we do what he wants. We make others respect and honor God when we do what he wants. God answered Jesus from heaven by a thunderous voice. God told Jesus that he would glorify his name. How did God glorify his name? God helped Jesus when he was beaten and crucified, but most importantly, he raised Jesus back to life. God brought glory to his own name when he brought Jesus back to life. God gave us hope when he brought Jesus back to life. Now we know that even if we die, we shall rise again. When you have a pure heart you only do what God wants. God also honors you by helping you see how powerful he is, just like he talked to Jesus from heaven.

**Dig Out The Answers**
1. What did Jesus say in the prayer to show that he had a pure heart?
2. What do we do to bring glory to God's name?
3. How does God honor those who bring glory to his name?
**In Your Own Words:** Write down what you learned.

**My Prayer:** Tell God to help you bring glory to his name.

**Today's Wise Words:** A pure heart brings glory to God's name.

125

## Jesus Makes Peace
### (See Day 47)

When did Jesus make peace? Judas Iscariot, one of Jesus' disciples, betrayed him. Judas Iscariot kissed Jesus so the Temple guard would know whom to arrest. They were about to arrest Jesus, take him away and kill him. Jesus' disciples wanted to fight back. They didn't want their master to be taken away and killed. One of Jesus' disciples struck the ear of the high priest's servant. How did Jesus make peace in today's story? Jesus told his disciples not to fight back. Jesus touched the servant's ear and healed him. Jesus did a good thing to a person who was about to arrest him. Do you think the servant ever forgot the kindness Jesus showed him? Probably Marcus, the servant whose ear Jesus healed, became a follower of Jesus later. When we are kind to those who are mean to us, we are making peace. Who knows? Our good deeds may bring them to Christ one day.

**Dig Out The Answers**
1. What was the kind thing Jesus did in today's story to make peace?
2. Write down some things you'll do to make peace.

**In Your Own Words:** Write down what you learned.

**My Prayer:** Ask God to help you make peace even in difficult times.

**Today's Wise Words:** Being kind to a person who dislikes you means you are being a peacemaker.

126

# Jesus Is Called the Son of God

**(See Day 47)**

**READ**

Mark
15:37-39

**Day 111**

When the centurion or the army officer saw how Jesus died, he said that Jesus was truly the Son of God. Do you know that people can tell by how you live that you are a follower of Jesus, too? God calls us his children when we make peace by telling others about Jesus and being kind. Did somebody ever tell you that he thinks you are a Christian because of a good thing you did? Have you also looked at someone's life and thought, this person must be a Christian? Let's continue to make peace so others will see we are children of God.

### Dig Out The Answers

1. What did Jesus do to bring peace between God and us?
2. What do you do to bring peace to others?
3. Who are called sons of God?

**In Your Own Words:** Write down what you learned.

**My Prayer:** How thankful I am that Jesus' death brought peace between God and us. Lord, let my life so shine that others can see that I am a Christian, in Jesus' name, Amen.

**Today's Wise Words:** I want others to look at my life and tell me, "You are a Christian!"

**READ**

Luke
19:47-48

**Day 112**

Was Jesus persecuted for doing good? Yes. As we read in today's passage, the chief priests and the teachers of the law wanted to kill Jesus. They realized that people not only listened to Jesus' words but also believed them. Jesus was persecuted for teaching about God's love.

Jesus knows that all who follow him will sometimes be persecuted. Many Christians are killed in so many countries for believing in Jesus. You must pray for them. Tell God to make them strong, so that they will continue to trust and follow Jesus. Jesus has promised to help us stand firm and continue trusting him.

Sometimes people will make fun of you because you believe in Jesus. Some might tell on you in class when you'd done nothing wrong. And some will not like to be your friend. Yet remember to be kind to all, because that might bring them to know Jesus, too. They will escape going to hell.

**Dig Out The Answers**
1. Are Christians being persecuted in the world today?
2. When you are treated badly what should you do?

**In Your Own Words:** Write down what you learned.

**My Prayer:** Dear God, let me trust Jesus and follow him even when I am treated badly, in Jesus' name. Amen.

**Today's Wise Words:** Jesus was persecuted - we may be persecuted too.

# Jesus' Townsfolk Are Jealous of Him (See Day 48)

## READ
### Mark 6:1-3

**Day 113**

Did people say all kinds of evil things against Jesus? Yes, just as you read from today's story. Jesus went back to the very town that he grew up in. He went to the synagogue, the place of worship, as he used to. He taught the word of God. The people were amazed at his teaching. But some became jealous. They huffed and puffed. They couldn't figure how the boy they grew up with could become this wise.

Jesus makes us wise when we obey him. Sometimes others become jealous because we are becoming wise and good. But this should not make us sad. We should thank God because if we are at all wise or good we owe it all to him.

### Dig Out The Answers

1. What do you do when others say evil things against you because you do the right thing?
2. What does God make us when we obey the word of God?

**In Your Own Words:** Write down what you learned.

**My Prayer:** God, please make me wise and good as I strive to obey your word. Teach me to be strong when others say evil things against me – help me always to be wise and good.

**Today's Wise Words:** Others may not always be happy I am growing in wisdom.

# Jesus' Brothers Tease Him
### (See Day 48)

**READ**

John
7:1-5

Was Jesus persecuted again and again? Yes. Jesus had to stay away from Judea. He wanted to avoid the Jews who were planning to kill him. When someone is planning to hurt you, avoid the person. Jesus avoided going to Judea because they wanted to harm him.

Jesus also knew he had to finish his work of teaching and healing. He wasn't yet done. Even Jesus' own brothers did not believe he was the Messiah. They gave Jesus bad advice. They told Jesus to go show off his miracles in Judea so he could become popular.

Sometimes people say things to us they know will get us in trouble. We must not listen to those who don't believe in Jesus nor should we take advice from them. They only intend to tease us when we get hurt. Jesus did not take his brothers' advice.

**Dig Out The Answers**
1. Why did Jesus avoid going to Judea?
2. What should you do about a person who intends to harm you?
3. What did Jesus' brothers do?

**In Your Own Words:** Write down what you learned.

**My Prayer:** Dear God, help me avoid people and places where I am likely to suffer harm. Amen.

**Today's Wise Words:** Even Jesus was teased.

# Jesus Escapes Threat
### (See Day 48)

**READ**
John
8:58-59

**Day 115**

Jesus was having a chat with the Jews. Jesus told them he was there before Abraham. Jesus was with God the Father in heaven before he came to earth. Abraham lived way before Jesus, but Jesus has always been. The Jews did not understand that Jesus was the promised Messiah and the Son of God. They couldn't understand that he was there before Abraham was even born, because Jesus has always been one with God. They became very angry, and picked up stones to stone him. But Jesus hid himself, and escaped.

When someone wants to hurt you, don't just stand there – escape. That's what Jesus did. Jesus knows that people may try to hurt us because we believe in him. We believe that Jesus is God. But it is good to slip away from such people when you have the opportunity to. Avoid people who want to hurt you because you are a Christian.

**Dig Out The Answers**
1. Why did Jesus say that he was there before Abraham?
2. Jesus came from heaven and Jesus is _____ with God.

**In Your Own Words:** Write down what you learned.

**My Prayer:** Father, I thank you that Jesus is one with you. I will continue to believe this even though others may not like it. Thank you, Father, in Jesus' name. Amen.

**Today's Wise Words:** Yes, Jesus was persecuted again and again.

131

# When Did Jesus Pray?
### (See Day 63)

(See Day 63)

**READ**
Luke
3:21-22

**Day 116**

Jesus practiced what he preached. That's what we have been discussing for the past several days. Jesus wants his followers to follow this example too. What did Jesus do when he was being baptized? He prayed. Have you been baptized yet? If you have, that's a good thing.

Those of you who are yet to be baptized should remember to pray as you are being baptized. A wonderful thing happened as Jesus prayed – the Holy Spirit descended on him. Do you know that every time we pray the Holy Spirit comes to strengthen us? That's why it's very important to pray often. The more we pray, the more we get strength and power to obey God. The Holy Spirit helped Jesus to do all the work the Father wanted him to. In the same way, the Holy Spirits helps you do God's work. So pray often, like Jesus.

### Dig Out The Answers
1. What happened as Jesus prayed?
2. What happens every time we pray?
3. Why does the Holy Spirit give us strength every time we pray?

**In Your Own Words:** Write down what you learned.

**My Prayer:** God, help me pray often, in Jesus' name. Amen.

**Today's Wise Words:** The Holy Spirit descended as Jesus prayed.

132

## Jesus Prays First Thing in The Morning (See Day 63)

**Day 117**

Today's story tells us that Jesus used to get up early in the morning to go talk to God in prayer. He went to a quiet place where he could be alone. Jesus teaches us a very important lesson here. The first thing Jesus did in the morning was to talk to God and commit the day into his hands. The Father was the most important person in Jesus'

life so he was the first person he talked to everyday. Also, only his Father had the power to help Jesus with all the work he had to do for the day. So Jesus always asked God to help him. It is a good thing to talk to God first thing when you wake up, thanking him and asking him to help you with all that you have to do for the day. And it is good to talk to God all by yourself.

### Dig Out The Answers

1. Why did Jesus talk to God first thing in the morning?
2. Why is it important for you to talk to God first thing in the morning?

**In Your Own Words:** Write down what you learned.

**My Prayer:** God, teach me to talk to you first thing in the morning, praising you and asking for your help for the day, in Jesus' name. Amen.

**Today's Wise Words:** Jesus prayed first thing in the morning.

# Jesus Did Not Judge Others – he came to save (See Day 76)

**John 8:3-11**

**Day 118**

To judge others is to find fault with them. Today's story shows us that Jesus did not judge others but came to save them. The Pharisees, and the teachers of the law brought a sinful woman to Jesus. The woman had taken somebody's husband. Grown-ups are not allowed to take the wife or husband of another person. Grown-ups who do that commit a sin called adultery. The woman who was brought to Jesus had committed adultery. The Pharisees wanted to see what Jesus would say about the sin of the woman. But Jesus told them to stone her if none of them ever sinned. And all of them left because they had all sinned. Because we all do wrong things every day, we must be careful not to make a habit of finding fault with others. What did Jesus tell the woman? Jesus told her to stop living a life of sin. Probably the woman became a follower of Jesus. Jesus did not condemn her; he saved her. Instead of finding fault with what people do or say, let's tell them about Jesus who is able to save them from their sins.

## Dig Out The Answers
1. Did Jesus condemn the woman in the story?
2. What did Jesus tell her and what do you think the woman did afterwards?
3. Instead of finding fault with people what do you tell them?

**In Your Own Words:** Write down what you learned.

**My Prayer:** Dear God, help me not to find fault with people, rather help me tell them about Jesus who is able to save them from their sins. Amen.

**Memory Verse:** *John 3:17: "For God did not send his Son into the world to condemn the world, but to save the world through him."*

**Today's Wise Words:** Jesus does not condemn us. He saves us.

# When Did Jesus Fast?
### (See Day 70)

**READ**

Luke
4:1-2

Day 119

Jesus did not only talk about fasting, he himself fasted. Fasting means going without food for a time. Jesus fasted for forty days. He practiced what he preached. Who led Jesus into the desert to fast? The Holy Spirit! The Holy Spirit helps Christians to fast. When we fast by our own strength we gain nothing from it. When we want to fast, we need to ask the Holy Spirit to lead us to do so. The Holy Spirit gives us the strength to fast. Sometimes, some skip breakfast and that is a half-day fast. Some may skip breakfast and lunch and break at suppertime. That is a whole day's fast. Others are also able to fast for many days. Since you are still young it is good to talk to your parents if you decide to fast.

**Dig Out The answers**
1. Who led Jesus into the desert to fast?
2. Why do we need the Holy Spirit's help when we decide to fast?

**In Your Own Words:** Write down what you learned.

**My Prayer:** God, thank you for teaching that I need to ask the help of the Holy Spirit when I feel ready to fast, in Jesus' name. Amen.

**Today's Wise Words:** Jesus was led by the Holy Spirit to fast.

135

# Jesus Provides Food for the Crowd

**Day 120**

*The Miracles of Jesus*
*The miracles of Jesus prove that Jesus is the Son of God and has complete power over everything that there is and ever will be. Amen.*

Today's story shows that Jesus has power to give us food when we need it. The crowds saw the many miracles Jesus performed. He healed the lame, the blind, the crippled and the mute. The crowds had been with Jesus for a while now, and Jesus knew they were hungry.

Jesus is very loving. He didn't want to send the crowds back to their homes hungry, because their homes were far away. Jesus then performed a miracle by feeding four thousand people and more. He did this by multiplying seven loaves and a few fish to feed this many people. This miracle shows that Jesus is able to give us food when we need it. He is able to provide food for the poor. Today you can pray for some poor people you know about who can't afford the food they need, and Jesus will miraculously help them. Jesus may use food others donate, money, or even perform a miracle just like the one we read about today.

**Dig Out The Answers**
1. Write down the diseases Jesus healed.
2. Why didn't Jesus send the crowd away hungry?
3. What did Jesus do to feed the crowd?
**In Your Own Words:** Write down what you learned.

**My Prayer:** Father God, I'm very sure you are able to provide food for me, and I ask you to help these poor people whom I know in _____; in Jesus' name.

**Today's Wise Words:** Jesus gives us daily bread.

136

# Jesus Is Never Tired of Providing for Me

Remember yesterday's passage? Jesus fed four thousand people and more with seven loaves of bread and a few fish. In this passage, Jesus fed about five thousand people with only five loaves of bread and two fish. Jesus performed this miracle of feeding thousands of people more than once. That tells you that Jesus is never tired of performing miracles in your life. So you must be willing to ask him for miracles in your life. The feeding of the five thousand people also shows that Jesus will never leave us to go hungry, but will find a way to provide food and the things we need.

### Dig Out The Answers

1. What did Jesus do with the loaves and fish before serving them to the crowd?
2. Were there leftovers? What does it tell you about Jesus?
3. Does Jesus care to provide your needs?

**In Your Own Words:** Write down what you learned today.

**My Prayer:** God, help me know that Jesus cares and is able to provide my needs.

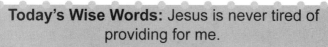

**Today's Wise Words:** Jesus is never tired of providing for me.

# Jesus Is Food that Endures to Eternal Life

**READ**

John
6:25-27

**Day 122**

Remember the crowd Jesus fed? They looked for Jesus till they found him. But Jesus knew why they were looking for him. They thought he would keep performing miracles to feed them. You may eat food everyday but you'll still die one day. Jesus doesn't want us to follow him just because he'll give us food to eat. Jesus wants us to follow him because we believe he is the Son of God who gives us *eternal life.*

Knowing Jesus as Lord and Savior is the most important thing in this life. Why? Because if you know him in this life you are sure to go to heaven and be with him after you die. You are sure Jesus is always with you and will help you through all the difficult situations you'll face in this world. Jesus is the friend who will never fail you. He is the best friend one could ever have.

## Dig Out The Answers

1. What should be the most important reason to follow Jesus?
2. What does Jesus do for those who follow him?
3. Why is Jesus the best friend you can ever have?

**In Your Own Words:** Write down what you learned.

**My Prayer:** Jesus, help me follow you because you give eternal life.

**Today's Wise Words:** Jesus is food that endures to eternal life.

# The Work of God

Yesterday, we read about the crowd that found Jesus after he'd fed them. Jesus had told the crowd to believe in him for eternal life. The crowd now asked Jesus what works they had to do to be able to have eternal life. And Jesus gave them the answer. Jesus wants all of us to know what the work of God is. The work of God is to believe in Jesus, that he is the Son of God. This is the most important work in the

world and nobody should miss it. You do believe that Jesus is the Son of God, who gives eternal life. No other work you do will take you to heaven except believing that Jesus is the Son of God.

**Dig Out The Answers**
1. What did Jesus say is the work of God?
2. Will any other work take you to heaven?

**In Your Own Words:** Write down what you learned today

**My Prayer:** God, help me know that believing in Jesus is the work of God. Amen.

**Today's Wise Words:** The work of God is this: to believe in the one he sent.

139

# Jesus – The Bread of Life

Jesus said that he is the bread of life. What does Jesus mean? We all know that we need food to stay alive. If you don't get food to eat for a long time, you will fall sick and die. So, we need food or bread to eat to stay alive in this world. But you know a person is made up of spirit, soul, and body! These are what make you a person.

The food we eat only feeds our bodies. But we also need to feed our spirits and souls. These two never die. Your body may die but your soul and spirit never do. The kind of food that feeds the soul and spirit is called spiritual food. And Jesus is that spiritual food that can keep your soul and spirit from dying.

How do the spirit and soul die when it's been said that they never die? Anyone without Christ is dead. The spirit or soul without Christ is dead. When you accept Jesus as your Lord and Savior, "the bread of life" gives you life. Apart from Jesus, there are other spiritual foods out there in the world, but they are all lies from the devil. Be careful, and never believe in them. They only lead to death, and finally hell. Only Jesus gives eternal life. Only Jesus can bring you to heaven.

## Dig Out The Answers
1. What are the three things that make up a person?
2. Which parts of a person need spiritual food?
3. Which part of a person needs physical food?
4. Who is the only true bread or food for our spirits and souls?

**In Your Own Words:** Write down what you learned.
**My Prayer:** Father God, let me hold on to Jesus because he is the only one who gives my soul and spirit food that will keep my soul and spirit alive. Amen

**Today's Wise Words:** Jesus is the bread of life.

# Jesus and the Miraculous Catch

We are still learning that Jesus has power and authority to provide our daily needs. Jesus taught us to pray to God our Father for our daily needs. Jesus shows in this story that he is able, as the Son of God, to provide our daily needs. Jesus knows everything. He knew exactly where the fish were in the lake. So he could tell Simon Peter to let down his fishing net into the lake. And oh! what a big catch they had!

Simon Peter was a fisherman and he needed to catch fish, sell, and make money so he could take care of his family. Jesus knows how to prosper the work of your parents or guardians so they can take care of you. Through your parents' work, Jesus provides your daily needs. Jesus is willing to show your parents how to work well so they can make enough money to take care of you, just as he did for Simon Peter.

**Dig Out The Answers**
1. What did Jesus tell Simon Peter to do?
2. What happened when Simon Peter obeyed?
3. Do you think Simon Peter made enough money from the sale of the fish to take care of his family?
4. Do you think Jesus can lead your parents in their work too?

**In Your Own Words:** Write down what you learned.

**My Prayer:** Today, pray that Jesus will help your parents in their work, so they'll make enough money to take care of you.

**Today's Wise Words:** Jesus cares and blesses the work my parents do.

141

## Jesus and Another Miraculous Catch

Day 126

After Jesus rose from the dead, he appeared to his disciples. This was how it happened. Simon Peter and some of the disciples went fishing. They fished the whole night but caught nothing. Early in the morning, Jesus appeared on the shore, and told them where to cast their nets. And wow! what a large number of fish they caught! That was when they realized it was the Lord standing on the shore ("the Lord" is another way we speak of Jesus).

Sometimes we are given projects to do at home or school. We try our best, but it just doesn't come out right. It is good to turn to the Lord at such times in prayer. Jesus knows exactly how to help you even with your projects. Sometimes too we think we've done a particular job for so long we can't go wrong, but we do get stumped. It happened to Simon Peter and the disciples. They'd been fishermen all their lives so you'd expect them to be experts by then. Even they needed Jesus' help. This story teaches us to depend on Jesus in all we do. He is able to meet our need to do our jobs and chores well everyday. Doing our chores and jobs well is a daily need, too.

**Dig Out The Answers**
1. How did Jesus show in the story that he is always ready to provide help in all we do?
2. Did the disciples do what Jesus asked them?
3. If you want Jesus' help, how should you respond to what he tells you?
**In Your Own Words:** Write down what you learned today.

**My Prayer:** God, help me obey all Jesus tells me when I ask him to help. Amen.

**Today's Wise Words:** It is the Lord! Follow his instructions.

# A Miracle for a Man Born Blind

Jesus proves again that he is indeed the Son of God. He has power to make blind people see. The disciples thought the man was born blind because he might have sinned (done something wrong), or perhaps his parents had sinned. Jesus told the disciples that was not the reason. The man was born blind so God would show his power by making him see. And

that's exactly what Jesus did. He made him see. Jesus put mud mixed with saliva on the blind man's eyes and asked him to go wash in the Pool of Siloam. The blind man obeyed and he could see. For the first time he saw the world. How wonderful!

There are certain problems that we may have in our families – sickness, a parent losing a job, not doing well in school, losing a friend, accidents and the like. Jesus wants us to remember that some of these problems are there because God wants to show his power in our lives. But we have to trust him. Go to him in prayer. Believe Jesus as you pray, and Jesus will perform a miracle in your family, today.

**Dig Out The Answers**
1. Why was the man in the story born blind?
2. What happened to him when he met Jesus?
3. What happens to our problems when we take them to Jesus?
**In Your Own Words:** Write down what you learned today.

**My Prayer:** Tell God in prayer about any problem you have and trust him to solve it for you.

**Today's Wise Words:** God shows his power in our lives even when we face problems.

143

## READ Jesus Opens Spiritual Eyes

**John 9:5**

**Day 128**

This verse was part of yesterday's passage. Would you like to memorize it? Jesus made a very important point here. Jesus said, "While I am in the world, I am the light of the world". Do you know that Jesus is still in the world? Yes, he lives in your heart if you have asked him to be your Lord and Savior. When Jesus comes to live in your heart, he helps you see. That's exactly what he did for the blind man in yesterday's story. As we discussed a few days ago, a person is made up of spirit, soul and body (physical). Jesus gave sight to the blind man's physical (body) eyes. In the same way, Jesus gives light to our spiritual eyes so we can see and know God.

We see God when we see that we are sinners and turn to Jesus to save us. We no more walk in darkness like blind men. To walk in darkness means to walk in your sins, not knowing that you need a Savior.

You are spiritually blind if you don't have Jesus in your life. Thank God, you have eyes that see this beautiful world. But most of all, thank God, you have spiritual eyes that see Jesus, because you have him in you.

**Dig Out The Answers**
1. Which set of eyes does Jesus give light to?
2. Is Jesus still in the world today? Where does he live?
3. The light that Jesus gives to our spiritual eyes helps us to see

_____.

**In Your Own Words:** Write down what you learned today.

**My Prayer:** Thank you Jesus that I can see this beautiful world. But most of all I thank you for giving light to my spiritual eyes so I can see and know God. Help others to see this light too.

**Today's Wise Words:** Jesus opens our spiritual eyes to see and know God.

# Neighbors Take Notice of a Blind man

When Jesus does something wonderful in your life, people take notice. This is what happened to the man born blind. His neighbors realized he had been healed of his blindness. They wondered how that happened, so they asked him. The blind man who could now see told them, "The man called Jesus…" The blind man who could now see openly honored Jesus. He wasn't shy or afraid to tell them that Jesus was the one who had healed him. God is happy when we openly honor him before our friends and family. God is happy when we tell others the good things he does for us everyday. So, even as you go to school today, or play with your friends, remember to honor Jesus by telling about the good things he does for you.

### Dig Out The Answers

1. Was the man born blind shy to tell who had healed him?
2. We _____ God when we tell others about the good things he does for us.
3. What other things can you do to honor God?

**In Your Own Words:** Write down what you learned today.

**My Prayer:** God, teach me to honor you, by telling others what you do for me, in Jesus' name, Amen.

**Today's Wise Words:** Openly honor God when friends question what he is doing in your life.

# The Pharisees and the Sabbath

**READ**
John
9:13-17

Do you remember the Pharisees? (See Day 18). They did not like Jesus because he pointed out all the things they were doing wrong. God wants us to obey him in *his* way, not our own way. The Pharisees wanted to keep the Sabbath their own way, not God's way. The Sabbath is Saturday for the Jews. God expected all Jews to rest on this day. Christians keep the Sabbath on Sunday, because Christ Jesus rose on Sunday, the first day of the week.

The Pharisees were angry that Jesus had made the blind man well on a Sabbath. Do you think they should have been angry? Of course not! They should have been glad that a man born blind could now see. They were angry because they did not understand that we keep the Sabbath by doing good to people in need, too. Jesus showed the Pharisees and the Jews the right way to keep the Sabbath – he made the blind see, healed the sick, preached the good news, fed the hungry, and did other good things.

**Dig Out The Answers**

1. What did Jesus do on the Sabbath?
2. What does Jesus expect you to do on the Sabbath?
3. How can you be wise and holy on the Sabbath?

**In Your Own Words:** Write down what you learned today.

**My Prayer:** Lord, help me keep the Sabbath like Jesus, doing what is good – sharing the word of God, praying for the sick, and doing good things, in Jesus' name.

**Today's Wise Words:** Keep the Sabbath God's way, not your own way.

# Parents of Blind Man Scared

The Pharisees hated Jesus so much that they couldn't see all the good things he was doing. Hatred blinds us from seeing all the good things around us. They still didn't believe that Jesus could give sight to a man born blind. They had to ask the man's parents. The man's parents told them that the blind man who could now see was indeed their son. "How is it that now he can see?" the Pharisees asked the parents. The parents were afraid of the Pharisees so they told them to ask their son themselves. But, God doesn't want us to be afraid to tell others the great things he does for us. Pray to God to give you boldness to tell even the "people you are most afraid of" about what Jesus has done for you.

## Dig Out The Answers

1. Why were the parents of the man born blind afraid to admit that Jesus was the one who healed their son?
2. When you are afraid to speak the truth about Jesus, what should you do?

**In Your Own Words:** Write down what you learned today.

**My Prayer:** Pray that God will give you boldness to tell about Jesus.

**Today's Wise Words:** Boldly tell what the Lord has done for you.

147

## READ

**Day 132**

John 9:24-34

# Testimony of the Blind Man

We will continue the story from yesterday. The parents of the man born blind were afraid to say that Jesus was the one who healed their son. So the Pharisees turned to their son to answer the question. The man born blind still insisted that it was Jesus who had made him see. The Pharisees called Jesus a sinner, but no sinner could do the miracles Jesus did. So we know the Pharisees said that only out of hatred and jealousy.

We must be careful not to say nasty things about people because we are jealous of them. The man born blind knew that nobody could do such a miracle unless he was sent from God. Do you also know that? Do you know that Jesus is holy and sent from God to save us and heal us? You know what happened to the man whose eyes were opened by Jesus? They threw him out of the synagogue, the Jewish place of worship. Sometimes you may lose a friend if you decide to walk with Jesus. But that shouldn't discourage you. Jesus, the mighty one, is able to take better care of you than anyone else in the world.

**Dig Out The Answers**
1. Did the blind man change his story because the Pharisees kept bothering him?
2. Even though someone may keep bugging you about your faith in Jesus, should that make you stop telling the truth about Jesus?

**In Your Own Words:** Write down what you learned today.

**My Prayer:** Pray that Jesus will help you put your faith in him even if you are bugged.

**Today's Wise Words:** Don't be jealous of Christian friends God is using to do great work.

148

# The Blind Man Meets Jesus

Jesus heard that the blind man he healed had been thrown out of church. He went looking for him. Jesus truly cared about this man and he cares for you, too. You must remember that the blind man had not seen Jesus, yet. He was blind when he met Jesus. Jesus asked him to go wash in a pool after putting mud mixed with spit on his eyes. He obeyed Jesus, and as soon as he finished washing in the pool, he could see. Jesus told him that he was and still is the "Son of God". The man believed in Jesus and worshipped him. Anyone who comes to believe in Jesus worships him. If Jesus is worshipped, then he is God. Jesus said, "I and the Father are one". Jesus is no ordinary man. He is the Son of God. Jesus also said something very important to the man who could now see, "I came to make the blind see". Remember that everybody in the world is spiritually blind. If you admit that you are blind and come to Jesus, he will open your eyes so you can see and know God. The Pharisees would not admit that they were blind so they refused to repent, and remained blind. Can *you* see?

**Dig Out The Answers**
1. What kind of blindness were the Pharisees suffering from?
2. What do you have to do to have your spiritual eyes open?
3. What did the man in the story do when he met Jesus?
4. Everyone who comes to believe in Jesus _____ him.
**In Your Own Words:** Write down what you learned today.
**My Prayer:** Lord Jesus, I thank you for coming to heal me of spiritual blindness.

**Today's Wise Words:** Those with eyes that see Jesus worship him.

## READ

**Mark 8:22-26**

# The Blind Man at Bethsaida

Jesus used spit to heal this blind man also, at Bethsaida. Isn't it nice that Jesus never turned any sick person away who came to him for healing? Likewise, Jesus will never turn you away when you come to him in prayer with a request. The blind man did not see clearly right away when Jesus spat on his eyes. The second time around, he could see clearly. The more Jesus touched his eyes the better he saw.

That's the lesson here. The more Jesus touches our spiritual eyes the better we see God. How does Jesus touch our spiritual eyes? He touches us when we read the word of God daily, obey it, and pray. When we do these things, the light of Christ in us shines brighter and brighter. The more we see God clearly, the more we enjoy our lives on earth. We have peace and lots of joy in all situations. So let's continue to walk in the light of Jesus. Don't forget that only Jesus performs such miracles. He has power to do anything. Believe in him!

**Dig Out The Answers**
1. What did Jesus do for the blind man?
2. What do we do in order to see God more clearly?
**In Your Own Words:** Write down what you learned today.

**My Prayer:** God, help me walk in the light of Christ, daily.

**Today's Wise Words:** The light of Christ in me gets brighter day by day.

# Blind Men Call Out to Jesus

Matthew
20:29-34

**Day 135**

This is another story of Jesus healing blind men. They sat down by the roadside calling out to Jesus to have mercy on them. Do you know that you can also call out to Jesus when you are in need? The crowd didn't want them shouting out for Jesus. But, did the blind men listen to the crowd? No! And you should never listen to what the world is saying about Jesus. The people in the world don't know Jesus. They don't know about his love and

goodness. Jesus heard the cry of the blind men. He touched their eyes and healed them. Immediately they could see, and they became Jesus' disciples.

Have you noticed that every time Jesus healed a blind man he became a follower of Jesus? Unless Jesus opens your eyes, you cannot see him to follow him. You can trust Jesus today to heal a friend or family member of physical blindness. Believe that he is able to do that. But, most important of all, pray that Jesus will open their spiritual eyes so they can follow him as Savior and Lord.

**Dig Out The Answers**
1. Why shouldn't you listen to the crowd out there in the world?
2. Will Jesus answer you if you keep calling for him like the two blind men?
3. Why is it important that Jesus opens your spiritual eyes?
**In Your Own Words:** Write down what you learned.
**My Prayer:** God, help me follow Jesus everyday, because he opened my eyes. Amen.

**Today's Wise Words:** Cry out; call out to Jesus when you need him.

151

## READ

# Walk in the Light

We have read stories about Jesus healing blind men. Blind men live in darkness. They don't see anything around them – the beautiful world or their loved ones. Jesus doesn't want anyone to walk in darkness. We all know the dangers of walking in darkness. There may be wild animals hunting for food, creepy crawlies that could sting, and other bad things. It is the same with those suffering from spiritual blindness. They too walk in spiritual darkness. Walking in spiritual darkness means you still live in your sins and have not received forgiveness from Jesus. The spirit in you needs light to be able to see. Jesus says that he is that light.

When Jesus comes into your life, all the spiritual darkness disappears. You see the difference between truth and lies. You can see God, know him, and go to him with your requests. Would you memorize this verse? *"I am the light of the world. Whoever follows me will never walk in darkness, but will have the light of life. "John 8:12 (NIV)*

**Dig Out The Answers**
1. Who is the light of the world?
2. Whoever follows me will never walk in ___.

**In Your Own Words:** Write down what you learned today.

**My Prayer:** Thank God for giving you the light of life.

**Today's Wise Words:** The light of Jesus drives away spiritual darkness.

# A Miracle for a Leper

Jesus did not only make the blind see, he also healed those who suffered from leprosy. Leprosy is a skin disease that spreads all over the body. It also destroys your appearance as it spreads over the body. A leper is somebody with leprosy. In Jesus' time lepers were very sad people, because there was no medicine that could cure them. A leper could not live in town because others could get the disease. Sooner or later, a whole town would have leprosy. To prevent this from happening, all lepers lived together at a place outside of town. They lived with the leprosy till they died. There was no hope. What a sad state!

In today's story, you'll remember that Jesus actually touched the leper. The leper was healed immediately, and Jesus did not get infected. Jesus had made a very important point here. He is the Son of God and has power to heal and not get infected. The leper wanted to be healed so he asked whether Jesus was willing to heal him, and Jesus said 'Yes'. He was willing to heal him, and he did. When you go to God in prayer, tell him what you want. But, remember to tell him that you will also accept what he wants in your life, because he is wise and knows what is best for you. That is how the leper in today's story did it.

**Dig Out The Answers**

1. Jesus didn't mind touching the leper, even though he looked yucky. What do you learn about the character of Jesus?

2. When you pray 'God, if you are willing, please give me what I ask,' it means that you trust that God knows what is best for you because he is _____.

**In Your Own Words:** Write down what you learned today.

**My Prayer:** Father, thank you that Jesus healed lepers and is still able to heal all who come to him.

**Today's Wise Words:** Jesus still says, "I am willing".

# A Cured Leper Tells About Jesus

We are continuing yesterday's story. The leper had been cured. He was so happy. Jesus told him to go show himself to the priest. During the time of Jesus, the priests were responsible for checking whether a leper had been healed or not. The priests followed the law God gave Moses. When the priest was sure a leper had been healed, the leper brought an offering to God. Now

you know why Jesus told the leper to go show himself to the priest. Jesus followed the rules or laws of his time. Jesus told the leper not to tell anyone about his healing because his great aim was to be a Savior from sin, not just a popular healer. Jesus wants to let everyone know he is the Son of God who saves from sin.

Christians do not do good things because we want to be popular, but because we want others to come to know Christ. In spite of what Jesus said, the cured leper went around telling about what the Lord had done for him, and that was good. It is good to tell others what Jesus does for us.

**Dig Out The Answers**
1. What should be the number one reason for doing good deeds?
2. What did the leper do when he realized he'd been healed?
**In Your Own Words:** Write down what you learned today.

**My Prayer:** God, help me do what is right because I want others to come and know Jesus.

**Today's Wise Words:** Jesus' great aim was to be a Savior, not just a popular healer.

154

# READ

Luke
17:11-14

**Day 139**

## Miracle for Ten Lepers

We now know that lepers couldn't live in towns, only on the outskirts. Also, they had to stay a safe distance from healthy-looking people. As we learned earlier, the disease is contagious, that is, it spreads from person to person. In today's story, ten lepers stood at a distance calling out to Jesus to heal them. They had heard that Jesus was passing by. Jesus heard their cry, took pity on them, and told them to go show themselves to the priest.

They believed Jesus, so they set out to go see the priest. And that was when it happened. They were all cured. Unlike the leper we read about two days ago, Jesus did no more than just speak to them, and they were healed. We are amazed at the different ways Jesus could heal.

When we ask God to do something for us, we should not expect him to do it the same way he did for some other person. God works in so many ways. Let's just trust him.

### Dig Out The Answers

1. What did Jesus do to heal the ten lepers?
2. Did the lepers do what Jesus told them?
3. What happened when they obeyed?

**In Your Own Words:** Write down what you learned.

**My Prayer:** Lord God, help me know that you heal in so many ways. Amen.

**Today's Wise Words:** "And as they went, they were cleansed."

155

## READ
Luke
17:15-19

# The Thankful Leper

Yesterday we read about the ten lepers who called out to Jesus to heal them. Jesus told them to go show themselves to the priest. Remember, why they had to go show themselves to the priest? Read the notes on Day 138. As they went on their way, they all got healed. But only one of the ten cured lepers came back to thank Jesus. He talked to Jesus face to face. By talking to Jesus face to face, he got to know Jesus better. Jesus told him that his faith had saved him, which meant, he had completely trusted Jesus, the Son of God. He was now a follower of Jesus. The others who did not come back to thank Jesus missed out on the most important thing of all – receiving Jesus as their Savior. When we go back to thank God for the things he does for us, we get to know him better, because God also talks back to us. It is very important to thank God when he answers your prayers.

**Dig Out The Answers**
1. How many lepers came back to thank Jesus?
2. What did the leper who came back to thank Jesus receive?
3. What do you do when God answers your prayer?
**In Your Own Words:** What did you learn? Write it down.

**My Prayer:** God, teach me to thank you whenever you answer my prayers, in Jesus' name.

**Today's Wise Words:** "Rise and go; your faith has made you well".

## READ

**Matthew 9:12-13**

**Day 141**

# Leprosy, Sin and the Doctor

For the past four days we have been reading stories about lepers. Jesus healed the lepers who asked him for help. In today's passage, Jesus tells us that those who are healthy don't need a doctor but rather those who are sick. And we all know that it's only when we get sick that we go see the doctor. What Jesus means is this: if you accept that you are a sinner, then he can save you from your sin. Jesus is the greatest doctor.

Did you know that the Bible says that in some ways sin is like leprosy? The wrong things we do are as disgusting as leprosy. And sin spreads just like leprosy, all over the body. Sin keeps spreading from one person to the other, from one town to the other, from one country to the other. Sin is contagious just like leprosy. Nobody can stop it from spreading except Jesus Christ. Jesus wants us to know that unless we see ourselves the way God sees us – as sinners – we cannot be saved. The only way sin stops growing in you, and stops spreading to others is to accept that you are a sinner. Then ask Jesus to forgive you and to become your Lord and Savior. Most likely, you have said this prayer before. You don't need to say it again. The day you said it, you became a child of God, because the blood of Jesus washed away all your sins and you are now clean.

**Dig Out The Answers**
1. What does the Bible compare our sinful actions to?
2. Does sin spread like leprosy? Is it contagious?
3. Who can stop sin from growing in you and spreading from person to person?
**In Your Own Words:** What did you learn? Write it down.
**My Prayer:** Thank you, Lord, that the blood of Jesus has washed away all my sins.

**Today's Wise Words:** "For I have come not to call the righteous, but sinners."

157

## The Prayer of the Tax Collector

**READ**

LUKE
18:13

**Day 142**

Would you memorize the prayer of the tax collector in this passage? Excellent! The tax collector in this passage saw himself as a sinner. He called out to God to have mercy on him. Do you remember the leper who told Jesus to have pity on him? The prayer of the leper is like the tax collector's prayer. They both needed healing.

As we discussed yesterday, our sinful actions look as disgusting as leprosy. But there is good news. Jesus is the doctor who heals us from sin. All those who come to Jesus will be washed clean in his blood. You must keep praying for your family members who don't see themselves as sinners. Pray that Jesus will open their eyes to see their need for salvation. When they come to Jesus, his blood will wash away their sins and they will become clean.

**Dig Out The Answers**

1. Why was the tax collector beating his breast?
2. What did the tax collector call himself?
3. What was his prayer?

**In Your Own Words:** What did you learn? Write it down.

**My Prayer:** Pray that your family members will all come to know Jesus.

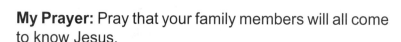

**Today's Wise Words:** "God, have mercy on me, a sinner".

158

# Cups Full of Dirt

Jesus was talking to the Pharisees and teachers of the law (see Day 18 and 25). He compared them to a cup that is clean outside but dirty inside. There are people who seem good to us, though they may not be Christians, but God still calls them sinners. Only God sees what is inside any person. And God who sees what is inside everybody says that we are all sinners, unless we come to Jesus to wash us clean in his blood.

Which part of the cup do you think should be kept clean first, the inside or the outside? Of course, the inside – you pour water or drink into the cup. You better be sure that the inside is clean, and then you can worry about the outside of the cup! Jesus says those who just want to look good on the outside and don't worry about the inside are spiritually blind. What you are inside is more important – the way you think and see the world. Why? Because the way you think shows in the things you do. Jesus called the Pharisees blind, because they were not aware of the wickedness and sinfulness of their hearts. God wants us to wash our hearts, the inside of us, first. When our spirits are washed in the blood of Jesus, we become clean inside and it begins to show outside, too. Inside, our spirits are washed and we begin to think like Jesus. Outside, it shows in the good things we do. Continue to pray for people who don't know Jesus.

**Dig Out The Answers**

1. Why does Jesus say those who want to look good only on the outside are blind?
2. How do you become clean inside?

**In Your Own Words:** What did you learn? Write it down.

**My Prayer:** Thank you, Jesus, that your blood has made me clean inside because I have asked you into my life. Now, I can see.

**Today's Wise Words:** What you are inside is more important.

159

We are still talking about how to be clean inside out. As we discussed earlier, the Bible compares our sinful actions to leprosy. Unless the blood of Jesus washes us clean, we will remain in our sins, die and end up in hell. Remember the Pharisees? They did not know what it meant to be clean. They thought they were made clean by obeying so many rules. Washing hands before eating, washing of cups, kettles, fasting, and long prayers were some of the rules the Pharisees followed carefully. As you read today, the Pharisees came and watched Jesus' disciples. They noticed that Jesus' disciples did not always wash their hands before eating. They didn't know God accepted people only when they have been made clean inside. Being a Christian is not about following rules. First you will be clean, when the blood of Jesus washes you; and from then on you obey the Holy Spirit.

It doesn't matter whether you kneel to pray or stand to pray. It doesn't matter whether you pray aloud or pray in your head. It doesn't matter whether there are shouts of Amens and Hallelujahs in your church or not. Those things don't save a sinner. Only Jesus can make you clean. Are you saved?

**Dig Out The Answers**
1. If you follow all the rules in your church, will you be made clean?
2. How do you become clean?
**In Your Own Words:** What did you learn? Write it down.
**My Prayer:** God, please help me know that I'm saved only because I asked Jesus to come into my life, not by following the church rules.

**Today's Wise Words:** Rules don't save; Jesus saves.

160

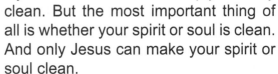

# The Heart and the Stomach

**READ**

Mark
7:17-19

Day 145

The disciples asked Jesus to explain how one becomes clean or unclean. Being clean means God has accepted you as his child, because you have asked Jesus into your life. Being unclean means you are not God's child, because you don't have Jesus in your life. It has nothing to do with germs. Of course, if you refuse to wash your dirty hands before eating, you may get germs into your body and fall sick. So you must be careful to keep your body clean. But the most important thing of all is whether your spirit or soul is clean. And only Jesus can make your spirit or soul clean.

Jesus explains that it's not what you put into your body that makes you unclean. Some of the things outside that we put into our bodies are food and drink. What makes us sinners or unclean is what comes out of our hearts. The wrong things we do are what make us unclean. Unless Jesus changes our sinful hearts, we are still sinners, no matter how many times we wash down or follow rules.

**Dig Out The Answers**
1. Will food or drink make you unclean?
2. What are the things which make us unclean and where do they come from?
**In Your Own Words:** What did you learn? Write it down.
**My Prayer:** Thank Jesus that his blood makes us clean.

**Today's Wise Words:** Jesus makes our whole life clean if we ask him.

**READ**

Mark
7:20-23

**Day 146**

# The Fruit of Sinful Hearts

Jesus talked about the things that come out the heart of sinners or wrongdoers. Do you know all people in the world are wrongdoers until they give their lives to Christ? Can you list some of the wrong things from our hearts that show in our actions? There are bad thoughts, stealing, killing, envy, bad language, swearing, lies, and many others. You realize that there's no way anybody can say they are clean before God. You can try to be good, but your own efforts will never make you good enough for God to accept you as his child. God is so good, so holy. He realized that there was no way anyone in the world would be clean. That's why Jesus came and died to save us. Jesus died on the cross so we would not die.

All who accept Jesus are washed in his blood. From then on, God sees their hearts as clean even though they may do wrong things sometimes. When Jesus makes a heart clean, that person is given power by the Holy Spirit to say "no" to sin and "yes" to living right.

**Dig Out The Answers**
1. List some of the evil things that come from our hearts.
2. Can anyone in the world stop sinning? How does God solve this problem?
**In Your Own Words:** What did you learn? Write it down.

**My Prayer:** God, I thank you for teaching me that my heart is full of sin, but Jesus' blood has power to make it holy. Amen.

**Today's Wise Words:** The heart without Jesus is full of sin.

162

## READ

### Joy in Heaven

**Luke 15:3-7**

**Day 147**

Jesus says that there is great rejoicing in heaven when a sinner turns to God. For the past few days we have been reading passages about how we can become clean. Now, Jesus tells us what takes place in heaven when one person turns to him. There's a great shout of joy in heaven. Why? Because one more person has escaped hell, one more person has come into the light; one more person is going to keep sin from spreading in the world.

The Father, the Son, and the Holy Spirit are one God, and all the angels join with God to rejoice when one person gets saved. We must have the same attitude. We rejoice when we hear that a family member or a friend has come to know Jesus. God, like a good shepherd, is always out there, calling out to people to follow him. You can work with God by praying and telling others about Jesus. God wants all Christians to be his special helpers.

**Dig Out The Answers**

1. What happens in heaven when one person comes to know Jesus?
2. Why do you think there is great rejoicing in heaven?
3. How do we become God's special helpers?

**In Your Own Words:** What did you learn? Write it down.

**My Prayer:** God, help me shout for joy when others come to know Jesus.

**Today's Wise Words:** There's rejoicing in heaven over one sinner who repents.

163

# Clean Your Dirty Feet

**Day 148**

Jesus says in this passage that people who have a bath and then go out for a walk only need to wash their dirty feet when they come back in. What did Jesus mean?

When you take a bath you become clean. Right! In the same way, when we are washed in the blood of Jesus we become clean, our whole person – spirit, soul, and body. You only have to ask Jesus to come into your life once, and that's that. When he comes in, he washes you from all your sins and you become clean once and for all. It's just as if you've taken a bath. That's what Jesus meant by a person who has had a bath.

Now, what does it mean to wash your feet? Even though God has forgiven us all our past, present and future sins, and we are on our way to heaven, we do not stop sinning or doing wrong things. God knows that sometimes we will give in when tempted. When we sin, it is as if we *dirtied* our feet – little lies, disliking somebody, not sharing, not doing your chores, being mean, talking back to your parents and the like. We wash our dirty feet by going to God in prayer and telling him that we are sorry. We then ask the Holy Spirit to help us not to do the same wrong things all over again. When we do that, it means we have "washed our feet". Remember to tell God you are sorry whenever you do the wrong thing.

**Dig Out The Answers**
1. How does a person become clean?
2. How does a person become clean through Jesus?
3. How do we dirty our feet? What do we do to wash our feet?
**In Your Own Words:** What did you learn? Write it down.
**My Prayer:** God, remind me to say sorry when I do wrong things, in Jesus' name.

**Today's Wise Words:** Wash your dirty feet by confessing your sins often.

# The Word Makes You Clean

**Day 149**

**John 15:3**

Jesus says in this verse that you are clean because of *the word* he has spoken to you. The word of God is the Bible. How does the word of God make you clean? As we said before, even though we are Christians we do sin, sometimes. When we do, we go to God in prayer and tell him we are sorry, and then we become clean. Good!

How do you know you are doing the wrong thing? We

know what is right from wrong when we make a habit of reading the word of God. The more you read the word of God and do what it says, the more you are able to say "no" to sin. The more you know and obey the word of God, the more you enjoy being a Christian. So continue to stay clean and happy as a Christian, reading the word of God and obeying it.

### Dig Out The Answers

1. According to Jesus, what makes us clean?
2. How does the word of God help you stay clean?

**In Your Own Words:** What did you learn? Write it down.

**My Prayer:** God, help me read the Bible, so I can stay clean, in Jesus' name. Amen.

**Today's Wise Words:** The word of God makes me clean as I obey it.

# Friends of a Paralyzed Man

The friends of a paralyzed man heard that Jesus was in Capernaum. A paralyzed man cannot walk. They wanted their friend to walk again. They decided to take their friend to Jesus. But when they got to the house there was a big crowd. They couldn't enter the room where Jesus was. They decided to get their friend through the roof of the house. It was a hard and dirty work they had to do. What wonderful friends the paralyzed man had! Finally, they lowered their friend through the roof. When Jesus saw their faith, he told the paralyzed man that his sins were forgiven. There's an important lesson here for us to learn. It was the faith of the paralyzed man's friends that brought him to Jesus. In the same way God wants us to bring our family members and friends to hear Jesus, so that their sins will be forgiven, just like he did for the paralyzed man. You can do this by inviting family and friends to church, or crusades, pray for them or talk to them about Christ. Like the friends of the paralyzed man, sometimes we may need to do some hard and even dirty jobs for our friends in order to bring them to Jesus. You may need to help them clean up the backyard, or help out with the dishes and other chores, so that you can go to a church service together. And sometimes you may need to be patient with their rudeness, meanness, and ugly jokes, which could be hard on any one. Will you be a wonderful friend today?

**Dig Out The Answers**
1. Why did the friends bring the paralyzed man to Jesus?
2. What did the paralyzed man receive when he was brought to Jesus?
**In Your Own Words:** What did you learn? Write it down.
**My Prayer:** Pray for others to come and know Jesus.

**Today's Wise Words:** Show your faith by bringing others to Jesus.

166

# Jesus Has Power to Forgive Sins

**Mark 2:6-12**

**Day 151**

We are still reading the story of the paralyzed man and his friends. Jesus told the paralyzed man that his sins were forgiven. The teachers of the law thought Jesus was making himself equal to God by forgiving sins. They knew only God had power to forgive sins. But Jesus knew what they were thinking and there and then Jesus showed them, as the Son of God, he really did have power to forgive sins. He turned to the paralyzed man, told him to take his mat and go home. The paralyzed man's sins were forgiven, and so he received healing. He could walk again, and all who were there were amazed. Jesus is still able to make the lame *walk* today, so you pray and trust God for any you know who can't walk. In the same way, a person without Jesus is paralyzed spiritually. But when such a person accepts Jesus as Lord and Savior, he is able to *walk in the truth* and follow Jesus daily. Nobody can *walk* the way to heaven unless his sins are forgiven. The way to heaven is through Jesus Christ alone. Are you walking with God? Or are you paralyzed?

**Dig Out The Answers**

1. What did Jesus do for the paralyzed man to show that he has power to forgive sins?
2. What happened to the paralyzed man when Jesus talked to him?
3. What do you do to be able to walk with God?

**In Your Own Words:** What did you learn? Write it down.

**My Prayer:** Thank God that you can walk with him because you have Jesus. Pray for healing for the sick.

**Today's Wise Words:** Walk with God.

167

# Walk by Day

**READ**

John
11:9-11

Day 152

Jesus is saying in this passage that there are twelve hours in a day that we all have to do our work. Nobody can make the day any longer or any shorter. Jesus had work to do while here on earth and he did it. When you read verse 11, it tells you that Jesus was getting ready to go and raise Lazarus from the dead. That was the work he had to do then. You also have work to do while you are alive and God wants you to do it while there is light. Jesus is the light that helps you do the work of God. What is the work of God? The work of God is to believe that Jesus is the Son of God who saves us from our sins. Have you done that work? Darkness refers to a life without God. Those who walk in darkness walk in disobedience because they have not accepted Jesus as Lord and Savior. Nobody sees well in darkness, you will stumble and hurt yourself. This is what happens to those who don't have Jesus in their lives. They don't know where to turn to when they have problems, so they stumble, fall, hurting themselves over and over again. What do you think happens when Jesus forgives your sins? You follow him. Do you think the paralyzed man whose sins were forgiven followed Jesus? Yes. He began walking "in daylight", meaning he was walking with Jesus. When we walk with Jesus, we see clearly where we are going, because he leads the way.

**Dig Out The Answers**
1. Why is it important to walk by daylight? 2. Who is that light?
3. What happens if you walk in darkness?
4. What does it mean to walk in darkness?
5. What is the work of God?
**In Your Own Words:** Write down what you learned today.
**My Prayer:** God, help me continue to follow Jesus so I can finish all the work God wants me to do on this earth, in Jesus name.

**Today's Wise Words:** God has work for me to do in this world.

## READ

**John 8:23-24**

**Day 153**

# Jesus Is from Above

Jesus was talking to the Pharisees. Jesus told them, "I am from above", which meant, he came from heaven. Jesus came from his Father in heaven. Who does Jesus claim to be? The Christ. Christ is the same as Messiah. God promised to send Christ to come and save us from our sins. So, if you don't believe that Jesus has come to save you from your sins, you will die in your sins. You will die in your sins means God is not your

Father so you'll not make it to heaven. Remember, the story we read two days ago! Jesus showed that he had authority to forgive sins. He forgave the paralyzed man his sins, and so he could walk again. Jesus came from heaven to save us from our sins by dying on the cross. Have your sins been forgiven?

### Dig Out The Answers

1. Who does Jesus claim to be?
2. Why did Jesus come down to earth from heaven?
3. What do you have to do so you won't die in your sins?

**In Your Own Words:** What did you learn? Write it down.

**My Prayer:** God, I thank you for sending Jesus, so I won't die in my sins. Amen.

**Today's Wise Words:** Jesus came from heaven.

169

# Jesus Sets Us Free

**Day 154**

Would you like to memorize John 8:36? *"So if the Son sets you free, you will be free indeed."* Wonderful! Jesus teaches a very important lesson here. He says that everyone who sins is a slave to sin. A slave does only his master's will. If we are slaves to sin, the only thing we do is sin, doing wrong things. What Jesus is saying is this: until he sets us free, we are all slaves to sin, just like the paralyzed man we read about a few days ago.

How does Jesus set us free? He sets us free from slavery by forgiving us our sins. Yes, when you ask Jesus to forgive your sins, he washes you in his blood, and you are set free. You are free to do what is right by walking with Jesus. You are no more a slave, but a child of God. Do you know that only the children belong to a family and not the slave or servant? When you become a child of God, you belong to the family of God, and you are free!

## Dig Out The Answers

1. Who is a slave to sin?
2. Who can set you free from being a slave to sin?
3. What do you do to become part of God's family?

**In Your Own Words:** Write down what you learned.

**My Prayer:** You belong to the family of God if Christ lives in you. If so, thank God that you are no more a slave to sin. Amen.

**Today's Wise Words:** The Son (Christ) sets us free

# Leave Your Life of Sin

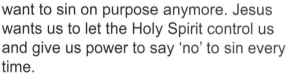

The important sentence in this passage I want you to think about is this – *"Go now and leave your life of sin."* Jesus spoke these words to a certain woman who was caught doing the wrong thing. Jesus forgave her and told her to stop living a life of sin. For the past two days we have been talking about Jesus forgiving us our sins. The question now is; how do we live after we have been forgiven? Jesus tells her and us not to

want to sin on purpose anymore. Jesus wants us to let the Holy Spirit control us and give us power to say 'no' to sin every time.

When we listen to the Holy Spirit, it means we are *walking* in the light and in the truth.

Do you think the paralyzed man who was forgiven and healed went back to his old way of life, doing wrong things all over again? I don't think so. He went away rejoicing, and trying to *live* and *walk* right. Today, decide to obey the word of God at all times. You may slip into sin sometimes, and when you do, say sorry to God. But make a clear effort to turn away from that sin and ask the Holy Spirit to help you live right.

### Dig Out The Answers

1. What does Jesus want us to leave when we are forgiven?
2. Who gives us power to live right?

**In Your Own Words:** What did you learn? Write it down.

**My Prayer:** God, help me leave my life of sin and live right in Jesus' name. Amen.

**Today's Wise Words:** Go now and leave your life of sin!

## READ

# The Centurion's Servant

**Matthew 8:5-7**

**Day 156**

When Jesus entered a town called Capernaum, a centurion (an officer of the Roman army) came to ask him for help. His servant was sick, paralyzed and suffering. He wanted Jesus to heal him. Isn't this army officer a kind man? He was humble too – he could have just sent one of the soldiers who worked under him, but he came himself to Jesus. An army officer or a centurion was the boss of a hundred soldiers.

When you are made leader of a group, remember to be kind to all the members, and don't boss over them. Be ready to help out when any of them has a problem just as the army officer did for his servant. See how Jesus was willing to go immediately with the army officer to heal his servant. No matter what problem you have, remember to go to Jesus. He is always willing to help you just as he helped the army officer in today's story.

### Dig Out The Answers

1. What was the kind thing the army officer did?
2. What did Jesus do about the army officer's request?
3. What does Jesus' answer teach you?

**In Your Own Words:** Write down what you learned.

**My Prayer:** God, teach me to be kind whenever I'm made the leader of a group, in Jesus' name, Amen.

**Today's Wise Words:** Be a kind leader not a bossy one.

# The Faith of The Centurion

**READ**
**Matthew**
**8:8-13**

This centurion was no ordinary man. He had so much faith in Jesus that he only wanted Jesus to speak, and he was sure the words of Jesus would make his servant well again. Do you remember how God made the world? Yes. God just spoke words, and everything you see around came to be. That's how great God is. That's how great Jesus is. The centurion understood one important thing – Jesus is the boss over diseases and all that there is. As an army officer, he knew that the soldiers under him had to obey his commands. He understood that a boss had to be obeyed. So, if Jesus indeed is the boss over everything, of things seen and things not seen, then everything will have to obey Jesus' commands.

Did the disease leave the centurion's servant when Jesus spoke? Yes, of course. Jesus proved again that he has authority over diseases as the Son of God. Now that you know that Jesus is indeed the boss over everything, be bold and take your worries to him. He is more than able to help you.

**Dig Out The Answers**
1. What did the centurion have that surprised Jesus?
2. Why did he have this much faith in Jesus words?
3. If Jesus is the boss of everything then everything has to _____ him.

**In Your Own Words:** What did you learn? Write it down.

**My Prayer:** If you know of someone who is terribly sick, ask Jesus to heal him or her.

**Today's Wise Words:** Jesus has power to heal people suffering from terrible diseases.

# Have Faith in God

We read about the faith of the army officer or centurion yesterday. Jesus was very pleased that he had faith. Faith is very important to the Christian. It helps us obey and not panic when faced with difficult situations. In today's verse, Jesus tells us to have faith in God. It is good to trust your father, or mother, brother, sister or friend, but for the big things you need to have faith in Jesus alone.

God may use your father, brother, sister, friend or relative to do things for you. Yes. But Jesus tells us to put our faith in God alone. Would you like to memorize this verse? *"'Have faith in God', Jesus answered."* Mark 11:22 (NIV)

## Dig Out The Answers

1. Who should you put your faith in?
2. Why do you think it's very important to put your faith in God?

**In Your Own Words:** What did you learn? Write it down.

**My Prayer:** God, help me put my faith in you alone, in Jesus' name. Amen.

**Today's Wise Words:** Have faith in God alone!

174

## READ

John
14:8-12

# Have Faith in Jesus

Jesus says in this passage that the Father is in him, and he is in the Father. That means he and his Father are one. And because Jesus and God the Father are one, we can have complete faith in him. The *words* Jesus spoke showed in the miracles he performed. The miracles Jesus performed were his *works*. The words Jesus spoke and the works that followed proved that Jesus came from God. So, we must believe in him. Jesus didn't say one thing then turned around to do something else. Whatever he said, he also did. Jesus promised that when we put our faith in him, we'd do what he did and even greater things. This is what Jesus meant by "doing greater things" - we together as believers would be his hands and feet, going throughout the world and telling people the good news.

When Jesus was on earth, he was only one person. When he ascended into heaven, he sent the Holy Spirit into our hearts. And now, we (Christians) go so many places preaching the word. Many lives are saved. But it is still Jesus working through us by His Holy Spirit. Have faith in him!

**Dig Out The Answers**

1. From the passage, what does Jesus want us to believe about him?

2. When Jesus was on earth what did he do?

3. Jesus promised that we'd do the things he did and more. List some of things he wants us to do.

**In Your Own Words:** Write down what you learned.

**My Prayer:** God, teach me to put my faith in Jesus, so I can do "greater things". Amen.

**Today's Wise Words:** "You'll do greater things because I am going to the Father."

## Jesus' Miracles Bring People to God

What did the crowd do? They put their faith in Jesus. Why? They saw the miracles that Jesus performed. Jesus made the blind see and the lame walk. He healed lepers and many other sicknesses. The miracles Jesus performed proved that Jesus was really the Christ, the "anointed" Savior of the world ("Christ" or "Messiah" means anointed.) But do you know the greatest miracle of all? When Jesus comes into someone's life, he changes that person. Did you ever hear of an uncle who was maybe a drunk who came to Jesus and stopped drinking completely? Did you ever hear of criminals in prison who gave their lives to Christ and have since stopped robbing banks, killing people and doing other bad things? The greatest miracle is that God can change the heart of people. Look at your own life and see how God helps you by his power to do what is right. These are the things that should help us continue to put our faith in Jesus, just as the crowd did in today's verse.

**Dig Out The Answers**

1. Why did the crowd put their faith in Christ?
2. Who is the Christ? What does Christ mean?
3. What is the greatest miracle of all?

**In Your Own Words:** Write down what you learned.

**My Prayer:** God, thank you that the greatest miracle in my life is that Jesus has changed my heart, so I can love you and do what pleases you. Amen.

**Today's Wise Words:** My changed life is a miracle.

# Jesus Heals in His Own Way

Jesus healed a man who could neither hear nor talk. The people who brought the deaf and mute man wanted Jesus to lay his hands on him. But Jesus did not do that. Rather, he put his fingers in his ears and spit on his tongue. Then he prayed and said, "Be opened!" When we go to God, we sometimes want to tell him how to answer our prayers. But that is not the right way. Jesus healed the deaf and mute man not by laying his hands on him, as his friends wanted him to, rather he put his fingers in his ears, and spat on his tongue. God heals us using different means that seem best to him. All we have to do is to ask him to heal us when we are sick or when someone dear to us is sick. Jesus has power to heal any disease, the way he wants. Have faith in him.

## Dig Out The Answers

1. What did Jesus do to heal the man in the story?
2. Jesus healed the man his own way and not the way those who brought him wished. What does this teach you about what you ask in prayer?

**In Your Own Words:** What did you learn? Write it down.

**My Prayer:** God, help me know that Jesus heals me, or my dear ones *his way*, whenever I ask him.

**Today's Wise Words:** Jesus heals his way, not my way.

Yesterday, we read about the deaf and mute man Jesus healed. The man began hearing and speaking clearly. He was a happy man that day. The people around were amazed. They were happy about the miracle Jesus had performed. They said, "He has done everything well".

You should remember everyday that Jesus does everything well. Things done *well* are things done without mistakes or shoddiness. So, when you take anything to the Lord in prayer, have faith that he is going to answer it well. When your life is in Jesus' hands, remember that everything is well with you. Jesus does everything well. The crowd that saw the miracles he performed could say that. You should also be able to say that Jesus does everything well when you look at what he is doing in your life.

### Dig Out The Answer

Jesus does all things well, and because my life is in his hands, it is _____.

**In Your Own Words:** What did you learn? Write it down.

**My Prayer:** Father God, help me understand more and more that Jesus does all things well. Amen.

**Today's Wise Words:** Jesus does everything well.

178

# Sing Praises to God

**Day 163**

Remember the story about the deaf and mute man that Jesus healed? Good. Jesus healed his hearing and his speech. When the Holy Spirit comes into our lives, he heals our spirits. He touches our spiritual tongues, so we can tell others about God. We are not mute anymore. Today's passage tells us why Jesus heals our spiritual tongues. So, we can speak and sing of God's great love. Jesus

wants us to tell others about his love, that he never fails, and that he can always be trusted. Speak and sing about God's power, goodness, and love, with your tongue.

**Dig Out The Answer**

Why does Jesus heal our spiritual tongues?

**In Your Own Words:** Write down what you learned.

**My Prayer:** God, help me sing and tell of your love, goodness and faithfulness.

**Today's Wise Words:** Sing of the Lord's great love forever.

# READ

**John 8:47**

## I belong to God

Jesus says in this verse that we hear what God says when we belong to him. Those who hear God understand his word and obey it. You don't hear God if you don't belong to him. Those who have accepted Jesus as their Lord and Savior belong to God. Just as Jesus healed the physical deafness of the man we read about a few days ago, he also heals the spiritual deafness of all who come to him to save them, so they can hear God's word, understand it and obey it. What a wonderful Savior! Remember that the Holy Spirit keeps

working in the hearts of those who are not saved, so they also can hear and come to Jesus to save them.

**Dig Out The Answers**

1. When you are spiritually deaf you don't hear what God _____.
2. He who belongs to God ___ what God says.

**In Your Own Words:** What did you learn? Write it down.

**My Prayer:** God, I thank you for healing me of spiritual deafness, so I can hear what you say, understand and obey it, in Jesus' name.

**Today's Wise Words:** I hear God because I belong to him.

# Jesus Walks on Water

After Jesus had fed the five thousand men, he sent his disciples away on a boat to Bethsaida, and he himself went up on a mountain to pray. The disciples tried all night to row their boat, but a howling wind prevented them from rowing. Jesus knew that they were having problems so he went to help them out. He did an amazing thing: he walked on the water.

The disciples thought it was a ghost and got scared. Often, we imagine scary things when we are afraid. Remember that because Jesus is always with us, a ghost or an evil spirit cannot do us any harm. Jesus told them, "Take courage! It is I. Don't be afraid". Did you ever hear of someone walking on water? Only Jesus could. Jesus has power over nature – sea, rivers, mountains, wind and rain, and all the things in nature you can think of. When you go swimming or fishing in the lake, Jesus is with you. When you go skiing on the mountain, Jesus is with you. When you go camping in the woods, Jesus is with you. So if you run into a problem, call on him, and he will find his own way to help you out.

**Dig Out The Answers**

1. What did Jesus do here to show that he has power over nature?

2. What does this teach you about Jesus?

**In Your Own Words:** What did you learn? Write it down

**My Prayer:** Father, I thank you that you created everything in the universe by your Word, and that Jesus is the Word and created it all with you. Thank you that you have complete power over the universe, which you made. Amen.

**Today's Wise Words:** The winds obey Jesus.

# Jesus' Authority Over the Storm

Jesus and his disciples were in a boat again. An angry storm swept over the boat. Well, it looked like they were about to drown. The disciples were very afraid. But Jesus was sleeping. The disciples went and woke him up. They said, "Lord save us. We're going to drown." Jesus got up and told the winds and the waves to be calm. And it was so. What a Savior! Jesus shows again in today's story that everything in nature is under his control. All nature has to obey him, because he created them. You can also call out to Jesus if you find yourself in a storm, or flood, tornado, hurricane or a thunderstorm. He has promised to help, when you call to him.

## Dig Out The Answers

1. What did the disciples do when they found themselves caught in a furious storm?
2. What do you do when faced with a problem?
3. What did Jesus do when they called to him?
4. Jesus' action teaches you that he is ready to _____ in time of trouble.

**In Your Own Words:** Write down what you learned.

**My Prayer:** God, I thank you that Jesus has power over the winds and waves. Amen.

**Today's Wise Words:** Jesus is able to save me in a storm.

# A Miracle for a Little Boy

**Day 167**

One day a man brought his only son to Jesus to heal him. The boy was suffering from an unusual disease. An evil spirit used to attack the boy, and used to make him scream and foam on the mouth till he looked dead. Jesus' disciples could not heal the boy while Jesus was away because they didn't have much faith. When Jesus arrived he told the demon or evil spirit to stop attacking the boy. The evil spirit obeyed Jesus and left the boy alone. The little boy was well again. There are evil spirits out there, which sometimes make people sick, but Jesus has power over them. Evil spirits or demons are fallen angels that work with the devil who is also called Satan. All they do is evil, evil, evil. When you call to Jesus, they leave because they are afraid of Jesus. When you have Jesus in your life, evil spirits are afraid to touch you. Always call to Jesus when you are afraid and he will help you.

**Dig Out The Answers**

1. Why couldn't the disciples heal the boy attacked by the evil spirit?
2. What did Jesus do to heal the boy?
3. Does Jesus have power over evil spirits or demons?
4. Because Jesus has power over evil spirits I should not be __.

**In Your Own Words:** Write down what you learned.

**My Prayer:** God, help me not to fear evil spirits, because Jesus has complete power over them. Amen.

**Today's Wise Words:** Evil spirits obey Jesus.

183

# Jesus Casts Out a Mute Demon

Jesus drove out a demon from a man who was mute. The evil spirit or demon in the man made him lose his speech. He couldn't talk. Just like in yesterday's story, Jesus told the demon to leave the man, and it did. What an amazing Savior, Jesus is! Evil spirits can make people deaf, blind, unable to talk (mute), and can cause other diseases. Jesus still uses Christians today to drive out demons from people so they can live for Jesus. Jesus is still alive and working through Christians. This Jesus we serve has power over all evil. Put your trust in him, and you will not be afraid.

## Dig Out The Answers

1. What caused the man in today's story not to be able to talk?

2. What did Jesus do to heal him?
3. What does this teach you about Jesus' power?

**In Your Own Words:** Write down what you learned.

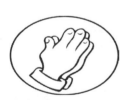

**My Prayer:** Father God, thank you that Jesus drove out demons that made people mute, and he still does miracles today. I ask you to touch and heal all who are mute, in Jesus' name. Amen.

**Today's Wise Words:** Demons can make people sick but Jesus has complete power over them.

184

# A Woman Finds Jesus' Hideout

**READ**
Mark
7:24-26

Here is another story that tells of Jesus' power over evil spirits. Jesus had gone to a place where he could be alone and probably have time to teach his disciples. But Jesus couldn't keep that secret for long. Before he knew it, a certain woman had found out, and there she was, kneeling and begging Jesus to come drive a demon out of her daughter. Only Jesus can drive a demon out of

people. Jesus is more powerful than all the evil, and evil spirits in the world. The woman who came to Jesus knew for certain that Jesus was able to drive out the demon from her daughter.

Do you also know for certain that Jesus is able to help you no matter how difficult a problem you bring to him? When we come to Jesus with a problem, we must believe with all our hearts that he is able to do what we ask. Jesus is the boss over everything in the world or universe – what we can see, and what we can't see. What a powerful Savior!

**Dig Out The Answers**
1. Why did the woman come to beg Jesus?
2. Do you think she believed Jesus could do something about her problem?
3. When we come to Jesus we must _____ that he is able to help us.

**In Your Own Words:** Write down what you learned today.

**My Prayer:** Lord God, I thank you that Jesus is everywhere now and I don't have to go looking for him to help me. I just have to pray. Amen.

**Today's Wise Words:** Jesus is only a prayer away.

# The Faith of the Gentile Woman

This is what Jesus said to the woman who came begging him to drive away an evil spirit from her daughter. Jesus said to the woman, *"the children must first be fed. It isn't right to take away their food and feed it to dogs."* You are wondering what Jesus meant by that. The *children* Jesus was referring to are the Israelites, also called Jews. Why did Jesus refer to the Jews as God's children? God chose the Jews, taught them his laws and his ways.

For a long time, only the Jews knew what God is like – his works, his character, his laws or commandments. Many came to learn about God through the Jews. The rest of the people in the world are called Gentiles. The *dogs* in Jesus' answer refer to the Gentiles who did not know the true God, until later. Jesus is not calling the Gentiles dogs. He was only using that as an expression. Jesus loves us all, whether Jews or Gentiles. Jesus was only testing the faith of the Gentile woman who came begging him to drive a demon from her daughter.

The woman refused to be put off, and she replied, *"but even the dogs under the table eat the children's crumbs"*. What did the Gentile woman mean by that? She meant that through the Jews, the Gentiles would also be blessed with miracles. This Gentile woman had faith that Jesus, who was a Jew, had come to bless both Jews and Gentiles together. He was not only going to feed the *children* and leave the *dogs*. I am sure many times you've dropped food to the cat or dog under the dining table. By doing that you are blessing your pet with food. The woman's answer showed that she had faith in Jesus. Do you have faith in Jesus to do what you ask him in prayer, too?

**My Prayer:** God, help me know that, sometimes you may not answer my prayers right away because you want to test me to see whether I have faith in you, in Jesus' name.

**Today's Wise Words:** Jesus loves both Jews and Gentiles.

# Jesus Casts a Demon Out of a Girl

Today we will finish the story about the woman who came begging Jesus to drive out a demon from her daughter. Yesterday, we read about the woman's faith in Jesus. She believed that Jesus came to save and bless both Jews and Gentiles. She had faith that even though she wasn't a Jew, Jesus was willing to bless her with a miracle too. Jesus was so pleased that this Gentile woman had faith in him. Jesus told her that because of her faith, her request had been granted, the demon had left her daughter.

Do you notice that, in this story, the girl was not brought to Jesus? The girl was at home and not with the mother, and yet Jesus was able to drive the demon out. It teaches us a wonderful lesson about Jesus. Even though we do not see Jesus physically standing or sitting by us, he is able to do what we ask him in prayer. It doesn't matter how far away the person you are praying for is, Jesus is everywhere and has the power to do anything you ask him to do, anywhere in the world, according to his will.

**Dig Out The Answers**
1. Did Jesus do what the woman asked for?
2. Which part of the story tells you that Jesus can heal somebody far away from where you ask?

**In Your Own Words:** Write down what you learned.

**My Prayer:** God, I thank you that Jesus can go anywhere in the world to help those I pray for. Amen.

**Today's Wise Words:** Jesus touches people I pray for, even if they are far from me.

187

# Jesus Has Authority Over Death

A ruler came to Jesus to help him. His daughter had died. He wanted Jesus to bring her back to life. What faith the man had! He was sure that Jesus was boss over death too. If Jesus told "death" to leave his daughter, "death" would have to obey, and his daughter would live again. Jesus got up immediately and went with him.

How loving Jesus is! When we are faced with big problems, he helps us. Do you believe Jesus can bring a dead person back to life even in our day? Yes. Many miracles take place in so many parts of the world when the good news is preached. Many are healed and some who are dead are brought back to life. If Jesus can wake a dead person up, then you must trust him to take care of you, no matter what. He is the boss even over death. Hallelujah!

**Dig Out The Answers**
1. What did the man ask Jesus' help for?
2. What did Jesus do? What does Jesus' action teach you?

**In Your Own Words:** What did you learn? Write it down.

**My Prayer:** God, I thank you that you have power to bring the dead back to life. Amen.

**Today's Wise Words:** God can bring the dead back to life.

# READ

## Dead Girl Brought to Life

**Matthew 9:23-26**

**Day 173**

Jesus went with the ruler all the way to his house. When they got to the house, there were people mourning for the girl. There were flute players and a big crowd. They were having a funeral ceremony. Jesus told them the girl was not dead, but only asleep. The crowd laughed at Jesus. The crowd didn't know that Jesus had power over death.

It happens to us, too. You may be faced with a problem and you believe Jesus is able to help you. But others tell you Jesus can't help. We must not believe what people tell us about Jesus. Let's read the Bible and know what Jesus is able to do and trust him to help us with all our problems. Jesus put the crowd outside, took the girl by the hand, and Voilá! She woke up! Jesus has power over death. Hallelujah! The news spread everywhere. So, you go spread the news, too – Jesus brings back the dead to life.

### Dig Out The Answers
1. Was Jesus able to bring the dead girl back to life?
2. What does that teach you about Jesus?

**In Your Own Words:** What did you learn? Write it down.

**My Prayer:** Thank Jesus that he still has power to bring the dead back to life.

**Today's Wise Words:** Know that Jesus has complete power over death.

**READ**

John
11:1-6

Day 174

# Lazarus Falls Sick

Mary, Martha and their brother Lazarus were Jesus' friends. Yes – Jesus made real good friends while here on earth. Jesus wants to be your friend, too. Jesus really loved Mary, Martha and Lazarus. So when Lazarus fell ill, Mary and Martha sent word to Jesus. Why do you think they sent for Jesus? They knew that Jesus was able to make him well. Yet, when Jesus heard that his friend Lazarus was sick, he did not go immediately. It makes you kind of wonder why. You'd think Jesus should have gone immediately, especially when it was such a close friend. Jesus knew that Lazarus would live again after this sickness. Jesus knows everything. Jesus wanted to wait because he wanted to bring glory to God.

What does it mean to bring glory to God? We bring glory to God when we obey him and not ourselves or the world. Jesus does not always answer our prayers immediately. Jesus waits for the right time to answer our prayers so all will see what a great, loving, and powerful God he is. So don't worry when God seems to keep long in answering your prayers. When he answers, you and all around you will see what he has done. And this will let others come to know Jesus too. God's time is the best.

**Dig Out The Answers**
1. Why doesn't Jesus always answer prayers immediately?
2. What does it mean to bring glory to God?
**In Your Own Words:** Write down what you learned.
**My Prayer:** God, help me trust you even if you don't answer my prayers as soon as I would like, in Jesus' name. Amen.

**Today's Wise Words:** God answers prayer to bring glory to his name.

# Jesus Talks about Lazarus' Death

**Day 175**

At the right time, Jesus told his disciples about Lazarus. Lazarus was dead. But Jesus knew that he wasn't going to stay dead. Remember what Jesus said about Lazarus yesterday – "his sickness won't end in death". Jesus told his disciples that he was going to wake him up. But Lazarus was dead, so what did Jesus mean by what he said, "his sickness won't end in death"?

Sometimes, that's how things look. They look dead. It seems like your sister would never share, or that friend of yours will never play with you again. Or, maybe you find it difficult to pay attention in class, or maybe your writing is so bad. You think those things will never change. But trust Jesus, who is able to solve all problems. What Jesus says actually happens. Only Jesus can solve the difficult problems you face as you grow up. Trust his word. If Jesus says something is not dead, believe it, it's not dead.

## Dig Out The Answer
1. Why should you trust what Jesus says about a problem rather than what others say?

**In Your Own Words:** Write down what you learned.

**My Prayer:** God, I thank you that your word always comes true. Amen.

**Today's Wise Words:** When Jesus says all is well with you, believe it.

191

# Martha Meets Jesus on the Way

**READ**

John
11:17-22

**Day 176**

We are still on the story of Lazarus. We read that Jesus arrived in Bethany four days after Lazarus had been buried. You'd think that Jesus was really too late. Probably the body of Lazarus was already going bad, beginning to rot. But Jesus is never late. Don't ever think that it is too late to ask Jesus for anything. Don't ever give up. Martha heard that Jesus was on his way. She went to meet him. She told Jesus that if he had been there, Lazarus wouldn't have died. Martha didn't understand this: God is still with us even when bad things happen to us.

There are bad things in the world, because people sin or keep doing wrong things. That's why Jesus came into the world. Jesus came into the world to save us, protect us and get us out of sin and trouble. That's why you need to go to him to help you when you have a problem. And one day, Jesus is coming back to take us into heaven, where you won't find any bad thing. Heaven is the happiest place, so look forward to it.

**Dig Out The Answers**
1. Why are there bad things in the world?
2. Why did Jesus come into this bad world?
3. Is Jesus with you in this world where bad things happen everyday?
**In Your Own Words:** Write down what you learned.

**My Prayer:** God, help me understand that you are always with me, even when bad things happen to me. Amen.

**Today's Wise Words:** Jesus' answers to our prayers are never late.

192

# Jesus – the resurrection and the life

**READ**
John
11:23-27

**Day 177**

We are still reading the story about Martha, Mary, and Lazarus. Martha had told Jesus that if he had been there Lazarus would not have died. Jesus told Martha that Lazarus was going to be brought back to life. But Martha did not understand what Jesus was saying. She didn't believe that Jesus was going to raise Lazarus right away. She was thinking of a time in the future where God would raise all who are dead back to life. Jesus told her, "I am the 'resurrection' and 'the life'". Jesus is the resurrection means Jesus is the only one who brings the dead back to life. Jesus is the life means only Jesus gives eternal life. Jesus told her that all who put their faith in him would live forever. Jesus is the Son of God, the Savior. That's why he has power to raise the dead. That's why when you put your faith in him you'll live forever with him in heaven. Martha knew that Jesus was the Son of God, our Savior. Jesus is the way to life.

**Dig Out The Answers**
1. Only Jesus can bring the dead back to _____ .
2. Those who put their faith in Jesus will never

_____.
3. Did Martha believe Jesus to be the Son of God?
**In Your Own Words:** Write down what you learned.

**My Prayer:** God I thank you that Jesus is the way to life. Amen.

**Today's Wise Words:** Believe Jesus when he says your problem has been solved.

# READ

## Jesus Wept

Martha went and told her sister, Mary, that Jesus had come over. Mary went to see Jesus, weeping as she went. She fell at Jesus' feet and told him that Lazarus wouldn't have died if he had been there. Jesus was touched by Mary's sadness.

Jesus was a good friend to Mary and Martha. He saw their sadness and wept along with them. Remember that Jesus is always with you, weeps with you when you are sad, and he is happy with you when you are happy. That's what good friends do for each other. Are you being a good friend to your friends at school or church? Be a good friend, today.

Jesus asked them to take him to the tomb where Lazarus had been laid. Guess what happened next?

**Dig Out The Answers**

1. What did Jesus do to share in Mary and Martha's sadness?
2. What does Jesus' action teach you about friendship?

**In Your Own Words**: What did you learn? Write it down.

**My Prayer:** Lord Jesus, teach me to be a good friend like you.

**Today's Wise Words:** Jesus weeps with me when I weep.

194

# Lazarus Is Raised Back to Life

A big miracle was about to take place in Bethany, but not in Martha and Mary's house. No! It was going to happen at the tomb where Lazarus had been laid. Jesus asked that the stone to the tomb be rolled away. This was a job for strong men. The job was done in no time. The

crowd was anxious to see what would happen next. What was Jesus going to do? First, Jesus prayed to his Father, thanking him for what he was about to do through him. Jesus asked the Father to perform this miracle so that those gathered there would know that he was the Son of God.

It is good to thank God for the things we ask for even when we haven't received them yet. Jesus knew that the Father always heard him when he prayed. Jesus always knew what his Father wanted, and those were the only things he did. As a child of God you too can know what God wants from you, by reading the Bible daily. When you know what God wants, you can pray and receive answers.

Jesus called out in a loud voice, "Lazarus, come out." And Lazarus walked out of the grave into the open. Praise the Lord! Jesus has power over death!

**Dig Out The Answers**
1. What was the first thing Jesus said in his prayer?
2. What should you also do whenever you go to God in prayer?
3. Did the Father listen to Jesus, and what happened?
**In Your Own Words:** Write down what you learned.
**My Prayer:** God, teach me to know what you want, and help me thank you when I pray, in Jesus' name.

**Today's Wise Words:** Thank God for hearing prayers that he has not answered yet.

# Why Did Jesus Perform all These Miracles?

**READ**
John
20:30-31

Today's passage tells us why Jesus performed all these miracles. Jesus performed many other miracles too, but not all of them were written down. Why did he perform all these miracles? The answer is, so that we will believe that he is the Christ, the Son of God. By believing in him, we will have life.

What does it mean to have life? To have life is to be in the presence of God here on earth, and then forever in heaven. What is the presence of God? The presence of God is the Holy Spirit. When you ask Jesus to come into your life, he sends the Holy Spirit into you to help you obey God and live a happy life. Those who refuse to accept Jesus into their hearts are dead, and will still be dead after their bodies die on earth. But, there is hope for all who are still living. They can still accept Christ today, and begin a good life here on earth and continue later in heaven when their bodies die. In heaven God will give us much more beautiful and perfect bodies that will never die. How wonderful!

**Dig Out The Answers**
1. Why did Jesus perform all those miracles?
2. By believing that Jesus Christ is the Son of God, you have _____.

**In Your Own Words:** Write down what you learned today.

**My Prayer:** Jesus, I thank you that you are the Son of God and because I believe in you, I can have life. Amen.

**Today's Wise Words:** Miracles point people to Jesus, the Savior.

196

# Jesus Is the Word

The miracles that Jesus performed showed that he was and still is the Christ, the Son of God. Yesterday, we also learned that by believing in him we have life. John, the man who wrote the verses you are reading today, gives another reason why we ought to believe that Jesus is Christ, the Son of God. Jesus has always been with the Father before anything came to be. Jesus, also called "the WORD", is God. Everything that was made in the universe was made through him.

This passage is telling us that Jesus is God, and created all things. That's why he was able to perform all those miracles. That's why evil spirits obeyed him by leaving those they attacked. That's why death obeyed him and even dead people came back to life. We believe firmly that Jesus is truly God. Because he is God he is able to save us from our sins. Say thank you to Jesus!

## Dig Out The Answers

1. Who made the universe and all that there is?
2. Who is called truly God in today's passage?
3. Why is Jesus the only one able to save us?

**In Your Own Words:** Write down what you learned.

**My Prayer:** Thank God for sending Jesus to be our Savior.

**Today's Wise Words:** Jesus is truly God.

## READ

**John 1:4-5**

**Day 182**

# Jesus Is Life

Yesterday we read that Jesus is truly God. That is why he is able to save us from our sins. Today, we learn another reason why Jesus is truly the Christ, the Son of God. Christ means "anointed" for a special work like being a king or a chief.

Jesus has life in him. A few days ago we talked about having life when you receive Jesus. Only Jesus is able to give us life, because he is the only one who has life. The life of Jesus has power in it. This power changes us, heals us, and delivers us from evil. The life Jesus gives has light in it, too. Light helps us see well. This light of Jesus that comes into our lives helps us see right from wrong. When you have light, you won't stumble in the dark. You have light and life if you have Jesus in your heart.

**Dig Out The Answers**

1. What does Jesus have that he alone can give to all who ask him?

2. How does the light of Jesus help us?

**In Your Own Words:** Write down what you learned.

**My Prayer:** Lord Jesus, I want to receive your gift of light and life. Amen.

**Today's Wise Words:** Jesus is true life, he has life, and he gives life.

198

# READ

## Jesus and Nicodemus

**Day 183**

Nicodemus was a Pharisee (See Day 18). Nicodemus had a question he wanted to ask Jesus. So one night he went to see Jesus. When you have a question for God, you read the Bible and pray. God uses the Bible to answer our questions. Nicodemus believed Jesus was sent from God, and he said so. Why did he believe that? He had heard and probably seen people Jesus had healed. Nicodemus was sure that only a man sent from God could perform these miracles.

When we read in the gospels about the many miracles Jesus performed, we also believe that God sent him into the world, like Nicodemus. When we look at the good character of other Christians, this also helps us to believe in Jesus. Jesus changes people. He saves them and helps them do what is right. The change in people's lives is the greatest miracle of all.

**Dig Out The Answers**
1. Why did Nicodemus believe that God sent Jesus?
2. Do you know of anyone who has received a miracle from Jesus?
3. What is the greatest miracle?
4. What do you do when you have a question about God?

**In Your Own Words:** Write down what you have learned.

**My Prayer:** Father, help me continue believing in Jesus, because you sent him.

**Today's Wise Words:** The Bible provides answers to questions we have about God.

199

# You Must Be Born Again

We are continuing the story of Nicodemus and Jesus. Jesus told Nicodemus that no one could see the kingdom of God unless that person was "born again". What did Jesus mean by "born again"?

If you invite Jesus to come into your heart he does come in. That makes a change in you, a big change, like being born all over again. How do you invite Jesus into your heart? First, tell Jesus you know you have done many bad things, and you tell him you believe that he came into the world to die for your sins. So ask him to forgive you all of your sins. Then ask him to be your Lord and Savior.

When Jesus becomes your Lord and Savior, it means he becomes the boss of your life. You follow him and obey him. So are you born again? Does Jesus live in your heart? If Jesus lives in your heart then you are born again and on your way to heaven.

**Dig Out The Answers**
1. What does it mean to be born again?
2. Are you born again? How do you know?

**In Your Own Words:** Write down what you learned.

**My Prayer:** Jesus, I ask you to come into my heart because you died to save me from sin. Be my Lord and Savior. Thank you, Holy Spirit, for helping me to receive Jesus into my heart. Amen.

*(If you have asked Jesus into your life before, just thank him for coming in.)*

**Today's Wise Words:** To be "born again" is to ask Jesus to come into your heart and give you a new start.

# Parable of the Sower Illustrated

### The Parables
*Parables were stories Jesus told to teach us great lessons.*

### Dig Out The Answer
Look at the hearts in the picture. Which one would be yours – the road, the rocky ground, the thorn bushes or the good soil?

**My Prayer:** God, make my heart good soil for your word to grow, in Jesus' name. Amen.

**Today's Wise Words:**          Jesus is the Sower.

# Parable of the Sower

Jesus tells the disciples the meaning of the parable you read yesterday. Jesus said the seed that the farmer scattered is the word of God. The word of God is all that God says in the Bible.

Do you remember the first seed fell on the path or along the road? The path or road stands for a certain kind of people. The birds stand for the devil. When people hear God's word, that Jesus has come to die to save us from sin, and they don't understand it, the devil snatches it away from them. There are people like that all around us. They've been hearing the word of God over and over again but they are still not saved. Jesus does not give up on such people. Jesus is still using Christians to preach the good news, hoping that they will hear and understand. We must pray for such people to pay attention to what they hear about Jesus, so they will be saved. Hearing the truth about Jesus, and believing it, is the only way to the kingdom of God. When you hear the word of God, and don't understand it, ask somebody who is able to explain to you. For example, you can ask your pastor at church, or your parents, or your teacher at Sunday school.

**Dig Out The answers**

1. The seed is the _____.
2. The birds stand for the ____who ____ the word from people who don't understand.
3. We must ____ for such people to _____ the word of God to be saved.

**In Your Own Words:** Write down what you learned.

**My Prayer:** God, help all these people who hear your word, to understand and give their lives to Jesus.

**Today's Wise Words:** Watch out! The devil steals God's word from people's hearts.

# Rocky Ground

Jesus describes another group of people. Remember the seeds that fell on rocky places, that quickly grew up but the sun scorched and killed them? Right. The rocky places stand for people who happily accept the word of God, but stop believing when they have problems, or when people treat them badly because they follow him. Have you sincerely asked Christ into your life? If so, Jesus wants you to hold firm to him even when friends make fun of you at school or in your neighborhood.

When you have a problem, or you need a good friend, or you want someone to play with, tell Jesus about it. Trust Jesus to help you when in trouble. We don't stop trusting him just because we have a problem. Those who stop trusting Jesus when they are in trouble are missing some of the blessings of God's kingdom. Jesus has all the power to help us in all our troubles. We must love Jesus and walk with him till the day we die. Jesus has promised to help us when we need him. We must remember to pray for those who have stopped believing in Jesus because they are facing many problems.

**Dig Out The Answers**

1. Is it okay to stop trusting Jesus when you are treated badly?
2. Can you really enjoy God's kingdom when you stop trusting Jesus as Lord and Savior?
3. We must keep ____ Jesus as Lord and Savior even in times of trouble.

**In Your Own Words:** Write down what you learned.

**My Prayer:** God, let me trust Jesus still as Lord and Savior even in bad times. Amen.

**Today's Wise Words:** Trust Jesus as Lord and Savior to the end.

203

# Thorn Bushes

The seeds that fell in the thorn bushes describe another group of people. These are also people who hear the word of God and believe immediately, but they don't believe with all their hearts. How do you know? Jesus tells us such people stop trusting him as Lord and Savior because they want to get rich, or because they are poor. Jesus wants us to trust him as both Lord and  Savior, whether we get richer or poorer. Jesus died for both the rich and the poor. Only Jesus can fix the problems that a rich kid may have, or the different problems a poor kid may have. We should never say that because Jesus is not helping me the way I want him to, he is no more my Savior and Lord. That would be a foolish thing to do. Jesus has saved us, and is preparing a wonderful home for us in heaven, where we will never need anything.

Do you know that those who stop believing in Jesus still don't get the help they need, anyways. So, it is better to trust Jesus, no matter what. He is able to help you now and bring you to heaven later.

**Dig Out The Answers**
1. Do you stop trusting Jesus because you are poor?
2. List some of the problems you think poor people have?
3. Only Jesus solves problems the best way, so it's best to ___ him everyday.
**In Your Own Words:** Write down what you learned.

**My Prayer:** God, never let me stop trusting you, even if I should have many needs, in Jesus' name. Amen.

**Today's Wise Words:** I'll trust Jesus with my big needs.

## READ

**Matthew 13:23**

# Good Soil

Jesus describes the last group of people as the good soil. Every one of us should like to be in this group. The seeds, which fell on good soil are those who hear the word of God, understand it and bear fruit. Every true believer or Christian bears fruit. What kind of fruit do they bear? The fruit a Christian bears is called the fruit of the Holy Spirit. The fruit of the Spirit is love, joy, peace, kindness, goodness, faithfulness, gentleness and self-control. The Holy Spirit comes and lives in all who accept Jesus as Lord and Savior. The Holy Spirit then helps us do what is good – loving and all that is listed above. This is how you know a person has come to know Christ. Ask the Holy Spirit to help you bear more fruit. The more we obey the Holy Spirit, the more we bear fruit.

**Dig Out The Answers**

1. The good soil are those who hear God's word, understand it and _____ fruit.
2. List the fruit of the Holy Spirit.
3. How do you bear more fruit?

**In Your Own Words:** What did you learn? Write it down.

**My Prayer:** God, help me bear more fruit because I understand your word and have given my life to Jesus. Amen

**Today's Wise Words:** Those who understand God's word bear lots of fruit.

# Parable of the Pharisee and the Tax Collector

This story tells about two men who went to pray in the Temple. The tax collector is the "good soil" that Jesus talked about in the parable of the Sower. The Pharisee is like the "rocky ground" in that same parable. Why is that so? The tax collector understood that he was a sinner who needed salvation. No one can come to Jesus unless he understands that he is a sinner who needs Jesus to save him.

The Pharisee thought he was good enough, and didn't need salvation. He was telling about all the good things he did. Such a person will not come to Jesus. Such people do not understand the word of God. They do not understand that good works cannot bring them into the kingdom of God, unless they give their lives to Jesus. Pray that God will help your relatives and friends who are not saved to understand that they are sinners and need Jesus to save them from their sins.

**Dig Out The Answers**
1. Who is the "good soil" in today's story?
2. The tax collector's heart is like "good soil" because he realized he was a sinner who needed to _____.
3. Who is the "rocky ground" in today's story? The Pharisee's heart is like "rocky ground" because he thought his _____ would bring him into God's kingdom.
**In Your Own Words:** Write down what you learned.

**My Prayer:** God, I thank you for helping me understand that I am a sinner who needs to come to Jesus, so I can be part of your kingdom.

**Today's Wise Words:** I must understand I am a sinner who needs Christ to save me.

# READ

## The Prayer that God Hears

**Luke 18:14**

**Day 191**

We are continuing the parable of the Pharisee and the tax collector. Jesus said that the tax collector's prayer was heard and not the Pharisee's. When we accept that we are sinners who need Jesus, God hears our prayer. The tax collector depended on God to save him. He was humble. The Pharisee's prayer was not heard, why? The Pharisee depended on his own good works to save him. He didn't depend on God's goodness. He was proud of the good things he did. But, do you know that God says all our good works are like filthy rags? The good things we do will never bring us into the kingdom of God. Like the tax collector, everybody in the world has to be washed in the blood of Jesus. Your sins must be forgiven and then you can be a member of God's kingdom. The tax collector went home "justified". Justified means, God had forgiven all his sins, and he had become righteous before God. Are your sins forgiven too?

**Dig Out The Answer**
Why was the prayer of the Tax collector answered?

**In Your Own Words:** Write down what you learned.

**My Prayer:** God, I thank you my sins are forgiven through Jesus, and I am now justified before you. Amen.

**Today's Wise Words:** God shows favor to the humble.

207

READ

Matthew
19:16-22

# The Rich Young Man

Day 192

The story is about a rich young man. This rich young man came to Jesus with a question. He wanted to know what good deeds he had to do so he could have eternal life. Jesus told him to keep the commandments. But the rich young man responded that he had kept all those commandments. So Jesus told him to go sell all that he had and give to the poor. Did he do that? No! He was very rich and didn't want to part with his riches. This rich young man's

heart is like the thorn bushes we talked about in the parable of the Sower. Remember, the seeds that fell in the thorn bushes are people who want to be rich and worry about their needs so much that they stop trusting Jesus as Lord and Savior. None of us would want to be like this rich young man. He would rather be rich here on earth, die, and go to hell. Is that wise? No! When we make Jesus our Lord and Savior, he is able to give us all that we need. You have to trust Jesus to do that for you. The rich man couldn't trust Jesus to meet his needs if he gave everything he had to the poor.

## Dig Out The Answers

1. What kept the young man from following Jesus?
2. The rich young man's heart is like the _____ where the seeds fell.

**In Your Own Words:** What did you learn? Write it down.

**My Prayer:** God, help the rich people in the world to depend on Jesus to save them from their sins, in Jesus' name. Amen.

**Today's Wise Words:** Riches cannot save.

208

# READ
## Matthew 13:24-30

## Wheat and Weeds Illustrated

Day 193

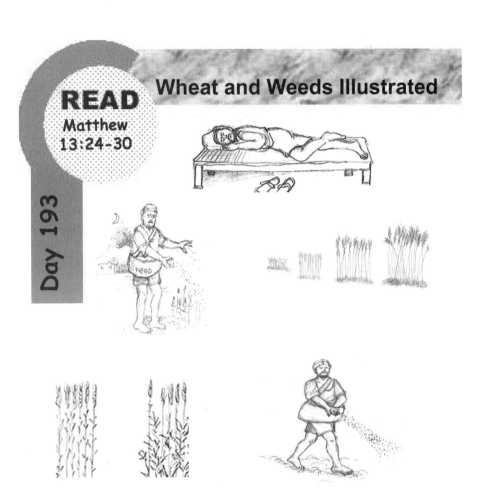

### Dig Out The Answers
1. Arrange the illustrations above in the order in which the story is told in the Bible. Use the numbers 1, 2, 3, 4, 5 and so on to show the order.
2. Is wheat something good?
3. Are weeds something good? Are you wheat or weeds?

**In Your Own Words:** Write down what you learned.

**My Prayer:** God, help me continue to grow as a good seed, in Jesus' name. Amen.

**Today's Wise Words:** The good seed are those who belong to God's kingdom.

209

# The Disciples Were Good Students

**READ**

Matthew 13:36

We read the parable of the wheat and weeds yesterday and arranged the pictures in the order that things happened in the story.

Today, we read that Jesus' disciples came to ask him about the meaning of the parable. They didn't understand the story Jesus told about the wheat and weeds.

Do you know that the disciples were good students?

Yes, they were. They asked Jesus for explanation whenever they couldn't understand what he taught. Jesus wants all of us to be good students. Jesus wants us to ask questions when we read a story in the Bible we don't understand. You can ask your parents, or Sunday school teacher, or pastor or any grown-up Christian you know. It is good to want to understand what God's word says. When we understand what God's word says, we can obey it better.

## Dig Out The Answers

1. Why were Jesus' disciples good students?
2. How can you become a good student of God's word too?

**In Your Own Words:** What did you learn? Write it down.

**My Prayer:** God, give me boldness to ask questions about things I don't understand in the Bible, in Jesus' name. Amen.

**Today's Wise Words:** Be a good student of God's word.

# READ

**Matthew 13:37-39**

**Day 195**

## The Church on Earth Now

We are trying to answer the question, "who make up the churches here on earth?" Today, Jesus explains the parable to his disciples.

Jesus tells us that *he* is the one who comes and sows the good seed in his field. The field is the world in which we live. But the field can also be the church that you attend. The good seeds are Christians. Remember that in the parable, an enemy comes to plant weeds while everyone is sleeping. You guessed correctly, the enemy is the devil. The devil comes and plants people who are not Christians in the church, so they can cause trouble in the church. These people bear bad fruit. They are happy to say bad things behind people's backs. They delight in breaking up friendships. They like finding fault with others. These people only pretend to be Christians. People who pretend this way are called hypocrites. They are in the church to cause trouble.

Christians are not supposed to behave this way in church or outside church. We are good seeds because Jesus lives in our hearts, so we bear good fruit. And when you find yourself doing any of the bad things listed above, go to God in prayer and ask him for forgiveness. Tell the Holy Spirit to help you not to do things that will hurt other Christians.

**Dig Out The Answers**
1. Who comes to plant evil people in the church? Why?
2. Christians must bear _____ fruit.
**In Your Own Words:** What did you learn? Write it down.

**My Prayer:** God, help me bear good fruit because I have Jesus in my heart. Amen.

**Today's Wise Words:** Not everybody who comes to church is a Christian.

211

## Jesus Cares for Hypocrites too

**READ**
Matthew
13:40-42

**Day 196**

Do you remember, in this parable, Jesus told the servants to wait till harvest time to pull out the weeds? Jesus is very patient and loving. Jesus knows that if you tried pulling out the weeds, the wheat could also be pulled out. Remember the weeds are the hypocrites, and the wheat refers to Christians.

Jesus cares for the weeds too, the hypocrites. A hypocrite may change and become a true Christian.

Imagine that one day you go to kids' church, and the pastor decides to send home kids he thinks are fake Christians. Don't you think he could make a mistake and even send Christians away too? Since we cannot see into the hearts of others, Jesus wants us to wait until he comes again. Only Jesus sees into the hearts of all people. When he comes again, all the hypocrites in the church and the world will be thrown into the fiery furnace. My, it's not good to be a hypocrite. It's good to follow Jesus with all your heart. Jesus even loves the hypocrite and wants him to be saved while there's time. Pray for hypocrites to become true Christians.

**Dig Out The Answers**
1. Why can't you look for hypocrites and drive them out of your church?
2. Jesus loves _____ too, and wants to save them.
3. What happens to hypocrites who never change?
**In Your Own Words**: Write down what you learned.

**My Prayer:** God, change the hearts of all hypocrites in the church, so they'll come and know Jesus as Lord and Savior.

**Today's Wise Words:** Jesus will one day send all hypocrites to hell.

## Wheat and Weeds

**READ**

Matthew 13:43

Day 197

Jesus is not yet done explaining the parable of the wheat and weeds. What happens to Christians when Jesus returns to earth? Christians are called "'the righteous'" here. The blood of Jesus washed away all their sins when they gave their lives to Christ, so God calls them righteous. All Christians are going to live with God forever in his kingdom. Think about the neatest things waiting for you in heaven that you can't even imagine. And the fun will never end. You are going to shine like the stars, because you'll never grow old. How marvelous! It is good to look forward to heaven everyday. It cheers you up.

**Dig Out The Answer**

Where will the righteous go when Christ returns to earth?

**In Your Own Words:** What did you learn? Write it down.

**My Prayer:** God, help me look forward to heaven everyday, in Jesus' name. Amen.

**Today's Wise Words:** The righteous will shine like the sun in God's kingdom.

213

# The Hidden Treasure Illustrated

### Dig Out The Answers

1. Arrange the illustrations above in the order in which the story is told in the Bible. Use the numbers 1, 2, 3 and so on to show the order.

2. What did the merchant do when he found the treasure?

3. What do you think is the greatest treasure in this life?

**In Your Own Words:** Write down what you learned.

**My Prayer:** Thank God for the gift of eternal life that is found in Jesus alone.

**Today's Wise Words:** The greatest treasure is eternal life found in Jesus alone.

## Parable of the Hidden Treasure

How should you look at the world, now that you are part of God's kingdom? Today's story tells us how. A man found treasure hidden in a field. He sold everything he had so he could buy the field where the treasure was hidden. Jesus is the treasure hidden in the field. A treasure is something very special and expensive. Why is Jesus special and expensive? Jesus is special and expensive

because he gives us eternal life. We get to live forever with him in heaven. When we come to know Jesus, it must mean everything to us. How do we live like Christ means everything to us? We show Jesus that he means everything to us by obeying him everyday. We talk to him more often in prayer. What do we have to give up? We give up on living in sin or doing wrong things – being selfish, wanting every toy we see in the store, getting all the latest fashion, spending our allowance only on ourselves and the like. Think about all the things you need to give up so you will enjoy Jesus more and more.

### Dig Out The Answers
1. Why is Jesus a treasure?
2. What makes Jesus special and expensive?
3. What do you have when you have Jesus?
**In Your Own Words:** What did you learn? Write it down.

**My Prayer:** God, I thank you that Jesus is the greatest treasure. Amen.

**Today's Wise Words:** Jesus is the greatest treasure.

# The Valuable Pearl
## Illustrated

## Dig Out The Answer

What do you think is the pearl of great value?

**In Your Own Words:** Write down what you learned.

**My Prayer:** God, I thank you that Jesus is the most important thing to me, just like the pearl of great value. Amen.

**Today's Wise Words:** Jesus is of very great value.

# READ **Parable of the Valuable Pearl**

What did the merchant go looking for? He went looking for pearls. Like the merchant, people are looking for something of great value that will make them happy. The merchant in the story found one pearl of very great value. He was overjoyed. He sold everything he had and bought it. In the same way, when people find Christ, they are overjoyed, and give up living in sin. Jesus is the greatest treasure in the whole world, When we come to him we must give up on sin. Can you think of things that lead you to do wrong things? All who find Jesus become happy people. Are you happy that you have Jesus in your heart? Are you happy that you are going to heaven? Are you happy that you always have a friend who will help you when in trouble? We can be really happy that we have a Savior and Friend like Jesus.

### Dig Out The Answers
1. What do we give up when we find Jesus?
2. Write down things you want to give up because you are so happy to have Jesus.

**In Your Own Words:** What did you learn? Write it down.

**My Prayer:** God, help me give up on sin because I have found Jesus. Amen.

**Today's Wise Words:** I am overjoyed because I have found Jesus.

# The Rich Young Ruler

Remember, you read this story a while ago in the book of Matthew. The question we want to answer is this: what did Jesus ask the rich young man to give up, so he could have eternal life? His riches. As we have been discussing for the past few days, Jesus wants us to leave behind the ways of sin and follow him. There are other things

that hold us back from following Jesus with all of our hearts. And for this rich young man, it was his riches. Is something holding you back from giving your life to Christ? Maybe you don't want friends to laugh at you. Maybe you are afraid of what your family and friends will say and do to you. Jesus wants us to give up being afraid of others and follow him. We must trust Jesus alone to save us and

make us happy. Pray for those who don't want to give up friends, family, or money to follow Jesus.

### Dig Out The Answers
1. What did Jesus tell the rich young man to do so he could have eternal life?
2. Have you given your life to Jesus?

**In Your Own Words:** Write down what you learned.

**My Prayer:** If you have given your life to Jesus, pray that you will trust him to take of you.

**Today's Wise Words:** Depend on Jesus alone to save you.

# Serving the Lord Is Never in Vain

**Matthew 19:27-28**

**Day 203**

Peter and the other disciples had left their fishing business to follow Jesus. That was all they had, and that was how they made money to feed their families. Levi, for example, gave up his tax collecting business. Peter asked Jesus, "We have left everything to be your followers. What will we get?" Jesus promised his twelve disciples that they would sit on twelve thrones and reign with him when he comes back to reign on earth one

day. Do you know that Jesus is coming back to earth one day to reign as king? Jesus assured his disciples that they did not give up their fishing business for nothing. He was going to give them great rewards. Did you ever read of Peter's or any of the disciples' families going hungry because the fathers worked for Jesus? No! Even here on earth Jesus supplied their needs. They would reign like kings with him, one day. So, remember that Jesus will reward you much more than all that you give up to follow him, no matter how small or big. But the greatest reward of those who obey Jesus is the peace of knowing that they do what he wants.

**Dig Out The Answers**
1. What did Peter and the other disciples give up to follow Jesus?
2. What did Jesus promise to give them in return?
**In Your Own Words:** Write down what you learned.

**My Prayer:** God, thank you that Jesus will reward me for all that I give up to follow him. Amen.

**Today's Wise Words:** Jesus rewards all his followers.

## READ

**Mark 10:29-31**

# Jesus Promises A Reward

We read this story yesterday in Matthew. Mark tells us what Jesus told Peter he'd give to all who follow him. Some people have to give up houses so they can become followers of Christ. Some have to give up mothers, fathers, brothers, sisters and all that they own to follow Jesus. Do you know in certain countries when you decide to follow Jesus your parents stop taking care of you? Some are driven away from their communities. They

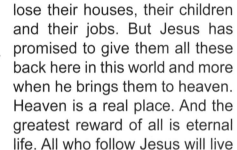

lose their houses, their children and their jobs. But Jesus has promised to give them all these back here in this world and more when he brings them to heaven. Heaven is a real place. And the greatest reward of all is eternal life. All who follow Jesus will live forever, enjoying their many rewards. When Christians are driven away from home, Jesus gives them people who are able to love them like real mothers, or fathers, or children. God even blesses them with new jobs so they are able to build new houses. So, if you lose a friend because you are a Christian, trust Jesus to give you another.

**Dig Out The Answers**
1. What did Jesus promise to give all who give up things to follow him?
2. What is the most important reward of all?
**In Your Own Words:** Write down what you learned.

**My Prayer:** Thank you Jesus for giving me eternal life, the greatest reward for following you. Amen.

**Today's Wise Words:** Jesus is able to give me back all that I lose for his sake.

## READ

Matthew
18:23-27

# The Forgiving King Illustrated

### Dig Out The Answers

1. Arrange the illustrations above in the order in which the story is told in the Bible. Use the numbers 1, 2, 3 and so on to show the order.
2. Identify the king and servant in the picture.
3. Why is he down on his knees before the king?
4. What did the king do?

**In Your Own Words:** What did you learn? Write it down.

**My Prayer:** Pray about what you learned.

**Today's Wise Words:** The servant was forgiven.

221

# The Forgiving King

Yesterday we arranged the parable of the forgiving king as it read in the Bible. A servant of a king owed him lots of money. Money you owe someone is called debt. The servant in the story owed the king about twelve million dollars. That was a lot of money. He couldn't pay the king. The king decided to sell the servant, his wife, and children to pay the debt. But the servant begged him. You know what the king did? He forgave the man all twelve million

dollars. That's lots of money to forgive. In the same way, God has forgiven all of our many sins, because we asked Jesus to come into our lives. The blood of Jesus paid the debt we owed God because of

our sin. God is very kind and merciful.

**Dig Out The Answers**
1. Who forgives the many, many sins we commit?
2. Who paid the debt we owed God? How did Jesus pay for the debt?

**In Your Own Words:** Write down what you learned.

**My Prayer:** God, I thank you that you are the king who forgives all my sins, because Jesus paid for them by dying on the cross.

**Today's Wise Words:** The servant was forgiven.

# The Unmerciful Servant Illustrated

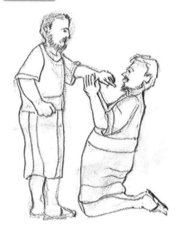

## Dig Out The Answers

1. What is the forgiven servant doing to the other servant?
2. Is it a good thing? Why is it a bad thing?

**In Your Own Words:** What did you learn? Write it down.

**My Prayer:** Pray about what you learned.

**Today's Wise Words:** Be kind and forgiving.

**READ**

Matthew
18:28-30

Day 208

Yesterday we studied the illustrations of the unkind servant. You remember this servant's debt was cancelled though it was a very, very huge amount – twelve million dollars! Another servant owed this servant only about seventeen dollars. This servant grabbed the other servant who owed him by the neck. He choked him and threw him into prison, even though he begged for mercy. The king had earlier forgiven this servant so much, yet he did not want to forgive only seventeen dollars. Sometimes, we forget how much God has forgiven us, and refuse to forgive wrong things done to us. God wants us to remember how much he has forgiven us, so we also will forgive others.

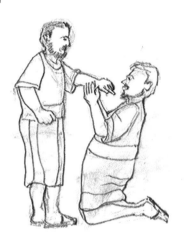

### Dig Out The Answer

What does God want us to remember to help us forgive others?

**In Your Own Words:** Write down what you learned.

**My Prayer:** God, help me remember how much you have forgiven me, so I can forgive those who wrong me, in Jesus name, Amen.

**Today's Wise Words:** Remember how much God has forgiven you.

# Parable of the Unmerciful Servant

**READ**

**Matthew 18:31-35**

The other servants of the king were so shocked when they saw how the forgiven servant treated the other servant who owed

him only seventeen dollars. They went and reported to the king. What did the king do? He threw the unmerciful servant into jail to be tortured. In the same way, God will punish those who refuse to forgive others of wrongs done to them. Does it mean you'll go to hell because you haven't forgiven your sister, brother or friend certain wrongs done to you? No. You will never go to hell if you have Jesus in your heart. The "unmerciful servants" are people who do not accept the debt Christ paid on the cross to save them from their sins. They do not understand that Jesus died to pay all their debt, so they are not able to forgive others, too. And because they do not understand, they do not become Christians. If you are a Christian, it means you understand that Jesus died to pay for your sins. You are forgiven, so you too can forgive others. Pray for those who still do not understand that Jesus paid their huge debt of sins by dying on the cross. And remember to be kind to those who owe you something.

**Dig Out The Answers**

1. The "unmerciful servant" stands for people who do not understand that Jesus paid all their debt of sins by _____ on the cross.

2. Jesus forgave us our sins so we can _____ others.

**In Your Own Words:** What did you learn? Write it down.

**My Prayer:** God, I thank you that Jesus paid all my debts on the cross. Amen.

**Today's Wise Words:** Jesus paid my debt of sin on the cross.

## READ

Luke 10:30-35

**Day 210**

**Dig Out The Answers**

1. Imagine you are a pastor in a hurry to go preach at church, would you stop to help somebody wounded by the roadside? Remember the congregation is waiting!

2. Imagine you are a helper at your church. You help set up the rooms for Sunday school. Your teacher depends on you to do this every Sunday. Would you stop on your way to church to help someone wounded by the roadside?

3. Imagine you meet a wounded person on the roadside who happened to be the one person that hates you in school. Would you help him?

**In Your Own Words:** Write

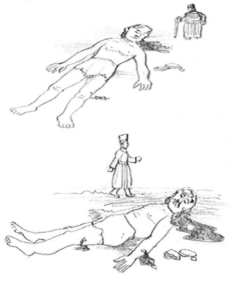
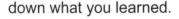

down what you learned.

**My Prayer:** Pray about what you learned.

# Parable Of The Good Samaritan

**READ**
Luke
10:30-35

We read this story yesterday. Remember! Jesus told this parable to show us how to be good neighbors. A neighbor is anybody you can help. A man lay half dead on the road. He'd been beaten by robbers and stripped naked. A priest came by, but didn't help him. So did a Temple helper, also called a Levite. But, look who came to help him – a Samaritan.

Do you know the wounded man on the road was a Jew? The priest and the Levite were also Jews. Did they help their fellow Jew? No! But the Samaritan did. Do you remember that Jews and Samaritans didn't like each other? (See Days 29 – 40) And yet this Samaritan was kind to the wounded Jew. Jesus shows by this parable that we should be willing to help anybody who needs our help, no matter how they talk or what they look like. Jesus has given Christians power through the Holy Spirit to be good neighbors. Those who belong to the kingdom of God should be good neighbors.

## Dig Out The Answers
1. Who is your neighbor?
2. Should you be good neighbors to only those who are kind to you?
3. Who gives you power to be a good neighbor?
**In Your Own Words:** What did you learn? Write it down.

**My Prayer:** Ask God to help you continue to be a good neighbor.

**Today's Wise Words:** Help those in need, whatever their background.

227

# Parable of the Good Samaritan

**Day 212**

When Jesus had finished the story, he asked the teacher of the law, "Which of these three men was a good neighbor to the wounded man?" You know the answer – the Samaritan, of course. Jesus told the teacher who had asked the question to go and do the same. Jesus wants all Christians to be good neighbors. Think of ways you can be a good neighbor at school, your neighborhood or church. Maybe, you could look out for kids new to your church and be their friend. You can be a friend to a new kid in school, too. You should learn to say "hello" to neighbors who live around your neighborhood. Being friendly to your neighbors makes you a good neighbor, too.

**Dig Out The Answers**

1. What did Jesus tell the teacher in the story to do?
2. What does Jesus want you to do?

**In Your Own Words:** Write down what you learned.

**My Prayer:** God, open my eyes to see ways I can help others, so I'll be a good neighbor, in Jesus' name.

**Today's Wise Words:** Be friendly

# The Widow and the Judge
## Illustrated

## Dig Out The Answers

1. Identify the judge and the widow in the illustrations.
2. Did the judge in the story fear God?
3. Why did the woman have to go many times to the judge?

**In Your Own Words:** What did you learn? Write it down.

**My Prayer:** Pray about what you learned.

**Today's Wise Words:** God is a just judge.

# The Widow and the Wicked Judge

**READ**

Luke
18:1-8

Day 214

Jesus told this parable to teach a lesson about prayer. This widow needed help, so she went to see the judge. A judge works in court where he settles problems between people. This judge did not fear God and didn't care about anybody. The judge was not a good person at all. The woman had to go to him many times. He got tired of the woman, so he decided to help her.

God is not like this bad judge. God is a good judge, so when you go to him, have faith that he will answer your prayer. If there is a problem between you and a friend, take it God in prayer. He will give you wisdom to solve it. Don't be discouraged. God is not like this bad judge in today's story, who didn't care about people. God cares about you and wants to do the best for you. So go to him in prayer whenever you have a need. All who belong to the kingdom of God must trust God to answer their prayers.

**Dig Out The Answers**

1. God is a just God because he ___ about you.
2. Because God cares about you, you can trust him to _____ your prayers.

**In Your Own Words:** Write down what you learned.

**My Prayer:** God, I know you are a good judge and ever ready to help me when I come to you in prayer, in Jesus' name. Amen.

**Today's Wise Words:** God cares about you.

# READ
## Matthew 25:1-5

# Parable of the Ten Virgins Illustrated

**Dig Out The Answers**

1. Identify the wise and foolish virgins in the illustrations above.
2. Why were the five virgins called foolish? Why were the other five called wise?
3. What do you suppose the oil means?

**Note This:** The Holy Spirit is like the oil in the lamp. You are wise if the Holy Spirit lives in you.

**My Prayer:** God, I thank you I have the Holy Spirit living in me.

**Today's Wise Words:** Wise people have the Holy Spirit.

# READ Parable of the Ten Virgins

Matthew 25:6-10

This parable teaches Christians to look forward to Jesus' second coming. Jesus is coming back to earth one day, but nobody knows when. Yesterday we studied the illustrations about the ten virgins. As you read yesterday, the ten virgins were waiting to meet the bridegroom so they could join him at the wedding banquet. A bridegroom is the man who marries a woman (the bride) at a wedding ceremony.

The bridegroom came back at midnight. All ten virgins were asleep. Remember, there was no electricity at that time. People used lamps to see around at night. All ten virgins woke up from sleep. The wise virgins trimmed their lamps, because their lamps were still burning, and then they followed the bridegroom to the wedding banquet. The lamps of the foolish virgins had gone out. The wise advised them to go buy some oil. And by the time they got back, the door to the wedding banquet had been shut. They couldn't get in. In this story, Jesus is the bridegroom. The wise virgins are Christians. All Christians have the Holy Spirit, who is like the oil in the lamp. Jesus wants all Christians to look forward to his second coming. You do that by making your light shine. Remember, the lamps of the wise virgins kept burning, giving light throughout the night. We make our light shine by the good deeds we do in this dark world.

**Dig Out The Answers**
1. What does this parable teach us?
2. How do we make our light shine as we wait for Jesus' second coming?
3. What do you put in a lamp to keep it burning?
**In Your Own Words:** What did you learn? Write it down.
**My Prayer:** God, let my light shine till Jesus comes back. Amen.

**Today's Wise Words:** Give me oil in my lamp; keep me burning.

**Day 217**

# The Foolish Virgins

This parable also teaches us to become true followers of Jesus. Today, we read what happened to the five foolish virgins.

The door to the wedding banquet was shut when they came back. They couldn't get in. What a tragedy! The foolish virgins stand for people who go to church but never invite Jesus into their hearts. They will not make it to the great banquet that Jesus will be throwing for all Christians when he comes back. Jesus knows those who have the Holy Spirit in them, and only they will be allowed to the banquet in heaven.

A banquet is a great party. Would you want to be at the greatest of all parties? So, don't just go to church, make Jesus your Lord and Savior! Those who have Jesus in their hearts are wise. He wants you to look forward to his second coming by doing good deeds. Good deeds make us shine like lights in this dark world. Your light shines only when the Holy Spirit lives in you. The Holy Spirit is like the oil in the lamp.

**Dig Out The Answers**

1. Those who just go to church without inviting Jesus into their hearts are called _____.
2. How do you become wise?
3. What happened to the foolish virgins when Jesus, the bridegroom, returned?

**In Your Own Words:** What did you learn? Write it down.

**My Prayer:** God, thank you that I'm going to be at this great banquet because I have Jesus in my heart. Amen.

**Today's Wise Words:** Look forward to Jesus' second coming by letting your light shine.

233

## Parable of the Talents Illustrated

**READ**
Matthew
25:14-18

*Using the gifts God has given us*

Day 218

## Dig Out The Answers

1. What do you suppose the man with the one talent should have done?

2. What are you supposed to do with the gifts God has given you?

**Note This:** God has given every Christian a talent to use. A talent is a gift.

**My Prayer:** God, help me use the gifts you have given me, in Jesus name. Amen.

**Today's Wise Words:** God has given me a talent.

234

# Parable of the Talents

Jesus told this parable to teach us that God has given every Christian a gift or talent. We must all use the gifts we have, because one day God is going to ask how we used his gifts. The master of those servants returned from his trip. He called his servants to hear what they did with the money he gave them. The servants who received five and two talents each doubled their amounts. They traded with the monies they received from their master and they got more. The master was very pleased. He rewarded them. As you read in the story, the master gave different amounts to the servants. Likewise, God gives everyone unique gifts. God knows what you are able to do. So, do not complain about the gifts of others. God wants each of us to be happy with the gifts he has given us.

Some gifts God gives are opportunities to do good to others. Maybe, you are good in math, and there's a kid in class who is struggling to understand. You have the opportunity to help him understand. Or maybe you are good at making friends. You have an opportunity to make friends with that new girl at church or school. Or maybe a boy in your class is usually afraid to go to the washroom by himself. You are bold, so you have the opportunity to go along. Can you think of things you are good at doing? When you use the gift God has given you, it means you are being a faithful servant. And God is going to reward you greatly.

**Dig Out The Answers**
1. Find out the talent God has given you and use it.
2. When you use your gifts you are being a _____ servant.
**In Your Own Words:** Write down what you learned.
**My Prayer:** God, teach me to use my gifts so I can be a faithful servant, in Jesus' name. Amen.

**Today's Wise Words:** Use the gifts God has given me.

# Parable of the Talents

Yesterday we read about the two faithful servants who received rewards for using their talents. You know what happened to the servant who received one talent and buried it? The master took away his one talent and gave it to the servant who now had ten talents. When we refuse to use the talents God has given us, we lose them. You wouldn't want to lose your talent, so use it. God is happy when we use the talents he has given

us. Moreover, he will reward us greatly when we go to heaven to be with him. When we use our gifts, God gives us power to use them in many more ways. The more we use our gifts the more we see how great God is, and the more we get blessed.

### Dig Out The Answers

1. What happens if you don't use your gifts?
2. List the good things that happen when you use your gifts.

**In Your Own Words:** What did you learn? Write it down.

**My Prayer:** Dear God, help me use my gifts so I can see how great and good you are, in Jesus' name. Amen.

**Today's Wise Words:** Don't lose your gift; use it.

# Parable of the Faithful Servant

Jesus told this parable to teach us to work very hard even as we wait for his second coming. When you believe that Jesus is coming back soon, you'll want to get ready to meet him. And that is why Jesus wants us always to think and look forward to his second coming. The servant in today's story was faithful. He was the leader of the servants in his master's house, but he took good care of them. Do you know as a Christian you need to help other Christians know Jesus better?

How do you do that? When you read something from the Bible, talk over it with your Christian friends. You must pray for your Christian friends and help them when they are in need. When you do such things, and keep at them, you are being a faithful servant. Christians must be responsible for one another. Jesus is coming soon, and we must prepare to meet him by living right.

### Dig Out The Answers

1. How do you get ready for Jesus' second coming?
2. Think of things you have learned from the Bible that you will be doing to get ready for Jesus' second coming.

**In Your Own Words:** Write down what you learned.

**My Prayer:** God, I believe that Jesus is coming back one day, so help me get ready by living right and doing the work you want me to do, in Jesus' name. Amen.

**Today's Wise Words:** I must help other Christians know Jesus better.

# READ

## Parable of the Wicked Servant

Matthew 24:48-51

Jesus told this parable to teach us that there are people who say they are Christians, but are not looking forward to his coming back again. They think it's taking forever for Jesus to come back, so they stop believing that he is coming back at all. The wicked servant in today's story tells it all. See how badly he treated his fellow servants, and he ate and drank with drunkards.

This wicked servant is not a Christian. He only pretended to be one. All true Christians believe that Jesus is coming back one day, even though no one knows when. Jesus doesn't want any of us to perish, so he warns us to think and look forward to his coming. Pray for Christians to always look forward to the Lord's second coming.

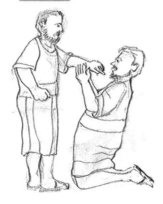

### Dig Out The Answer

1. All true Christians believe that Jesus is _____ back to earth one day.

**In Your Own Words:** Write down what you learned.

**My Prayer:** God, keep me looking forward to Jesus' second coming. Amen

**Today's Wise Words:** Jesus is coming back.

# READ    Parable of the House Owner

Jesus told this parable to teach us to share God's word and talk about the things he does for us. Jesus compared his disciples to a good house owner. The "treasures" in the story refer to God's word. God's word is a great treasure and we must share with others. A good house owner has both new and old "treasures" in his storeroom.

If you have a storeroom in your house, you know there are usually both old and new things in there. The more we read God's word, the more truths we discover for ourselves. Jesus wants us to hold on to the things we learned earlier as well as the truths we discover later. They are all God's word and we must use them by obeying them. One day you

are probably going to teach and preach God's word like Paul, or sing gospel songs, or teach Sunday school. For all of these jobs, you need to know the word of God, and it's good you are studying it right now. Live and learn!

## Dig Out The Answers
1. What do the "treasures" in the story refer to?
2. What are we supposed to do with God's word?
**In Your Own Words:** What did you learn? Write it down.

**My Prayer:** God, teach me to study your word, live it and share with others.

**Today's Wise Words:** Hold on to and share both old and new truths you discover in the Bible.

239

# The Growing Seed Illustrated

**READ**
Mark
4:26-29

Day 224

## Dig Out The Answers

1. Arrange the illustrations above in the order in which the story is told in the Bible. Use the numbers 1, 2, 3, 4, and so on to show the order.

2. Jesus compared the word of God in our hearts to seed scattered on the ground.

3. Did the man who scattered the seed do anything to make the seed sprout?

**Note This:** The word of God grows in me by the power of the Holy Spirit.

**My Prayer:** God, I thank you that your word changes me through the work of the Holy Spirit.

**Today's Wise Words:** The word of God in me grows.

## READ

**Mark 4:26-29**

Day 225

# Parable of the Growing Seed

Jesus told this parable to teach us that the word of God in our hearts has power to change us. Jesus compared the word in our hearts to seed scattered on the ground. The man who sows the seed doesn't know how the seed sprouts, becomes a plant, and produces grain. It is the same with the word of God in our hearts. Nobody knows how the word of God changes us and makes us bear fruit, but we see the good changes in our lives.

The power in the word of God is the Holy Spirit. We only have to believe the word of God, and the Holy Spirit works in our lives and changes us. The Holy Spirit helps you bear good fruit – love, joy, peace, patience, kindness, goodness, faithfulness, gentleness and self-control. Just as the small seed became a plant bearing lots of grain, so will you also continue to grow in the Lord and bear much fruit. The Holy Spirit is doing this in your heart right now.

**Dig Out The Answers**
1. Who uses the word of God in our hearts to change us?
2. Though we start small like a seed, we will _____ and bear fruit.
**In Your Own Words:** What did you learn? Write it down.

**My Prayer:** God, I thank you that your Holy Spirit uses the word in my heart and changes me into a better person each day, in Jesus' name. Amen.

**Today's Wise Words:** The Holy Spirit is the power in the word of God.

# Parable of the Mustard Seed Illustrated

*God's Kingdom On Earth Continues To Grow*

## Dig Out The Answers

1. What does Jesus compare the mustard seed to?
2. Do you think the kingdom of God is growing on earth?

**Note This:** The kingdom of God is growing on earth.

**My Prayer:** God, I thank you that your kingdom is growing here on earth, and I am glad that I am part of it because I have Jesus in my heart. Amen.

**Today's Wise Words:** The kingdom of God is growing.

242

# READ

## Parable of the Mustard Seed

**Mark 4:30-32**

Jesus told this parable so we'd always know for certain that the kingdom of God would continue to grow on earth, and bless many people. God is all-powerful and more than able to make his kingdom grow on earth. Jesus compared the kingdom of God to the smallest of seeds – the mustard seed. The mustard seed, though one of the smallest garden seeds, grows into a big plant. Do you know that the Christian church started with only one hundred and twenty

people? Today, you see many Christians scattered all over the world. There are churches in almost all countries of the world. The kingdom of God continues to grow. And just as the mustard seed grows into a plant bigger than any other garden plant, so does the kingdom of God. The kingdom of God is the greatest of all kingdoms. You must be glad to be part of this kingdom.

**Dig Out The Answer**
The kingdom of God is the _____ of all kingdoms.
**In Your Own Words:** Write down what you learned.

**My Prayer:** Thank God his kingdom is growing on earth.

**Today's Wise Words:** The kingdom of God is the greatest.

# Children Are Special

Jesus teaches in today's passage that all children are special. You must remember this everyday. All children have angels of God watching over them. These angels stand in the presence of God, waiting to do what God commands them to do for you. Isn't this great? So, whenever you are afraid or sad, call to God, and he will quickly send you help. God loves little children dearly, and all grown-ups must love and protect them too.

**Dig Out The Answers**

1. Are there angels in heaven just for children?

2. What does that make you feel?

**In Your Own Words:** What did you learn? Write it down.

**My Prayer:** God, I thank you that my angels in heaven see your face, ready to obey what you tell them to do for me, in Jesus' name. Amen.

**Today's Wise Words:** I have angels standing in God's presence in heaven.

**READ**
Matthew
18:12-14

Day 229

# Parable of the Lost Sheep Illustrated

## Dig Out The Answer
What do you do when you lose something you cherish?

**Note This:** Once you become a child of God, Jesus makes sure you don't wander away forever.

**My Prayer:** God, I thank you that Jesus will look for me when I wander away. Amen.

**Today's Wise Words:** I am precious to Jesus.

245

# Parable of the Lost Sheep

See how the shepherd went looking for the one sheep that got lost. It's the same way Jesus goes looking for you when you wander away into sin. Do you know that sin or wrongdoing keeps us away from Jesus? It's just like wandering away. Even though we may do wrong things, we are still Christians, and Jesus loves us the same. When we keep doing the wrong things over and over again we lose our joy. Sin steals our joy. We are not happy as children of God. Jesus

wants us to be happy, so he lets the Holy Spirit speak into our hearts so we will stop doing wrong things. When we listen to the Holy Spirit and tell Jesus we are sorry, that means we have come home, and stopped wandering. We again enjoy our life in Jesus.

**Dig Out The Answers**

1. Wrongdoing makes us _____ away from Jesus.

2. Jesus looks for us like the lost sheep by letting his _____ talk to us about our sin.

3. How do we become happy again?

**In Your Own Words:** Write down what you learned.

**My Prayer:** God, I thank you that you'll always bring me home to yourself when I wander into sin, in Jesus' name.

**Today's Wise Words:** God will keep me safe in Jesus.

## READ
Luke
15:11-19

# Parable of the Prodigal Son Illustrated

**Dig Out The Answers**

1. An inheritance is your share of all that your parents own, given to you after their death. Have you ever spent all your allowance on something silly?
2. How did that make you feel?
3. What is the foolish thing the younger son did in the story.

**Note This:** I can do foolish things sometimes, but I am still a child of God.

**My Prayer:** God, help me avoid doing foolish things, in Jesus' name. Amen.

**Today's Wise Words:** Don't do foolish things.

Jesus told this parable to teach us that he loves us as his children, even if we wander away sometimes. The younger son, also called the prodigal son, left home for a country far away, where he spent all his inheritance. An inheritance is your share of all that your parents own, given to you after their death. When the prodigal son came to his senses, he decided to go back home to his father. And this is true of every child of God. When we do wrong things, we are not happy. We go back to God the Father and say we are sorry. That's exactly what the prodigal son decided to do. As a child of God, you are never happy when you wander away into wrongdoing. You always want to come back and tell God you are sorry. This is a mark of a true child of God.

### Dig Out The Answers

1. What did the prodigal son decide to do?
2. What is the mark of every true child of God who sins?

**In Your Own Words:** Write down what you learned.

**My Prayer:** God, I thank you that your Holy Spirit will prompt me to come back when I wander into sin, in Jesus 'name. Amen.

**Today's Wise Words:** Every Christian comes back to God when he wanders into sin.

# READ

## Parable of the Prodigal Son

**Luke 15:20-24**

**Day 233**

Today's passage teaches us that God is always ready to forgive us our sins when we ask him. As you read from the story today, the father went out to meet his son while he was still a long way from home. This father loved his son so much he always looked forward to his coming home. God loves us that much, just like the father in today's story. God is always waiting with open arms to receive us home when we wander away. The father in the story was so happy, he threw a party

for his son. Can you imagine the joy in heaven when we turn away from wrongdoing and obey God? Let's make God happy by turning away from sin and doing what is right.

**Dig Out The Answers**
1. What did the father in the story do to show that he loved his son?
2. How does God show his love to us when we sin and say we are sorry?
**In Your Own Words:** Write down what you learned today.

**My Prayer:** God, I thank you that you love me so much, you are ready to forgive me the moment I say I am sorry for the wrong things I do, in Jesus' name. Amen.

**Today's Wise Words:** God waits with open arms to receive me home when I wander away.

249

# READ — Parable of the Prodigal Son

**Luke 15:25-28**

Today's passage teaches us to be happy when a fellow Christian turns away from wrongdoing. The older brother of the prodigal son got angry that his father was throwing a party for the younger brother who had squandered all his share of the inheritance. An inheritance is your share of all that your parents own, given to you after their death. Some of us behave like this older brother. We are not particularly happy when our parents give more attention

to a brother or sister who needs more help than we do. It takes some children a longer time to learn to do the right things. God wants us to be patient with them. He wants us to be happy when they get a little more attention, and rejoice when they finally make it. We must have the love of God in our hearts for such children. Who knows? One day another child may have to be patient with you when you find it difficult to learn a particular lesson.

**Dig Out The Answers**

1. Why was the older brother angry in today's story?

2. What are you supposed to do for kids who seem to take a longer time to learn?

**In Your Own Words:** Write down what you learned.

**My Prayer:** God, please teach me to be patient with kids who take a longer time learning to do certain things right, in Jesus' name. Amen.

**Today's Wise Words:** Be patient and loving toward kids with a learning problem.

# READ

Luke
15:29-32

## Parable of the Prodigal Son

Day 235

Today's passage teaches us that God still loves us even when we don't seem to understand his patience for his other children.

See how the father tried to explain to the older brother why it was important to celebrate the homecoming of his younger brother. We all behave like the older brother, sometimes. We do not understand why God should bless that mean kid with neat toys and a neat house. We don't understand why that kid gets away with throwing tantrums. We don't understand why that kid gets a happy sticker for all the mistakes on his work, while we get nothing better for getting a perfect score.

Like the father in today's story, God wants us to be happy with such kids, despite all their faults. We don't lose anything, because we are still part of God's kingdom. And all the good things in God's kingdom are still ours.

## Dig Out The Answer

How can you show kindness to kids you think are not deserving of it?

**In Your Own Words:** Write down what you learned.

**My Prayer:** God, teach me to understand that you love all your children, both the obedient and the disobedient, in Jesus' name. Amen.

**Today's Wise Words:** God loves me even when I don't understand all that he does.

## Parable of the Net

**READ**

**Matthew 13:47-50**

**Day 236**

Jesus told this parable to teach us that there will come a time when God will cast all sinners into hell. The fishermen in today's story caught all kinds of fish in their net. What did they do with the bad ones? They threw them away. In the same way, on judgment day, God will cast all sinners into hell. Hell is real, and heaven is real. All Christians will go to heaven. All sinners will be thrown into hell, because they did not believe that Jesus is the Son of God, and that he died to save them from their

sins. If you have asked Jesus to come into your life already, know that you are on your way to heaven. If not, it's not too late. Ask Jesus to forgive you your sins, and invite him to be your Lord and Savior.

**Dig Out The Answer**
What will happen to those who did not believe in Jesus?

**In Your Own Words:** Write down what you learned.

**My Prayer:** God, I thank you that I'm on my way to heaven, because I have Jesus in my heart. Amen.

**Today's Wise Words:** Heaven is real. Hell is real.

# READ
## Luke 16:19-21

# The Rich Man and Lazarus Illustrated

## Dig Out The Answers

1. What do you think the rich man should have done for Lazarus?

2. Write down things you plan on doing for the poor.

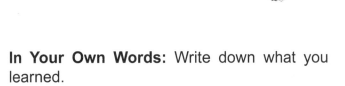

**In Your Own Words:** Write down what you learned.

**My Prayer:** God, teach me to be kind to the poor and not to look down on them. Help me not to overlook their needs. Amen.

**Today's Wise Words:** Be kind to the poor.

**READ**
Luke
16:22-23

# The Rich Man and Lazarus Illustrated

**Dig Out The Answers**

1. Where did the rich man go after he died? Is hell a nice place?

2. Where did Lazarus go after he died? Note: Abraham's side is heaven.

**Note This:** Lazarus went to heaven not because he was poor, but because he was poor in spirit. Those who are poor in spirit depend on God to save them from their sins. The rich man went to hell because he did not depend on God to save him from his sins.

**My Prayer:** Pray for your relatives and friends who are not saved yet.

**Today's Wise Words:** The poor in spirit will go to heaven.

# The Rich Man and Lazarus

**Luke 16:24-26**

**Day 239**

Today's story teaches us that no one can cross over from heaven to hell, or from hell to heaven, after death. The rich man was now in hell and suffering greatly. He begged father Abraham to let Lazarus give him a drop of water to cool his tongue. Hell is a terrible place. His prayer or request was not granted. By the time someone is in hell, it's too late to pray.

Jesus is God, so only he could tell us what happens after we die. And we must take what Jesus says

seriously. There's no place like purgatory to go to when you die. You go straight to heaven if you have accepted Jesus. The rich man could not cross over to Abraham's side nor could Lazarus cross over to hell. God has given everybody a chance to believe in Jesus while they are alive. Pray for others to come and know Jesus.

## Dig Out The Answers

1. Can any cross over from hell to heaven? Why?
2. Where do you think you'll go when you die?

**In Your Own Words:** What did you learn? Write it down.

**My Prayer:** Continue to pray for relatives and friends who are not saved.

**Today's Wise Words:** Jesus is the way to heaven

This part of the parable teaches us that people will not come to Jesus because someone rose from the dead to tell about how terrible hell is. In today's story, the rich man asked father Abraham for another favor. He wanted father Abraham to send Lazarus back to his brothers, to warn them not to come to hell. But father Abraham told him that the people back on earth had God's word that he spoke through Moses and the prophets of old. If they didn't believe God's word, neither would they believe even if someone rose from the dead.

Imagine somebody rising from the dead and telling all about hell! People will be frightened for a while. But then they will go right back to sinning after the fright is gone. Do you know Jesus rose from the dead and yet people still don't believe? God knows the hearts of all men. Only God knows the best way to bring sinners back to himself. And the best way is for people to hear and read the good news found in the Bible.

**Dig Out The Answer**
The best way to come to God is to hear and read _____.
**In Your Own Words:** Write down what you learned.
**My Prayer:** God, let people hear and read the Bible so they will be saved, in Jesus' name. Amen.

**Memory Verse:** Romans 10:17 *"So, faith comes from what is heard, and what is heard comes by the preaching of Christ".* (NRSV)

**Today's Wise Words:** Memorize the verse above.

**Day 241**

**Matthew 19:13-15**

Jesus blessed the children who were brought to him, as you read in today's story. Jesus loves children and Jesus loves you, too. In the story, the disciples tried to stop the parents from bringing their children to Jesus to bless them. They didn't think children were very important. Jesus stopped his disciples from turning them away. He made them understand that children were very

important, and needed as much attention and respect as adults. Jesus placed his hands on the little children and blessed them.

Do you know that Jesus is blessing you right now because you are his child? Jesus loves you very much so he keeps blessing you everyday. Blessings are good things that God brings into your life. Can you list some of the blessings in your life? And do you

know that you belong to the kingdom of God? You belong to God and he will take care of you. That's how special you are to God.

### Dig Out The Answers
1. What did Jesus do for the little children?
2. What does Jesus do for you too?
3. Little children belong to the _____ God.

**In Your Own Words:** Write down what you learned.

**My Prayer:** God, I thank you that Jesus blesses me everyday and I belong to the kingdom of God. Amen.

**Today's Wise Words:** Jesus blesses all little children.

257

**READ**

Jesus teaches us in today's story to love him better than anything in the world. That's what Jesus meant when he said, "If anyone comes to me, he must hate his mother, father, wife, children, sisters, brothers, and his very own life." You must love Jesus better than anything and anyone else in the world.

Suppose your brother or sister asks you to do something

that is not good. For example, she might tell you to play along with her instead of doing your homework. Would you rather listen to your sister or obey Jesus by doing the right thing? Whenever we do what Jesus says rather than the wrong things others want us to do, it means we love Jesus better. Do you know many children obeyed Jesus, became Christians, and didn't listen to other people who would rather not have them follow Jesus? These children showed that they loved Jesus better. Some children have also died along with their parents because they refused to say they were not Christians. By dying for Christ, they showed that they hated their own lives. They loved Jesus better.

**Dig Out The Answers**
1. What does it mean to hate your very life?
2. What are you going to do from today, to show that you love Jesus better?
**In Your Own Words:** Write down what you learned.
**My Prayer:** Dear God, help me love Jesus better than anything in the world. Amen.

**Today's Wise Words:** Love Jesus better than anything in the world.

# READ

**Day 243**

## Take Up Your Cross

Yesterday we learned that Jesus wants us to love him better than anything else in the world. Today Jesus teaches you to take up your cross and follow him. What does Jesus mean by taking your cross? Your cross is what you

suffer because you want to obey Jesus in all things. For example, you may feel like giving part of your allowance to missions instead of spending it all on yourself. Some kids give up their bikes for missionaries in poor countries. You may have to get up a little early to read your Bible instead of sleeping a little more. You may have to skip a friend's birthday party because you may be going to church that day. Jesus wants us to know that following him is not always going to be easy. You may suffer sometimes, but there are blessings that come to you because you love Jesus more.

**Dig Out The Answers**
1. What does Jesus mean by taking up your cross?
2. Can you think of some of the things you miss out on because you are a Christian?
**In Your Own Words:** Write down what you learned.

**My Prayer:** Dear God, help me when I have to miss out on certain activities because I am a Christian, in Jesus' name. Amen.

**Today's Wise Words:** Suffer for Christ cheerfully.

# Story of the Builder

Today Jesus compares following him to a man who decides to build a house without thinking of the cost. Do you know it costs lots of money to build a house? Anyone who wants to build a house must be sure he has enough money to finish it. When people start building a house and they don't finish, others laugh at them.

It's the same with following Jesus. The devil will laugh at you if you start with Jesus and walk away in the middle of it. Jesus wants us to follow him till we die.

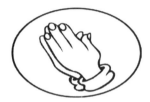

Just like the man in today's story, you are also building a house. The house you are building is your life. You are building your life on Jesus. Just as it costs a lot to build a house, so it will cost you a lot to build your life on Jesus. For example, you'll spend time reading the word of God everyday, instead of sleeping or playing all the time. Can you think of other ways you spend your time with Jesus instead of doing other things? Jesus teaches us in today's story to follow him to the end, even though it will cost us a lot.

### Dig Out The Answers
1. Think of things you won't do because you are a Christian.
2. Do these things cost you time, friends, money, or fun?
**In Your Own Words:** What did you learn? Write it down.

**My Prayer:** Dear God, give me power to walk with Jesus till I die. Amen.

**Today's Wise Words:** It costs to follow Jesus

# The Story of the King Going to War

In today's story, Jesus compares following him to a king going to war with another king. He had to be sure that he'd win the war otherwise he'd have to surrender to the other king. Do you know that war costs lives? When a country goes to war with another country, some of the soldiers die. Jesus wants us to know that just as soldiers die when they go to war, so will some Christians die when they follow him. Soldiers are brave, and Jesus wants us to be brave and stand up for him. As we said a while ago, there are so many countries where people are killed

for following Christ. You live in a country where you are free to practice Christianity. You must remember to pray for Christians in countries where following Jesus is a crime. Pray that Jesus will make them brave to continue to follow him till they die. Pray that God will also give you courage to stand up for Jesus anytime.

**Dig Out The Answer**
Why did Jesus compare following him to a king going to war?

**In Your Own Words:** What did you learn? Write it down.

**My Prayer:** Dear God, give courage to Christians who are dying for you, and give me courage to stand up for you, in Jesus' name. Amen.

**Today's Wise Words:** Stand up for Jesus.

261

# The Teacher of the Law

Today's story teaches us that we may have to do without certain things when we decide to follow Jesus. A certain teacher of the law made Jesus a promise, "I will follow you wherever you go". But Jesus told him that if he did follow him, he might not have a comfortable life, even a house to sleep in. For example, he might have to sleep out in the cold sometimes, if no one houses them. There are many missionaries all over the world

who don't own houses, cars, bikes and many of the things others own. They are willing to do without these, so they can preach the good news to the lost. If these missionaries chose to build houses, buy cars, and do other business, they would

not have any time to travel around preaching God's word, and many more people might die without Christ. Maybe one day, you may also want to be a missionary or preacher, and you'll have to do without many things, but God will provide for you.

**Dig Out The Answers**
1. What are some of the things missionaries might not have because they are preaching the good news?
2. Things you can do to help missionaries: pray for them, give/donate things they need.
**In Your Own Words:** Write down what you learned.
**My Prayer:** God, I thank you for missionaries who have given up houses, cars, and many other things, so they can preach the good news. Bless them and their families. Amen.

**Today's Wise Words:** Doing God's work will sometimes cost you comfort.

# The Man Who Wished to Bury the Dead

**READ**
Luke
9:59-60

**Day 247**

Today's story teaches us to follow Jesus no matter what goes wrong with any of our family members. Jesus told a man to come follow him, but the man wanted to go take care of his aging father first, then he'd come follow Jesus. Jesus told him to leave the care of his father to others and come follow him. The man did.

Do you know that when we put Jesus first, he takes care of the needs of our family members? Don't give

excuses for avoiding church services or any work at church. Do all your chores on time so you can worship with other believers. Don't find excuses for not doing your devotion. When you put Jesus first, he is sure to take care of your needs. Remember to take care of members of your family by helping out, but don't forget that Jesus is the one who helps us take care of our families and he'll provide help when we need it.

**Dig Out The Answer**
Why should you put Jesus first and not your family's needs?
**In Your Own Words:** Write down what you learned.
**My Prayer:** Dear God, help me not to give excuses to escape doing my devotion or to avoid helping out with work at church, in Jesus' name. Amen.

**Today's Wise Words:** Follow Jesus first, and he will take care of your needs.

## The Man Who Wished to Bid Farewell

**Day 248**

Today's passage teaches us to follow Jesus and never turn back. Following Jesus may sometimes cost us. We may not see certain friends for a long time. It happens to many missionaries who leave home for far away countries. In today's story, a certain man wished to follow Jesus but wanted to go and say goodbye to his friends and family back home first. Jesus told him that those who would want to follow him would have to obey him first rather

than their wishes. Those who would not are not fit to work for the kingdom of God. When you continue to obey Jesus, instead of following your wishes, you are walking with him. When you walk with him, it means you are serving in the kingdom of God.

**Dig Out The Answers**
1. Who are not fit to serve in the kingdom of God?
2. How can you make yourself fit to work in God's kingdom?

**In Your Own Words:** Write down what you learned.

**My Prayer:** God, teach me to obey Jesus instead of my own wishes, so I can work in the kingdom of God. Amen.

**Today's Wise Words:** I'll keep following Jesus so I'll be fit to serve in God's kingdom.

# The Twelve Apostles

Jesus went up to pray on a mountain. And he spent the night praying to God. In the morning he called all his disciples (disciples mean "learners" – are you a learner?). Jesus had many disciples. He chose twelve of the disciples to be apostles (apostles means "missionaries", people chosen for the job of telling others about Jesus – will Jesus call you too to tell others about him?).
The apostles were going to be leaders of the church.

Jesus knew the name of each disciple. Jesus knows you are his disciple, and knows you by name. Always remember that. Out of the many disciples that followed Jesus, he chose only twelve to be apostles. Sometimes, Jesus may choose somebody to do a particular job. We must all be happy for the person. Jesus knows what each of us is able to do very well, and he gives us exactly the jobs that we can do. Maybe you'd like to learn the names of the twelve apostles. Good.

**Dig Out The Answers**
1. How many disciples did Jesus choose to be apostles?
2. Are you a disciple of Jesus? What does disciple mean?
**In Your Own Words:** Write down what you learned.

**My Prayer:** God, I thank you that Jesus knows my name. Amen.

**Today's Wise Words:** I am Jesus' disciple. He knows my name

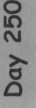

# READ

Mark
6:7-12

## Jesus Sends The Twelve

Today we read that Jesus sent out the twelve apostles on a preaching mission. The apostles were the leaders of all the disciples. Jesus gave them power to heal the sick, drive out

demons and preach the good news. We must know that Jesus has given all disciples power to do his work. You are Jesus' disciple so he has given you power to share the good news, and pray for those who are sick. You can share the good news with your friends at school. You can pray in the quietness of your room for family or friends who are sick. You don't have to be a preacher to be able to do all that. Though you are a child, you also have the power of the Holy Spirit to help the kingdom of God grow on earth in your own little way.

**Dig Out The Answers**
1. How can you help the kingdom of God grow in your own little way?
2. Who gives you power to help with the work of God?

**In Your Own Words:** Write down what you learned.

**My Prayer:** Tell God to help you preach the good news and pray for the sick in your own little way.

**Today's Wise Words:** I have the power of the Holy Spirit to share the good news and pray for the sick.

266

# Jesus Trains His Disciples

**READ**
Luke
10:1

Many people followed Jesus and some became his disciples. Jesus taught the disciples many truths about the kingdom of God. After teaching them for so long, Jesus sent them into the towns to practice what he had taught them. They went in groups of two. Jesus told them to preach the good news and heal the sick.

Are you learning from Jesus? Good. Jesus trains all his disciples. Jesus teaches you when you read the Bible.

You put what you learn in the Bible into practice when you do what it says. When you obey what the Bible says, it means Jesus is training you, just as he trained his first disciples or "learners". Jesus also uses our Christian parents, Sunday school teachers, and pastors to train us. They all teach us the word of God and how to put them into practice. Jesus is training you to be a good learner.

**Dig Out The Answer**
List some of the ways that Jesus trains you to become a good Christian.

**In Your Own Words:** Write down what you learned.

**My Prayer:** Dear God, help me read your word, know it and obey it. When I do all this, it means I'm allowing Jesus to train me to become a better Christian.

**Today's Wise Words:** Jesus wants us to be good learners.

## Disciples Should Pray for More Workers

**READ**

Luke
10:2

Day 252

Yesterday we read that Jesus taught a group of learners, and then sent them out to practice what they'd learned. Today, we read what Jesus told them to do as they set out into the towns. Jesus said to them, "the harvest is plentiful, but the workers are few." This is what Jesus meant by what he said: so many people want to hear the good news, but only few people are willing to go and share the good news. Jesus wanted his disciples to care that

there were all these people who didn't know God.

Jesus wants you also to care that there are so many people around you who don't know him. What do you do to show you care that the people around you don't know Jesus? Jesus told his disciples to pray that God would raise more Christians to preach the good news. And that's what you can do to show you care for the lost. Pray that God will send preachers to tell them the good news.

**Dig Out The Answer**
Why did Jesus ask his disciples to pray that God will send more people to preach the good news?
**In Your Own Words:** What did you learn? Write it down.

**My Prayer:** God, I pray that you'll send more preachers into the world to tell the good news, in Jesus name, Amen.

**Today's Wise Words:** God, send more preachers to tell the good news.

268

## READ

# Disciples to Be as Lambs

Yesterday we read that Jesus told the disciples to pray to God to send out more preachers to tell the good news. In today's verse Jesus added another thing. Jesus told them they were going into the towns "like lambs among wolves".

What did Jesus mean by that? Lambs are peaceful and patient. Those who don't want God and hate the word of God are the wolves. They would hate the preachers, scare them, and hurt them, but Jesus had

given the disciples the mighty power of his Spirit. Preachers will be peaceful like lambs, but by Jesus' power they will overcome these enemies. Do you know that many preachers are hated, and beaten and maltreated? But God gives them courage by the Holy Spirit who lives in them. Remember to pray that God will continue to protect all preachers.

**Dig Out The Answer**
Jesus' disciples are like lambs because they must be _____ and patient.

**In Your Own Words:** Write down what you learned.

**My Prayer:** Dear God, help me to be peaceful and patient when I share the good news with my friends, in Jesus' name. Amen.

**Today's Wise Words:** Be peaceful and patient like a lamb

269

**READ**

Luke
10:5-7

**Day 254**

Yesterday we read that Jesus told his disciples to be as lambs among wolves. They must be patient and peaceful even when God-haters are cruel to them. Jesus wasn't done telling the disciples what they were to do as they set out. The disciples were supposed to go from house to house preaching the good news. Jesus told them to stay in the houses of those willing to let them.

There's an important lesson here for all of us. Sometimes preachers are invited to your church from other countries, states or provinces. They may need a family to stay with. It's nice to remind your parents to let some of these preachers stay in your home. Jesus told his disciples that those who allowed them to stay in their houses would have peace. That's what we get when we host preachers in our homes. God blesses our homes because we are helping the work of God grow.

**Dig Out The Answers**

1. What blessing comes to your family when a preacher out-of-town stays in your home?

2. What are you going to do to help those who preach the good news?

**In Your Own Words:** Write down what you learned.

**My Prayer:** Dear God, teach me to help out when my parents decide to let a preacher stay in our home, in Jesus' name. Amen.

**Today's Wise Words:** Be happy to have preachers stay in your home

# Disciples Told to Preach and Heal

**Day 255**

Yesterday we read that Jesus told his disciples to bless the homes that accepted them. In today's passage Jesus told them to heal the sick and preach the good news of the kingdom of God. Was what the twelve did different from the seventy? No. Jesus gave them all power to do his work. Jesus hasn't changed. What he told the disciples then, he still tells all preachers. Jesus has given some preachers power to heal the sick and preach the good news.

Pray that God will give preachers faith to trust him to help them heal the sick, and tell the good news. You are also a disciple of Jesus, so trust Jesus to heal you when you fall sick. Trust Jesus to help you tell your family and friends about him, too.

**Dig Out The Answers**

1. What two things did Jesus tell the disciples to do?
2. Is Jesus still using preachers to heal the sick and preach the good news?

**In Your Own Words:** Write down what you learned.

**My Prayer:** Pray that God will help preachers trust him to use them to heal the sick and preach the good news.

**Today's Wise Words**: Preachers preach and heal in Jesus' name.

# READ

## The Disciples Return

Luke 10:17

**Day 256**

The seventy disciples went and did as Jesus had instructed them. They obeyed all that Jesus told them to do. They came back to Jesus very happy. They told Jesus that evil spirits obeyed them. They were able to drive evil spirits out of people in Jesus' name. Wow! There's power in the name of Jesus. See how happy the disciples were, because they had done everything Jesus asked them to! We are also happy children when we obey Jesus.

Another wonderful thing the disciples did was to come back to Jesus to report. It is good to go back to God at the end of each day and tell him all that happened during the day. Remember, you asked him to take care of you at the beginning of the day. Also, when our parents give us work to do, it is important to go back to them and tell them we are done. It shows respect and love.

**Dig Out The Answers**

1. Like Jesus' disciples, we must report back to God at the end _____.

2. What do you do when you complete work your parents had asked you to do?

**In Your Own Words:** Write down what you learned.

**My Prayer:** Pray that you'll obey Jesus so you will always be full of joy.

**Today's Wise Words:** Joy follows obedience.

## READ

# Jesus Praises God

**Luke 10:18-21**

**Day 257**

Yesterday we read about the disciples telling Jesus how evil spirits obeyed them when they preached the good news. Jesus told them that what should give them the greatest joy was that "their names are written in heaven" – they *are* citizens of heaven. Likewise, you should be happy each time you remember you are a citizen of heaven.

Jesus also added that he had given them power over all the power of the devil. Yes, as a disciple of Jesus, he has given you power to overcome all the power of evil and the evil one. Remember this whenever you are afraid.

What did Jesus do about all the good things the disciples told him? Jesus was full of joy and praised the Father. This is what we must do when God does something for us. We must be happy and praise him.

### Dig Out The Answers

1. What did Jesus do about all the good things the disciples told him?
2. What do you when God does something for you?
3. Jesus has given all who follow him _____ to overcome all the power of the enemy (devil).

**In Your Own Words:** Write down what you learned.

**My Prayer:** God, teach me to praise you for the all the good things you use me to do in the lives of other people, in Jesus' name. Amen.

**Today's Wise Words:** Praise God for all good things he uses you for.

273

# The Kind of Giving God Accepts

This passage teaches us that what we give to God must come from our hearts. Jesus sat in the Temple courts watching people give offering. Jesus saw the rich putting in lots of money. But he also saw a widow put in such a small amount of money. Jesus called his disciples and told them that the woman who gave the smallest amount of money gave more than the rich. You may ask - how could that be? The widow gave all the money she had

in the world. The rich gave lots of money, but they still had lots more at home.

Jesus wants us to give everything to him. But how can we give everything to God? We may have nothing left to live on. This is what Jesus wants from us. He wants us first to give him our hearts. When we give our lives to Jesus, it means we've given everything to God. Those who know the love of God give more to the work of God. They give their lives, things they own, and money to the work of God.

**Dig Out The Answers**

1. How do you give everything to God as an offering?
2. Those who know how sweet God's love is _____ more to the work of God.

**In Your own words:** Write down what you learned.

**My Prayer:** God, help me know more of your love so I can give more to your work, in Jesus' name. Amen.

**Today's Wise Words:** The love of God in my heart helps me give more offering.

# Jesus Teaches Us to Be Good Citizens

Jesus teaches us in today's story to be good citizens. The Pharisees wanted to create trouble for Jesus. They didn't like paying taxes to the government of which Caesar was the head. So they asked Jesus whether it was right to pay taxes to the government. Jesus used a coin to point out that it was important to pay taxes to the government, since the coin was made by the government.

Any government uses taxes to build good roads,

hospitals, schools, libraries and other things that we need in our cities and towns. You are a child, so you may not have to pay taxes to the government, but there are other things you can do to be a good citizen. For example, bike on the sidewalk and not on the neighborhood street. If you take your dog for a walk, be sure to clean after it. Don't throw out orange peels or food wrappers in the park or streets. Can you think of other things you can do to show you are a good citizen?

**Dig Out The Answer**
Find out some of the things you can do to be a good citizen.
**In Your Own Words:** Write down what you learned.

**My Prayer:** Dear God, teach me to be a good citizen, in Jesus' name. Amen.

**Today's Wise Words:** Be a good citizen.

275

# READ

**Matthew 17:24-27**

## Day 260

# Did Jesus Pay Taxes?

In today's story Jesus practiced being a good citizen. Jesus wants us to practice what we preach. The collectors of the two-drachma tax asked Peter whether Jesus paid taxes. Peter told them Jesus did. When Peter came back into the house, Jesus asked about the tax. Jesus then asked Peter to go catch a fish, open its mouth, collect

the money stuck in its mouth, and use that to pay their taxes. Peter did as he was told. Jesus was a good citizen. Jesus wants us to follow his example by obeying the laws of our countries.

### Dig Out The Answer

What did Jesus do to show he was a good citizen?

**In Your Own Words:** What did you learn? Write it down.

**My Prayer:** God, help me to be a good citizen like Jesus. Amen.

**Today's Wise Words:** Jesus was a good citizen.

# Jesus Teaches about His Second Coming

**READ**
Matthew
24:30-31

**Day 261**

This is what will happen when Jesus comes a second time. Jesus will come down from heaven. With a loud voice, he will command all Christians to meet him in the air. Read 1 Thessalonians chapter 4, verses 15 to 17. It tells what happens next. All Christians who are dead will rise up first and meet Jesus in the clouds. After that, all Christians who are still alive will join Jesus in the air. It doesn't mean we are going to stay in the air. We will pass through the clouds into heaven to be with Jesus. You may wonder how we are going to go up in the sky like that. It is just as Jesus ascended into heaven when he rose from the dead. Jesus will make every Christian fly up through the clouds into heaven. It will take less than a second for us to meet Jesus in the air and to go into heaven with him. Jesus is very powerful and able to do all things.

**Dig Out The Answers**
1. Which way is Jesus coming a second time?
2. What happens as Jesus descends from heaven with a loud call?
3. Where does Jesus take all Christians?

**In Your Own Words:** Write down what you learned.

**My Prayer:** Dear God, I thank you that if Jesus should come today, I'll join him in heaven because he is my Lord and Savior, in Jesus Name, Amen.

**Today's Wise Words:** Jesus will come down from heaven with a loud command, at his second coming.

# Kinds of Bodies that Go to Heaven

## READ
Matthew
22:29-30

**Day 262**

Take note of verse 30 in today's passage. Christians will be like the angels in heaven when Jesus comes again to take them home to be with him.

Read 1 John, chapter 3, verse 2. It also tells us that when Jesus appears we shall be like him. This new body is called a glorified body. These bodies won't die or grow old. This is the type of body we will fly over into heaven with when Jesus comes down from heaven with a great shout. Isn't this great? Bodies that can fly through space in seconds! Wow! Jesus will do all that for you when he comes to take you to heaven. Ask your pastor to tell you more about the resurrected body or glorified body.

## Dig Out The Answer

What kind of body will Jesus give you when he comes to take you to heaven?

**In Your Own Words:** Write down what you learned.

**My Prayer:** God, I thank you that I'll get a glorified body when Jesus comes to take me to heaven. I am happy that this body will never die or grow old, in Jesus name. Amen.

**Today's Wise Words:** At Jesus' return every Christian will get a glorified body.

## No One Knows When Jesus Is Coming Back

**READ**
Matthew
24:36

Day 263

Jesus teaches his disciples that no one knows when he is going to come back to earth. Jesus wants you to understand this too. Some people claim to know exactly when

Jesus is coming back, but what Jesus says here proves that they are mistaken. Do not believe such people. Jesus wants you to know that no one knows when he will come back to earth, only God the Father.

**Dig Out The Answers**

1. Can anyone tell when Jesus will come back to earth?
2. Only _____ knows the day and the hour Jesus will return to earth.

**In Your Own Words:** Write down what you learned.

**My Prayer:** Dear God, thank you for teaching me not to believe those who claim to know when Jesus is coming back to earth.
You are the only one who knows.

**Today's Wise Words:** Only God knows the day and hour Jesus will come back to earth.

# Signs – wars, earthquakes, and famines

**READ**

Matthew
24:6-8

Before Jesus comes back, there'll be lots of wars, earthquakes, and people starving to death in many places. Even though these things are happening we should not panic. These things must happen way before Jesus comes again. Jesus wants us to stand firm and trust in him even when these things are happening.

There are wars in so many countries around the world,

today. Earthquakes occur here and there. There's hunger in so many places around the world, but Jesus has not come back.

### Dig Out The Answers

1. List the things Jesus said would happen before he comes.
2. What are you supposed to do if you should see those things happen?

**In Your Own Words:** Write down what you learned.

**My Prayer:** Dear God, help me not to be scared when I hear of wars, or earthquakes or hunger. Rather, let me trust you to take care of my family and friends, in Jesus' name. Amen.

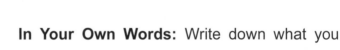

**Today's Wise Words:** Don't panic when you hear of wars, earthquakes and famine. Trust Jesus to take care of you.

**Day 265**

# Signs - False Christs

One other thing that will happen before Jesus comes is this: some people are going to say, "I am the Christ". They will perform fake miracles and signs to fool people. Just don't believe such people. Such a person can't be the Christ. Jesus Christ is in heaven right now. Remember that. Never believe anyone who says he is Jesus. Jesus doesn't look like any human now. Jesus has a different body now, a glorified body. Remember, when Jesus comes a second time, he'll come down from heaven for everyone to see.

## Dig Out The Answers

1. Should you believe anyone who says he is Christ? Why?
2. Where is Jesus now?

**In Your Own Words:** Write down what you learned.

**My Prayer:** Dear God, never let anyone fool me into believing that he is Jesus Christ, because Christ is in heaven right now. Amen.

**Today's Wise Words:** Don't believe anyone who says he is Jesus Christ.

## READ      Signs Before Jesus Returns

**Matthew 24:25-27**

**Day 266**

Jesus tells us in today's passage some other things we must watch out for. Some people will tell others that Jesus is over there in the desert or in some room, but you should not believe them. As we read before, when Jesus returns to the earth, he will appear from heaven and everyone will see him. It is very important to remember this. Never follow anybody who claims he saw Jesus at a certain place. Jesus is still in heaven. When he decides to come down from heaven, no one will miss it. All will see him come.

### Dig Out The Answers

1. What are some people going to tell others about where Jesus is?
2. Should you believe them? Why?
3. Where will Jesus appear? Is everyone going to see him when he appears from heaven?

**In Your Own Words:** Write down what you learned.

**My Prayer:** Dear God, I thank you that Jesus will come down from heaven to take me home. Help me not to be fooled by anyone who says Jesus is in the desert, the mountain, or some room, in Jesus' name. Amen

**Today's Wise Words:** Never believe anyone who says Jesus is somewhere on earth if you haven't seen the signs he gives.

# Watch for Jesus' Second coming

Why did Jesus tell his disciples about all the signs that would take place before his second coming? Jesus told them so they would keep watch and be ready when he appears. You are also a disciple of Jesus, and he is telling you the same thing – to watch and be ready.

What does it mean to keep watch? When we watch for the Lord's coming, it means we are looking forward to it. You must look forward to it more eagerly than you look forward to your birthday party or a trip to Disneyland. To look forward also means to *want* Jesus to come soon. What do you do as you watch? Would you want Jesus to pat you on the shoulders that you've been a good worker? So even as you watch for Jesus' second coming, be busy obeying the word of God by bearing fruit. Also help those who preach the word of God by praying and giving to them. Help out at your church too. When you do these things, you are getting ready for the Lord's coming.

### Dig Out The Answers

1. Why did Jesus tell his disciples about all the signs that would take place before his second coming?

2. What do you do to show you are watching and getting ready for the Lord's coming?

**In Your Own Words:** Write down what you learned.

**My Prayer:** Dear God, help me watch and get ready for Jesus' second coming. Amen.

**Today's Wise Words:** Watch and get ready for Jesus' second coming

283

# READ

**Mark 8:31-33**

## Jesus Rebukes Peter

Today's passage teaches that Jesus' suffering, dying and rising was God's plan to save us. You may hear some people claim that Jesus did not suffer, die and rise again. That idea is from Satan. Why does Satan make people think this way? He doesn't want them to be saved. The devil is working hard to take along, as many people as possible to hell, by making them believe this lie. He knows his time is short.

Today's story tells of how difficult it was for Peter to believe that Jesus would have to suffer, die and rise again. Jesus turned to Peter and said, *"Get behind me, Satan"*. Jesus knew that it was Satan who was trying to put that idea into Peter's head. Jesus corrected him because he loved him. Peter listened to Jesus because only Jesus knows the truth. Likewise, you must also listen to Jesus only by reading the Bible. Don't believe anything that goes against the Bible even if it sounds good. When somebody claims to quote what Jesus said, check it out by reading the Bible. You may also ask your Christian parents, pastor, or Sunday school teacher.

## Dig Out The Answers

1. What is one of the biggest lies Satan makes people believe?
2. How did God plan to save us?
3. Where do you go to check if what somebody said about Jesus is true or false?

**In Your Own Words:** Write down what you learned.

**My Prayer:** God, thank you for letting me understand that Jesus had to suffer, die and rise again to save me from my sins. This is the truth Jesus taught. Amen.

**Today's Wise Words:** Jesus' suffering, dying and rising is God's plan to save us.

# Jesus' Glory on the Mount

**Mark 9:2-10**

**Day 269**

Jesus had told the disciples that he would suffer, die, and rise again. They might have been very sad. They had thought he was coming to set up a kingdom on earth, right away. Could this be the Christ? They didn't understand that Jesus first had to suffer, die and rise again to save us from our sins. Only after that would he go back to heaven to reign in glory with the Father. Probably, they were sad and confused. Jesus wanted to show Peter, John and James that he was indeed the Messiah. He had and still has power to do everything and to reign on earth, but he had to save us first. He wanted them to know that he chose to die to save us, and nobody forced him to it. Jesus loves us very much. Jesus took them to the mountain. And there in front of them Jesus was completely changed. His clothes became whiter than anything they'd seen. They also saw Moses and Elijah with him. God spoke from the clouds and said, "Jesus is my son". Peter was so delighted he wished they stayed on the mountain forever. Just as Jesus showed his glory to Peter, John and James, he is willing to do that for you, too. Jesus shows his glory in our lives by answering our prayers, protecting us, leading us, performing miracles in our lives, and using us to bless others. Pray and ask Jesus to show you his glory.

**Dig Out The Answers**
1. What did Jesus look like on the mountain? What did the voice from heaven say?
2. How does Jesus show his glory in your life?
**In Your Own Words:** Write down what you learned.
**My Prayer:** God, let me see the glory of Jesus in my life. Amen.

**Today's Wise Words:** Jesus shows his glory in my life, too.

**Day 270**

# Jesus Tells About His Death and Resurrection

Today's passage teaches that Jesus is able to tell of things that will happen in the future. Jesus and his disciples were on their way to Jerusalem.

The disciples were afraid of what might happen when they got there. They knew the Jewish leaders in Jerusalem hated Jesus, and they remembered that Jesus had told them earlier that he would suffer. Now he told them once again what would happen to him there. He told of how he would be betrayed, found guilty by the chief priests, mocked, spat on, flogged and killed. But on the third day he would rise from the dead.

Nobody in this world can ever tell when he will die. Nobody else ever promised to rise from the dead and carried out his promise. Jesus is the only one who died and rose again, because he is God's Son. Believe everything Jesus teaches in the Bible, because it is the truth. Whatever the Bible promises will really happen. So be bold and live for Jesus!

**Dig Out The Answers**
1. List the things Jesus said would happen to him in Jerusalem.
2. Keep it in mind and compare to what actually happened to him when he was arrested.
**In Your Own Words:** Write down what you learned.

**My Prayer:** Dear God, I thank you that Jesus knows all about the future, so I can trust him to take care of me. Amen.

**Today's Wise Words:** Only Jesus could tell of his future suffering, death, resurrection and ascension.

# A Donkey for Jesus

**Day 271**

Jesus was about to enter Jerusalem. He told his disciples to go to the next village where they'd find a donkey that had never been sat on. The disciples must tell anyone who asked about the donkey that the Lord needed it. Did they find things just as Jesus had said? Yes. Jesus knows everything and you must trust him to take care of you. Did the owners refuse to give the donkey for Jesus' use? No. Likewise you should also be willing to use the things you have to serve Jesus?

You may give your used toys to the poor. You can volunteer to help clean your church. You can help out at a soup kitchen or food bank with your parents' permission. But most of all you can let Jesus use your heart so you can bear the fruit of the Holy Spirit.

## Dig Out The Answers

1. Did the donkey owners refuse to give their donkey to Jesus? What does this teach you?
2. Think of ways you can use the things you have to serve Jesus.

**In Your Own Words:** Write down what you learned.

**My Prayer:** Dear God, help me use the things I have to serve Jesus, in his name. Amen.

**Today's Wise Words:**
I'll use the things I have to serve Jesus.

# READ

## The Crowd Who Knew

John
12:17-19

**Day 272**

The disciples had the donkey ready for Jesus to ride into Jerusalem as we read yesterday. In today's passage we read about the crowd that came to meet Jesus. This was a special crowd. They had seen Jesus raise Lazarus back to life. They went out, telling others to come see Jesus, the one who raised the dead. They couldn't contain their excitement. Many more joined the crowd. And they all went out to meet Jesus. Even the Pharisees could not stop this crowd!

What would you tell others about Jesus – that he saved you from your sin, and you are on your way to heaven, that he answers your prayers! You can also tell your friends the great things the Lord has done for you and others. Get excited about Jesus, too. He is all-powerful!

**Dig Out The Answers**

1. What did the crowd that had seen Lazarus brought back to life do?

2. What do you do when Jesus does something for you or your family?

**In Your Own Words:** Write down what you learned.

**My Prayer:** Dear God, teach me to share the great things Jesus does in my life and in the lives of others with great joy and excitement, in his name. Amen.

**Today's Wise Words:**
Tell others about the miracles of Jesus.

288

# READ
## Hosanna to the Son of David!

**Luke 19:37-38**

What did the crowd do when they met Jesus? They praised him. Jesus must be Christ, the King, the crowd thought. They knew of a King who was to come and save them from their enemies. Nobody ever performed miracles like Jesus. Nobody ever taught about God like Jesus. They knew that this must be God's Son, the Christ, the Savior of the world. And they praised him. You must also praise Jesus every time you think about him. He has saved you, blessed you, he protects you and he will take you to a fun place called heaven. Praise the name of Jesus!

**Dig Out The Answers**
1. What did the crowd do when they met Jesus on the way?
2. You must also _____ Jesus for the wonderful things in your life.

**In Your Own Words:** Write down what you learned.

**My Prayer:** Lord Jesus, I praise you for the wonderful things in my life and the miracles you keep performing all around the world! Amen.

**Today's Wise Words:** Hosanna to Jesus! Praise the name of Jesus!

289

## READ

**Matthew 21:10-11**

# Who Is This Man?

Jesus entered Jerusalem. The crowd followed, praising him and shouting, "Hosanna". What a wonderful sight that was! The people living in Jerusalem got all excited with what was happening. They asked, "Who can this be?" The crowd answered, "This is Jesus, the prophet from Nazareth in Galilee". If someone asks you who Jesus is, what will you say? Would you say Jesus is the Christ, the Savior of the world? Would you say he is the

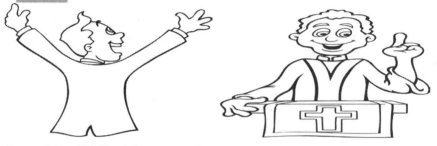

Son of God? Would you say he is also your prophet and your best friend? That would be right!

**Dig Out The Answers**
1. The crowd said Jesus _____ _____?
2. But Jesus is more than a prophet. Write all that you know Jesus to be.

**In Your Own Words:** Write down what you learned.

**My Prayer:** Dear God, I thank you that Jesus is more than a prophet. He is the Son of God, my Savior and Lord. Hallelujah! Amen.

**Today's Wise Words:**
This is Jesus, the Savior of the world.

**READ**

Luke 22:1-6

Day 275

Isn't this awful? Judas Iscariot pretended to be a friend of Jesus Christ, when all the time he was totally confused. As you know by now, the teachers of the law and chief priests didn't like Jesus at all. They were the enemies of Jesus. They didn't like the truth Jesus preached about God. They thought Jesus was getting popular and many would follow him instead of them. So, they became jealous of Jesus and wanted to kill him. That was a terrible thing. They couldn't arrest Jesus when he was teaching or healing, otherwise there would be a riot. They needed somebody who knew where Jesus was at particular times of the day, so they could arrest him quietly. Judas Iscariot, one of Jesus' disciples was sure to know this and he went to see them. Satan put this very evil idea into Judas Iscariot's heart to help the enemies kill Jesus. And Judas Iscariot listened to him.

Satan is the one who puts evil ideas into people's heads to say evil things against Jesus, his teachings, and those who follow him. As a Christian, you have the power of the Holy Spirit to say "no" to the bad ideas Satan wants to put in your head. You can also say, *"In the name of Jesus, get behind me, Satan!"* and the Lord will send him packing.

**Dig Out The Answers**

1. Who put the bad idea into Judas Iscariot's heart to help the enemies kill Jesus?
2. Who tempts people with evil ideas? What do you do when Satan tempts you?

**In Your Own Words:** Write down what you learned.

**My Prayer:** Dear God, let your Holy Spirit help me say "no" to every bad idea Satan tempts me with, in Jesus' name. Amen.

**Today's Wise Words:** Say "no" to every bad thought Satan tempts you with.

## READ

John 12:1-6

# Why Judas Betrayed Jesus

Today you read that Judas was actually stealing from the moneybag that belonged to the disciples. You also learned that Judas did not care for the poor. He only wished to have the perfume sold, so he could lay his hands on the money when it got into the moneybag, which he kept. Small sins grow, and in the end Judas loved money more than Jesus.

As a disciple he heard Jesus teach many truths but he was never quite convinced. He never gave himself completely to the Lord, so his heart was empty. Satan puts evil ideas into empty hearts. Judas' heart was empty so the devil was quick to drop the evil idea of betraying Jesus in it. What a tragedy, when someone comes so near to Jesus but never takes the final step of commitment.

A heart without Jesus is an empty heart. When Jesus lives in your heart, it's full of the Holy Spirit, so nothing else can get in. Keep Jesus' words in your heart and Satan will not have space to put evil ideas into your head. Those who listen to Jesus' words and believe will be delivered when tempted. The word of Jesus is the most powerful thing in the whole world. When you have him in your heart, the devil runs away from you.

**Dig Out The Answers**

1. Why was Judas' heart empty? What does the devil do with empty hearts?
2. A heart that Jesus lives in is full of _____.
3. When you have Jesus' word in your heart the devil _____ .

**In Your Own Words:** Write down what you learned.

**My Prayer:** God, I thank you that my heart is full of the Holy Spirit, so the devil cannot put evil ideas into it, in Jesus name. Amen.

**Today's Wise Words:** A heart that Jesus lives in is full of the Holy Spirit. No space for Satan.

# The Last Supper

We call it the "last supper" because it was the last time Jesus ate with his disciples before he died. It was also a special supper that all Jews ate at the Passover Festival. Jesus told Peter and John how to find a place for them to celebrate the Passover Supper. Did they obey Jesus? Yes. Did they find things exactly as Jesus had said? Yes. You can also trust every word in the Bible. When you obey God's word you will find happiness and peace, just as

Jesus promised to all who follow him.

### Dig Out The Answers

1. Did Peter and John follow the instructions Jesus gave about how to find a room for them to celebrate the Passover? Did they find it exactly as Jesus had said? What does this teach you?

**In Your Words:** Write down what you learned.

**My Prayer:** Dear God, teach me to believe and obey every word in the Bible, so I will be happy and enjoy peace, in Jesus' name. Amen.

**Today's Wise Words:**
Believe and obey Jesus' words.

# READ

## Celebrate the Last Supper

Jesus was very happy to eat this last supper with his disciples. Jesus enjoyed the company of his disciples. Likewise, you should also enjoy the company of other Christians. You must be happy to join kids' programs at your church, and enjoy what you do with other kids.

Jesus always gave thanks before eating. You must remember to thank God for all the food he provides for you. At this last supper, Jesus passed around a cup

of wine and pieces of bread to the disciples. He told them to keep having this kind of supper to remember him always. Christians should take part in "Communion" or "Lord's supper" given at church services. When you do that, you are obeying Jesus, and remembering him.

## Dig Out The Answers

1. Why did Jesus tell his disciples to keep having this kind of 'last supper'?

2. What should you do before eating any meal?

**In Your Own Words:** Write down what you learned.

**My Prayer:** Dear God, teach me to remember Jesus by taking part in the 'Last Supper' at my church.

**Today's Wise Words:** Eat the 'last supper/communion' to remember Jesus.

# Jesus Points Out the One Who'll Betray Him

**READ**
John
13:21-27

Jesus and his disciples were still eating the last supper. Jesus told his disciples that one of them was going to betray him. Betray means, one of the disciples of Jesus was going to work with the enemies of Jesus to have him killed. Remember Jesus had earlier told the disciples that one of them was a devil in John chapter 6, verse 70, and he meant Judas Iscariot! Jesus had always known who was going to betray him. The disciples were confused and wondered who that could be. Peter told John, who was sitting close to Jesus, to ask him. Jesus told John that it was the one he was about to give the piece of bread dipped in sauce. Jesus gave the piece of bread to Judas Iscariot. Judas left immediately after taking the bread, now bent on working with Jesus' enemies.

Jesus knows everything. You can trust him with your life. The other disciples did not understand what was happening. Judas Iscariot was the one who kept the moneybag that belonged to the group. They thought Judas was going to buy something they needed for the Festival. Remember, Judas used to steal from the moneybag! Small sins grow, and in the end Judas loved money more than Jesus. Judas Iscariot obeyed Satan instead of Jesus.

**Dig Out The Answers**
1. Did Jesus know who was going to betray him? What does it teach you about Jesus?
2. What were Judas' small sins? What do you do about small sins?
**In Your Own Words:** Write down what you learned.
**My Prayer:** Holy Spirit, give me power to overcome small sins, so they will not grow in my life. Amen.

**Today's Wise Words:** Small sins grow.

Day 279

295

# Jesus Tells about Peter's Denial

READ
John
13:36-38

Day 280

After Judas Iscariot left, Jesus told his disciples he would be going away. Peter wanted to know where Jesus was going. He was confident that he would never leave Jesus, but instead, he would follow him and even die with him. As already said, Jesus knows all things. Jesus knew that Peter would be too scared to say he knew him when he was captured. Likewise, Jesus knows all about what you can do for him and what you can't do for him, and yet he loves you all the same.

Jesus loved Peter, even though he knew Peter was about to say he didn't know Jesus in just a little while. You may do the wrong thing sometimes, but that doesn't mean Jesus will stop loving you. Once you have given your life to him, he always loves you.

## Dig Out The Answers

1. Does Jesus love you even though he knows all the wrong things you'll do now or in the future?

**In Your Own Words:** Write down what you learned.

**My Prayer:** Dear God, thank you that you know all the wrong things I will do but you still love me all the same. Amen.

**Today's Wise Words:** Jesus loves me even though he knows all the wrong things I'll do.

# READ

**Luke 22:31-34**

# Jesus Prays for Peter

Jesus told Simon Peter that Satan was going to tempt him sorely but he had prayed for him. Jesus prayed that Peter's faith would not fail. Jesus knows all the temptations that you will face throughout your life. He is sitting at the right hand of the Father in heaven and praying for you that your faith in him will not fail even if you should sin. And when Jesus prays, it will be done. Nothing can take you away from Jesus. You are kept by the *power of God* and *the prayer of Jesus*. Hallelujah!

Be assured that Jesus is able to bring you to heaven one day.

## Dig Out The Answers

1. Does Jesus know every single temptation that the devil will bring in your life?
2. What does Jesus do about this?
3. What are the two things that keep you in the faith?

**In Your Own Words:** Write down what you learned.

**My Prayer:** Mighty God, thank you that my faith will never fail, because your power and the prayer of Jesus keep me safe, in Jesus' name. Amen.

**Today's Wise Words:** The power of God and the prayer of Jesus keep me in the faith.

# Jesus Comforts His Disciples

Jesus comforts us when we are sad. Today's verse teaches us this. Jesus had earlier told his disciples at the last supper that one of them would betray him. He also told them he would be going away. They were a very sad lot. The disciples had left everything to follow Jesus. They had hoped that Jesus was coming to establish a kingdom in which they would rule with him. They didn't understand

that Jesus came into the world to die and save us from sin. Jesus comforted them and told them to trust him.

Sometimes we also get sad. You may be sad because your friend moved away, or you moved away to a different city. You may be sad that your granny died. Jesus wants you to trust God to make you happy again. Jesus knows how to fix all your problems.

## Dig Out The Answer
What does Jesus want you to do when sad?

**In Your Own Words:** Write down what you learned.

**My Prayer:** Dear God, help me talk to you when sad, because you are able to make me happy, and fix my problems as well, in Jesus' name. Amen.

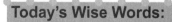

**Today's Wise Words:**

Jesus cheers me up.

**READ**
**John 14:2-4**

**Day 283**

Jesus is preparing a place for us in heaven. The disciples had given up everything to follow Jesus. Now Jesus was going away. They thought they had followed Jesus for nothing. But they were wrong. Jesus was preparing a better place for them in heaven. The things we miss here on earth are nothing compared to what Jesus is preparing for us in heaven. Imagine for a moment what God is preparing for children in heaven - the best of rides, playground, toys, space travel and all that you can think of is nothing compared to what is waiting for you in heaven. Can you imagine a jeweled city, streets of gold, tree of life, zillions of saints, worship, a great banquet (party), the Lord God Almighty, the Lamb, the river of life? Nobody can imagine it yet. And the fun part is that the fun will never end.

Here on earth, you can go for rides, or to Disneyland only for a short while, but in heaven the fun and joy never ends and you'll never get hurt. Don't be sad when you can't go to certain places or do certain things because you are a Christian. Think of all the fun things waiting for you in heaven. We live only a short time on earth, but in heaven we will live forever.

**Dig Out The Answers**
1. What is Jesus doing in heaven for all those who love him?
2. Write down what you think heaven will be like?
**In Your Own Words:** Write down what you learned.
**My Prayer:** God, I thank you that Jesus is preparing a fun place for me in heaven.

**Today's Wise Words:** Jesus is preparing a fun place for me in heaven.

# Jesus Is the Way to God

Today's passage teaches us that Jesus is the only way to God. Thomas, one of Jesus' disciples, asked him to show them the way to the place he was going. Jesus is the way to God, and Jesus wanted his disciples to understand that. Jesus died, rose again and went back to the Father. Those who love God will also accept Jesus as the way.

Have you accepted Jesus as your Lord and Savior? Good. Now, you know the way to God.

### Dig Out The Answers

1. Where was Jesus going?
2. How can you go to the Father in heaven?

**In Your Own Words:** Write down what you learned.

**My Prayer:** God, I thank you for sending Jesus to show me the way to you. Amen.

**Memory Verse:** *"Jesus answered, I am the way and the truth and the life. No one comes to the Father except through me." John 14:6 (NIV)*

**Today's Wise Words:** No one comes to the Father except through Jesus.

# Jesus Promises the Holy Spirit

**READ**

John
14:16-17

Day 285

Jesus promised to ask the Father to send the Holy Spirit, and true to his word, the Holy Spirit lives today in every Christian. Jesus can be trusted for everything. The disciples thought they'd miss Jesus if he went away. But Jesus promised

to send the Holy Spirit to be their friend. The Holy Spirit is also called the Comforter. He comforts us when we are troubled. He is also called the Spirit of Truth, because he teaches us the truth about Jesus. Jesus told them that the Holy Spirit would live with them and in them. True to Jesus' words, today the Holy Spirit lives with and inside every Christian.

**Dig Out The Answers**

1. Who did Jesus promise to send the disciples when he goes away?

2. Is the Holy Spirit living in your heart, and with you as a friend?

**In Your Own Words:** Write down what you learned.

**My Prayer:** God, I thank you for sending the Holy Spirit to live in my heart. Amen.

**Today's Wise Words:** Jesus has sent the Holy Spirit as he promised.

301

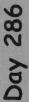

## READ
John 14:21

# What It Means to Love Jesus

Today's verse teaches us that those who love Jesus obey him. What Jesus commands us to do is found in the Bible. When we do what the Bible says, it means we love Jesus. Do you remember some of the things the Bible teaches us to do? (See Days 52 – 82) Ask God to help you obey them. When you obey God's word, you see and know Jesus better.

### Dig Out The Answer

How do you show your love for Jesus?

**In Your Own Words**: What did you learn? Write it down.

**My Prayer:** God, let me love Jesus by obeying him. Amen.

**Today's Wise Words:**
Love Jesus by obeying him.

# READ    What the Holy Spirit Does

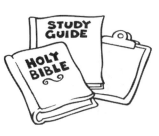

**John 14:25-26**

**Day 287**

Jesus told the disciples what the Holy Spirit would do. The Holy Spirit teaches all things about Jesus, and reminds us of all that we read in the Bible. Whenever you read the word of God and understand what it says, it is the Holy Spirit living in you, and teaching you. Whenever you remember a scripture verse you learned a while ago, it is the Holy Spirit

who has reminded you. It is clear that without the Holy Spirit we wouldn't understand God's word.

Before you read the Bible everyday, ask the Holy Spirit to help you understand what you are about to read. You are able to obey God's word when you understand it.

## Dig Out The Answers

1. What are the two things the Holy Spirit does for a Christian?
2. What should you do before reading your Bible everyday?

**In Your Own Words:** Write down what you learned.

**My Prayer:** Father God, remind me to ask the Holy Spirit to teach me as I read the Bible daily. Amen.

**Today's Wise Words:** When I read about Jesus the Holy Spirit teaches me, and later he reminds me of what I have read.

# Jesus Gives Peace

Today's passage teaches that only Jesus gives peace. Jesus gave his disciples peace. You may ask, what is peace? We have peace when we know that Jesus loves us in both good and bad times. We are sure that he'll never leave us and this helps us to be calm in all our troubles. Even if we should die, we are sure that we are going to a better place. Jesus knew that bad things would happen to the disciples after he'd returned to his Father. There are so many bad and wicked things in this world, that's why Jesus put his peace in the heart of every Christian.

It's like going to a dark room knowing that dad is already there. Though it's dark, you are not afraid because you know your dad is in there and he will protect you from all harm. That's the way it is with Christians. The world is one dark place, but Jesus is here with us, so we are confident that he'll protect us. What a wonderful Savior we have!

## Dig Out The Answer

Why has Jesus put peace in the heart of every Christian?

**In Your Own Words:** Write down what you learned.

**My Prayer:** God, I thank you that Jesus has put his peace in my heart. Amen.

**Today's Wise Words:** Jesus gives peace to all who follow him.

# READ

## Jesus Is the True Vine

**John 15:1-2**

**Day 289**

Jesus wants us to bear the fruit of the Holy Spirit. As we learned earlier in our devotional, the fruit of the Spirit is love, joy, patience, kindness, goodness, faithfulness, gentleness and self-control. Jesus is the truth, and those who follow him think and act like him.

Jesus is the true vine. Christians are the branches on the true vine. The branches that are part of the vine bear fruit. Every Christian who is truly in Christ bears fruit. God the Father is the gardener, and he prunes the branches that bear fruit. God does this by helping Christians stop some bad habits and sins in their lives, so they can bear more fruit. Can you think of some bad things you used to do that you have stopped?

God cuts off dead branches that bear no fruit. Dead branches are not attached to the vine, that's why they are dead. They don't draw food from the stem of the vine. There are people who say they are Christians, but are not because they have not invited Jesus into their lives. They are dead branches. Soon everyone notices that they were just pretending to be Christians, because they don't bear fruit. Nobody can fool God. When you follow Jesus with all your heart, you will bear fruit and keep bearing more and more.

**Dig Out The Answers**
1. Who is the true vine? Who are the branches?
2. What happens to branches that don't bear fruit?
**In Your Own Words:** Write down what you learned.
**My Prayer:** God, I thank you that because I have asked Jesus into my life, I am a branch on the true vine, and that you'll help me bear fruit of the Spirit, Amen.

**Today's Wise Words:** Jesus is the true vine, and Christians are the branches.

# Depend on Jesus to Bear Fruit

**READ**
John
15:4-6

**Day 290**

Jesus teaches that we cannot bear the fruit of the Spirit unless we depend on him. The branches draw food from the vine so they can bear fruit. We also need to draw power from Jesus, who is the vine, so we can bear fruit. That's what Jesus meant by "remain in me". We depend on Jesus by talking to him in prayer many times during the day. When we talk to him, he gives us

power to do what is right. We depend on Jesus by reading the word of God daily. When we know and do what Jesus says, we remain in him. We also depend on Jesus when we share what we know about him with other believers and unbelievers. All these things help us remain in Jesus, and we are able to bear more fruit.

## Dig Out The Answers

1. Why is it important to "remain in Jesus"?
2. List some of the things you do to help you remain as a fruit-bearing branch on the vine.

**In Your Own Words:** Write down what you learned.

**My Prayer:** God, help me depend on Jesus to bear fruit, because I can do nothing without him. Amen.

**Today's Wise Words:** Depend on Jesus and you'll bear more fruit.

306

## Benefits of Depending on Jesus: answered prayers

**READ**

**John 15:7**

**Day 291**

One of the benefits of depending on Jesus to bear fruit is that God will answer your prayers. How does that happen? You remember that when Jesus lives in you, you begin to think and act like him. The more you obey the word of God, the more you become like Jesus. The more you become like Jesus, the more you are able to know what God wants to do in your life. When you know what God wants to do in your life, you talk to him about it in prayer. And because it's God's will, your prayer is answered. It's wonderful to pray and get answers. Sometimes God says "no" to our prayers, and that's also an answer. It may be because what you are asking for will harm you instead of blessing you. And because God is wise and loves you, he'll rather not let you have it. Sometimes, God may want you to wait for a while before giving you what you asked for in prayer. When we depend on Jesus, and remain in him, God will answer our prayers.

**Dig Out The Answers**
What is one of the things God does for those who depend on Jesus to bear fruit?
**In Your Own Words:** Write down what you learned.
**My Prayer:** Dear God, help me depend on Jesus to bear fruit, so I'll receive answers to my prayers. Amen.

**Today's Wise Words:** Depend on Jesus to bear fruit and God will answer your prayers.

307

**READ**

John 15:8

**Day 292**

When we depend on Jesus to bear fruit, we bring glory to God. Those who depend on Jesus to bear fruit will bear much more fruit. This is what God does for those who depend on Jesus.

When you bear much more fruit, God uses you for greater things, and you bring glory to his name. When others look at your life, they can say that God is good, great and powerful, and they may think of giving their lives to God, too. When this happens, it means you are bringing glory to God because you are bearing much more fruit. If you want to bear much more fruit, then keep depending on Jesus.

**Dig Out The Answers**

1. How do you bear much more fruit?
2. How do we bring glory to God?

**In Your Own Words:** Write down what you learned.

**My Prayer:** Dear God, help me bear much fruit so I'll bring glory to you, in Jesus' name. Amen.

**Today's Wise Words:** Bring glory to God by bearing much more fruit.

**READ**
John
15:9-10

**Day 293**

When we depend on Jesus to bear fruit, we enjoy God's love more and more. God will never stop loving you, but we can stop loving God. The one thing we can do to continue loving God is to bear fruit. When you see how wonderful it feels to forgive, be kind, gentle, and at peace, you also feel deeply how precious God's love is.

Do you know fruit-bearing keeps you out of trouble?

It keeps out bad company or bad friends. When you avoid bad friends, you'll likely not get into trouble with teachers or your neighbors. When you bear fruit, you'll likely not disobey your parents and watch that horror movie, which gives you nightmares later. You feel blessed and loved by God when you see all the benefits you enjoy because you bear fruit. God loves you, and wants to keep you from trouble; that's why he wants you to bear fruit and enjoy his love and protection.

**Dig Out The Answer**
What do you enjoy when you keep on bearing fruit?

**In Your Own Words:** Write down what you learned.

**My Prayer:** Dear God, help me continue to bear fruit so I can enjoy your love more and more, in Jesus' name. Amen.

**Today's Wise Words:** Depend on Jesus to bear fruit and you'll enjoy God's love.

309

READ

John 15:11

Day 294

# Benefits of Depending on Jesus: Joy

When we depend on Jesus to bear fruit, we have lots of joy. Wouldn't you rather be full of joy than sadness? Now, Jesus shows us how to be full of joy everyday – we must depend on him, remain in him, let the words of Jesus live in us. We bear fruit when we depend on Jesus. Others see the fruit in our lives - love, joy, patience, kindness, goodness, faithfulness, gentleness and self-control. Our good lives may draw others to come and know Jesus. We are glad when others come to know Jesus because of us. Don't you feel glad when you do good deeds instead of wrong things? Now that you know how to be full of joy, continue to depend on Jesus to bear fruit.

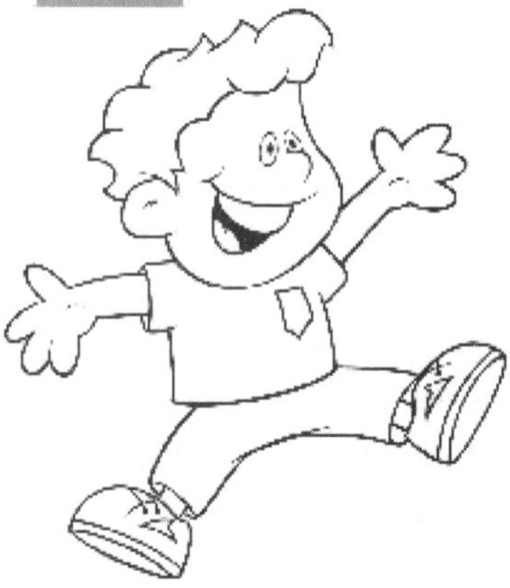

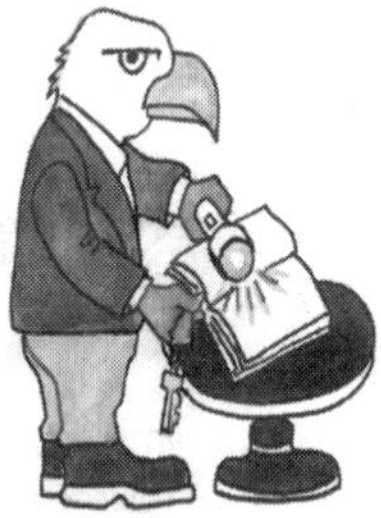

**Dig Out The Answers**

1. How do you become full of joy?

**In Your Own Words:** Write down what you learned.

**My Prayer:** Dear God, help me continue to depend on Jesus, so my joy will always be full. Amen.

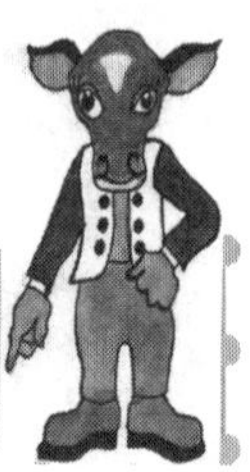

**Today's Wise Words:** Depend on Jesus to bear fruit and you will be full of joy.

# READ

**John 15:12**

## Jesus Commands Us to Love

Jesus wants us to love other Christians. Do you know that when the church started a long time ago, many joined because of the way the Christians loved one another? All Christians belong to one family, and Jesus is the head of that family. Think of your Christian friends. Are there ways you can love them better than you are doing now? List some things you'll start doing to show your love to them.

Some of the things you can do to show your love to other Christians are: be nice to them no matter how they look, don't talk behind their back, comfort them when they are sad, listen when they have a problem, pray with them, don't laugh at their mistakes but encourage them and share with those in need.

**Dig Out The Answers**

1. What does Jesus command us to do?
2. List the things you'll begin doing to show your love to other Christians.

**In Your Own Words:** Write down what you learned.

**My Prayer:** Dear God, help me love other Christians by being kind to them, in Jesus' name. Amen.

**Today's Wise Words:** Love other Christians dearly.

# READ

## Jesus Calls Us Friends

**John 15:13-14**

**Day 296**

Jesus calls you his friend. He died for you because you are his friend. What do you do for him if he is your friend? Jesus wants you to obey him. Jesus is not asking every Christian to die for him. Not many Christians will be killed because they believe in Jesus. You live in a country where you can worship Jesus freely. Thank God for that and obey the word of God, so you can show others that Jesus is your friend.

### Dig Out The Answers

1. What does Jesus call you?
2. What does Jesus want his friends to do?

**In Your Own Words:** Write down what you learned.

**My Prayer:** Thank God that Jesus is your friend.

**Today's Wise Words:**

Jesus is my friend.

# READ

## You Are More than a Servant

**John 15:15**

**Day 297**

Jesus calls "friends" all those who believe in him. And because Jesus is our friend, we are not servants or maids. Do you think your parents will be willing to tell a maid important things in your family? No. It's the same with Jesus and us. Because we are Jesus' friends, he is willing to show us everything we need to know about God. The only way you can know God is to become a friend of Jesus. How does Jesus tell us all about God? The Holy Spirit helps us understand God's word when we read it. You call somebody a friend because you know the person. In the same way, you can call Jesus your friend because you know him from what you read from the Bible.

## Dig Out The Answers

1. What does Jesus do for us because we are his friends?

**In Your Own Words:** Write down what you learned.

**My Prayer:** Dear God, I thank you that I am Jesus' friend, and he teaches me all that I need to know about you. Amen.

**Today's Wise Words:** Jesus tells me all about God, the Father, because we are friends.

313

John
15:16

Day 298

Jesus chose you to bear fruit – fruit of the Holy Spirit. Understand that you are a Christian because Jesus chose you. Isn't this wonderful? Before you were born, Jesus had already chosen you, and he is going to keep you safe till he brings you to heaven. So keep reminding yourself that Jesus chose you to be his disciple because he loves you. Why did he choose you? Jesus chose you and put his Holy Spirit in you so you would bear

fruit. Keep this in mind everyday. Jesus chose you as his disciple so you would bear fruit.

**Dig Out The Answers**
1. Why did Jesus choose you?
2. What is the fruit of the Holy Spirit?

**In Your Own Words:** Write down what you learned.

**My Prayer:** Dear God, I am happy to know that Jesus chose me to bear fruit. Help me do so, in Jesus' name. Amen.

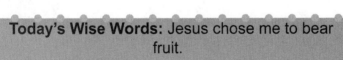

**Today's Wise Words:** Jesus chose me to bear fruit.

# The World Hates Christ's Followers

Jesus wants you to know that when you follow him you are not going to be popular in the world. Many people in the world do not like Jesus and his way. And they don't like people who follow the way of Jesus. The way of Jesus says that all are sinners, but the people in the world don't want to think that they are sinners. The way of Jesus says that Jesus is the Son of God who died to pay for our sins. The people in the world don't want to hear that. They think they can do enough good things to make it to heaven without Jesus' help. They don't want to accept that only the blood of Jesus can wash away their sins and bring them to God in heaven. Some people in the world don't want to accept that God made the world. They are angry with God and with themselves. But God loves the people in the world. The good news is being preached and many are turning to Jesus. It's good to remember that when you follow Jesus the world will not like you. But God is more important. The world will soon be destroyed and those who have Jesus will live in a new earth and heaven. You don't want to be destroyed along with the world.

## Dig Out The Answers
1. What did Jesus say the world would do to Christians?
2. What will happen to the world in the long run?
**In Your Own Words:** Write down what you learned.
**My Prayer:** God, give me power to walk with Jesus even though the world would hate me, so I'll not be destroyed along with the world, in Jesus' name. Amen.

**Today's Wise Words:** You won't be popular in the world if you are a Christian.

# A Servant Is Not Greater than His Master

Jesus continues to warn us that the world will treat us badly because we follow him. Jesus wants us to understand that if they did it to him, they'd do to us. We are not greater than Jesus who is our Master. Jesus gives two reasons why the people in the world treat Christians badly. The first thing is that they don't know God, the Father. Secondly, they don't want to know about their sins or wrongdoings. They'd rather keep their sins secret.

When we come to Jesus, his light shows us that we are wrongdoers, and then we turn to him to forgive us and save us. There are those in the world who don't want that, so they treat Christians badly. Praise God, Jesus showed you that you are a sinner, gave his blood to pay for your sins, and now you are on your way to heaven. Pray for people you know who are still refusing Jesus, that, they may come to him, too.

**Dig Out The Answers**

1. Write down the two reasons why those in the world hate Christians?

2. What do you do about family and friends who are still in the world?

**In Your Own Words**: What did you learn? Write it down.

**My Prayer:** Dear God, I thank you for my salvation. Save those in the world who do not know you, in Jesus' name. Amen.

**Today's Wise Words:** Jesus is the Master, and I am the servant.

# The Holy Spirit Is a Person

**John 15:26**

Jesus teaches in this verse that the Holy Spirit is a person. The Holy Spirit has titles like "Comforter or Counselor", and "Spirit of Truth". Jesus also teaches here that the Holy Spirit is not a power or a thing. The Holy Spirit is the Spirit of God, just as Jesus is the Son of God. Because the Holy Spirit is one with the Father and the Son, he does exactly what the Father and Jesus would do.

Don't get confused. God is one, but we know him as the Father, secondly as Jesus, and thirdly as the Holy Spirit. He is the same one God, and he wants us to understand this.

The Holy Spirit does a number of things for the Christian. He teaches us about Jesus. He gives us power to obey what we read from God's word. He reminds us of what we know about Jesus when we are in difficult situations. He comforts us through times of suffering. When the Holy Spirit does all this work in our lives, he is making us witnesses for Christ. The things the Holy Spirit helps us do tell unbelievers that Jesus is God and only he can save.

**Dig Out The Answers**

1. Write down some of the names of the Holy Spirit.
2. What do you learn from the notes above about what the Holy Spirit does in your life?

**In Your Own Words:** Write down what you learned.

**My Prayer:** God, I thank you that the Holy Spirit is God the Spirit, who teaches, gives me power to do what is right, and comforts me when I am suffering, so I can be a witness for Christ. I love you, Holy Spirit, for all the work you do in me, in Jesus' name. Amen.

**Today's Wise Words:** The Holy Spirit is God.

## READ

**John 15:27**

# Tell Others about Jesus

**Day 302**

Jesus told his disciples to tell others about him (telling others about Jesus is witnessing or testifying.) But how were they going to do it? Jesus promised that the Holy Spirit from God would make Jesus real to them. You are able to tell others about Jesus only when the Holy Spirit lives in you and teaches you about him. You must call on the Holy Spirit to help you

know Jesus more. That's his work and he is happy and ever ready to help you. Jesus wants all Christians to be his witnesses.

**Dig Out The Answers**
1. Who helps us testify about Jesus?
2. What does Jesus want all Christians to do?

**In Your Own Words:** Write down what you learned.

**My Prayer:** Dear God, help me by your Spirit to be a better witness for Jesus daily. Amen.

**Today's Wise Words:** Tell others about Christ.

# Jesus Tells of What Is Yet to Come

Jesus told his disciples how much they were going to suffer because of him. Jesus is God and knows everything. So he was able to tell the disciples all that would happen to them. He told them how they'd be driven out of the places where Jews worshipped, and even killed. He told them all that so they would not be discouraged and stop following him in times of trouble.

Do you know that all that Jesus said came true? The apostles were beaten and put in prison. Some were killed, just as Jesus had said.

There are many Christians around the world who are in prison, beaten, and killed, but they never stop following Jesus. If all that Jesus said is coming true, then it is also true that he is the Son of God, Savior of the world, and coming back to take us to heaven to live with him forever. It is also true, that Jesus will cast all those who reject him into hell on judgment day.

Every promise in the Bible will come true. It's very important to trust Jesus, and obey him with the help of the Holy Spirit. Jesus loves you and wants to bless you from now on and forever.

### Dig Out The Answers

1. Did the words of Jesus to the disciples come true?

2. Why is Jesus able to tell of things that will happen in the future?

**In Your Own Words:** Write down what you learned.

**My Prayer:** Dear God, help me hold on to Jesus, no matter what, because he has power to bless me and bring me to heaven one day. Amen.

**Today's Wise Words**: Jesus knows all that will happen in the future.

# Look on the Brighter Side

The disciples were sad after hearing all that they'd suffer for Christ. Sometimes, we are also sad because of things others do to us or things we miss out on because we are Christians. But Jesus wants us to look on the brighter side. Jesus had earlier told the apostles of how they'd sit on twelve thrones and reign

with him when he comes back to earth. He had also told them earlier that he was going to prepare a place for them. These are great rewards, but the disciples had already forgotten all these good things and they were thinking only of the sufferings ahead of them.

Whenever you miss out on something because you are a Christian, just remember Jesus' promise that you'll reign with him one day. Remember the fun things, especially for children, that Jesus is making ready for you in heaven, and be happy. When you do that you are looking on the bright side. Be happy, you are a prince or a princess in the kingdom of God.

**Dig Out The Answer**
Jesus doesn't want us to think so much about what we miss out on in the world but rather _____.
**In Your Own Words:** Write down what you learned.

**My Prayer:** Dear God, whenever I am sad, help me think of the wonderful things Jesus is preparing for me in heaven.

**Today's Wise Words:** Be happy about fun times ahead in heaven.

# Jesus Has Our Best Interest at Heart

Jesus teaches us in today's verse that he always does what is best for us. Jesus is love and will never do anything that will hurt us or leave us without hope. Jesus can be trusted. He wanted his disciples to understand this. Jesus had to go away so the Holy Spirit would come and help the disciples. See how blessed we are because the Holy Spirit lives in us, teaches us, and gives us power to do what is right. He even gives us gifts to work for Jesus

We all behave like the disciples at times. We worry about a few things that go wrong. We forget that Jesus loves us and only allows things in our lives that will bless us the best. Of course, bad things happen to Christians sometimes, but we must remember to trust Jesus to deliver us from them. The things that Jesus allows into our lives sometimes may be difficult and sad. You may not understand why you couldn't have that toy, or game. You may not understand why God had to take Grandma or Grandpa away. But remember, all Jesus allows into our lives bless us one way or the other. Trust him.

## Dig Out The Answers

1. Why was it important for Jesus to go back to heaven?
2. How are we blessed today because we have the Holy Spirit?
3. Jesus allows only the _____ to happen to you. Trust him.

**In Your Own Words:** Write down what you learned.

**My Prayer:** Thank God that he does only the best for you.

**Today's Wise Words:** All Jesus allows into my life bless me one way or the other.

# The Holy Spirit and the People of the World

John 16:8

Day 306

Jesus told the disciples the kind of work the Holy Spirit would do for the people of the world. The Holy Spirit makes people understand that they are sinners. He makes them understand that sin is ugly and filthy. He makes them understand that sin has made them foolish, and separated them from God who is holy.

The Holy Spirit makes the people of the world understand that no one avoids sin because it is our nature to sin. He also makes people understand that all who go on sinning will end up in hell.

God loves all the people in the world, that's why he sent the Holy Spirit to help us understand how awful sin is, so we can turn to Jesus to save us.

Do you know that if you have given your life to Jesus it is because the Holy Spirit made you understand that you are a sinner? Praise the Holy Spirit for doing this work in your life.

### Dig Out The Answers
1. What does the Holy Spirit show people about sin so they can come to Jesus?
2. What did the Holy Spirit show you about your sin so you could come to Jesus?
**In Your Own Words:** Write down what you learned.

**My Prayer:** Thank you, Holy Spirit, for working on my heart to help me become a Christian. Amen.

**Today's Wise Words:** The Holy Spirit makes people understand that they are sinners.

# Unbelief - the greatest sin

Jesus teaches that the greatest sin in the world is refusing to accept him as Savior. Unbelief was the sin of the teachers of the law in Mark chapter 3, verses 28 – 30. They did not believe in Jesus even though they saw the miracles he performed. The teachers of the law even accused him of casting out demons by another demon. Thank Jesus for saving you. You have obeyed the greatest commandment of God to accept Jesus as Savior. Only the Holy Spirit can make people understand that the greatest sin is refusing Jesus. The Holy Spirit convinces sinners like us to believe in Jesus.

If you are a Christian today, it is because the Holy Spirit opened your heart to understand that the greatest sin is not accepting Jesus as Savior. Once you understood that, you gave your heart to Jesus. Pray that the Holy Spirit will work on the hearts of those who don't believe, helping them to understand that their greatest sin is refusing to accept Jesus as Lord and Savior.

**Dig Out The Answers**
1. What did Jesus say is the greatest sin?
2. Who makes people understand this?
3. What happens when people understand this?
**In Your Own Words:** Write down what you learned.

**My Prayer:** Thank you Holy Spirit for opening my heart to understand that not accepting Jesus as Savior is the greatest sin. I have given my life to Jesus since then, and pray that others will too, in Jesus name, Amen.

**Today's Wise Words:** The Holy Spirit makes people understand that not accepting Jesus is the greatest sin.

# The Holy Spirit and Righteous Jesus

**READ**
John
16:10

Day 308

Jesus teaches that the Holy Spirit will open the heart of people to understand that he is a righteous man, and through him, all who come to him will be made righteous. You are right with God, now that you have Jesus in your heart. God calls you righteous. The Holy Spirit did this work in your heart. When Jesus rose from the dead and ascended into heaven he sent the Holy Spirit as he promised. The Holy Spirit lives in the heart of all Christians today and Jesus is now with the Father in heaven. Jesus is in indeed the Son of God.

**Dig Out The Answers**
1. The Holy Spirit convinces and makes people understand that Jesus is _____ .
2. What does it mean to be righteous?

**In Your Own Words:** Write down what you learned.

**My Prayer:** Thank you, Holy Spirit, for teaching me that Jesus is perfectly righteous, and that God also makes righteous all those who trust in him. Amen.

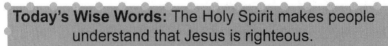

**Today's Wise Words:** The Holy Spirit makes people understand that Jesus is righteous.

# The Holy Spirit and the Judgment of the Devil

**READ**

John
16:11

The Holy Spirit helps people understand that the power of the devil has been destroyed. The devil is called the prince of this world. The devil has lost his power over people because God has found him guilty. The Holy Spirit shows us that the devil is a liar and deceiver, so we can turn to Jesus to save us. How was the devil judged? Jesus cast demons out of people while on earth. He showed that he had power

over the devil and his demons. Jesus overcame the temptations of the devil. Jesus showed the devil that he could not lead him to sin like other men. Jesus conquered the devil. So you also can say "no" to the devil when he tempts you because the Holy Spirit helps you. Jesus died and rose again, showing that death no more has power over those who believe in him. The Holy Spirit makes people understand that Jesus has complete power over the devil. Believe it. You are safe in the hands of Jesus.

### Dig Out The Answers

1. List some of the things Jesus did while here on earth to show that he had power over the devil?

2. What does the Holy Spirit help people understand in today's verse.

**In Your Own Words:** Write down what you learned.

**My Prayer:** God, I thank you that Jesus has complete power over the devil, so I am very safe in your hands. Amen.

**Today's Wise Words:** The Holy Spirit makes people understand that Jesus has conquered the devil.

325

# Pray in Jesus' Name

**READ**
John
16:23-24

Day 310

Jesus teaches us to pray in his name. What does it mean?

When we pray in Jesus' name it means we want God to answer our prayers according to his will, not ours. Why? Because God knows what is best for us.

Why does God answer our prayers? God answers our prayers so we will be full of joy. Jesus is praying for you in heaven right now. When you ask in his name, he then tells God about it, and God gives you what you asked for according to his will.

That's the way God wants us to pray – to ask in Jesus' name.

### Dig Out The Answers
1. In whose name do we pray?
2. Why do we have to pray in Jesus name?
3. Why does God answer our prayers?

**In Your Own Words:** Write down today's lesson.

**My Prayer:** Dear God, let me remember to always pray in Jesus' name. Amen.

**Today's Wise Words:** Ask in Jesus' name.

READ
John
17:1-5

## Jesus Prays for Himself

**Day 311**

Jesus prayed at the last supper. Jesus prayed for himself because he was about to suffer and die. He did this in front of his disciples. It is good to pray for yourself when you are in trouble and need help. Jesus' prayer tells us that he was with his Father before he came to earth. It also teaches that the Father gave him authority to give eternal life to all who believe in him. Jesus said he had finished all the Father asked him to do. You must also do all that God asks you to. When you do, it means you are bringing glory to God. Jesus asked his Father to answer his prayer by bringing glory to him. The Father answered Jesus' prayer by raising him from the dead, taking him to heaven and giving him the name above every name.

At the name of Jesus everything has to bow. That's why the devil runs away when you mention the name of Jesus. That's why when you pray in Jesus' name, you stop doing wrong things. There is power in the name of Jesus, and it stops the power of sin from driving you to do the wrong things. Jesus prayed and the Father answered. You must also pray and he will answer you too.

**Dig Out The Answers**
1. Jesus has authority to give _____ _____ to all who come to him.
2. Jesus was with ____ before he came to earth.
3. What did Jesus do to bring glory to God's name?
**In Your Words:** Write down what you learned.
**My Prayer:** Dear God, help me bring glory to your name by doing all that you ask me to, very well, in Jesus name, Amen.

**Today's Wise Words:** Jesus brought glory to God by finishing well all that God asked him to.

# Jesus Prays for His Disciples

Jesus now prayed for his disciples. Jesus was happy to tell God all that he had taught his disciples.

He told God how the disciples believed all that he taught them, and how they were sure that he was truly the Son of God. The disciples had been good students.

Can Jesus say the same about you to God? Be a good follower of Jesus, everyday! Jesus is happy to talk to the Father about you when you follow and obey him. Jesus is sitting at the Father's right hand in heaven right now, praying for you. Make him glad by following him like the disciples did.

**Dig Out The Answers**

1. What did Jesus happily tell God about the disciples in prayer?

2. The disciples believed that Jesus was sent from _____.

**In Your Words:** Write down what you learned.

**My Prayer:** Dear Father, make me a good follower of Jesus like the disciples, so he will tell you about me as he told you about them. Amen.

**Today's Wise Words:** The disciples made Jesus happy because they obeyed.

328

## Disciples Bring Glory to Christ

**Day 313**

We are still reading Jesus' prayer for his disciples. At this point there were only eleven of them because Judas Iscariot had left to tell the enemies of Jesus where he was. Jesus says in the prayer that his disciples belong to God. You also belong to God if you have given your life to him. Jesus also says in the prayer that all who belong to the Father are his, and all who belong to him are also the Father's. This tells us that Jesus is one with the Father. Jesus then asks the Father to let his disciples bring glory

to him. As we said before, we bring glory to God when we obey him. Jesus prayed that his eleven disciples would obey him all the time. Jesus prays this same prayer for you, too.

### Dig Out The Answer
Jesus asked in prayer that his eleven disciples would bring glory to him. How do you bring glory to Jesus?

**In Your Own Words:** Write down what you learned.

**My Prayer:** Dear Father, I thank you for teaching me that I belong to you because I believe in your Son, Jesus. Amen.

**Today's Wise Words:** I belong to the Father because I believe in Jesus.

**READ**

Day 314

We are still reading Jesus' prayer for his disciples. The Father knows everything and yet Jesus prayed about what was going to happen. It teaches us a lesson about prayer. Even though God knows everything, we should still go to him in prayer and tell him our problems. This shows that we trust him to help us. Jesus asked his Father to keep the disciples safe from the evil one, and to keep them all one. What does it mean "to be one"? Jesus wants his

disciples to love one another and continue to believe all that he taught while here on earth. There are times when quarrels break out among Christians because some start believing wrong teachings, which were not taught by Jesus. The power of Jesus protects those who believe and follow his teachings, helping them to love one another and spread the good news. Follow the teachings of Jesus carefully, so you can work "as one" with other believers.

### Dig Out The Answer

Jesus asked the Father to protect or keep his disciples safe and to keep them _____.

**In Your Own Words:** Write down what you learned.

**My Prayer:** God, help me talk to you in prayer about my problems even though you know them already, in Jesus' name. Amen.

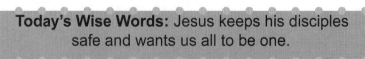

**Today's Wise Words:** Jesus keeps his disciples safe and wants us all to be one.

330

# READ

## Joy for all Disciples

**John 17:13**

**Day 315**

Jesus was still praying for his disciples. In today's verse, Jesus asked that his disciples might have joy in their hearts. The world is full of evil and wickedness. Jesus knows that Christians may suffer in the world and may sometimes be sad. That's why he asked his Father to fill his disciples with joy – joy that comes from knowing that they belong to God, that they are special, that they are going to reign with Jesus one day, and that Jesus is preparing a better place for them. Jesus wants you to live and follow him with great joy because you are special, dearly loved, and he is preparing a wonderful place for you in heaven, where you'll reign with him.

**Dig Out The Answer**
Jesus asked the Father to fill his disciples with _____.

**In Your Own Words:** Write down what you learned.

**My Prayer:** Dear God, fill me with joy so I can live happily for Jesus everyday. Amen.

**Today's Wise Words:** God fills me with joy.

# You Do Not Belong to the World

**READ**
John
17:14-16

Jesus is still praying for his disciples in today's verse. Jesus' prayer teaches that his disciples do not belong to the world. You also do not belong to the world. Those who belong to the world belong to the devil. Those who belong to Jesus are just passing through this world. Christians are here in the world to tell others to come and follow Jesus. Jesus also prayed that God would keep his disciples from the evil one, the devil. It is good to ask God to keep you from the evil one.

**Dig Out The Answers**
1. Do you belong to the world?
2. What are Christians to do while they live in the world?

**In Your Own Words:** Write down what you learned.

**My Prayer:** Dear God, help me understand that I don't belong to the world. I am here in the world to tell others to come and know Jesus. Amen.

**Today's Wise Words:** I don't belong to the world. I belong to God.

# I Am Set Apart

Jesus is still praying for his disciples. In today's passage, he asks his Father to set his disciples apart by his word. Jesus' teaching is called the truth or the word. *Set apart* means the same thing as *sanctify* or *make holy*. People set things apart that are special. Everybody who comes to believe in Jesus is set apart by God for the special

job of telling others about Jesus by the fruit they bear. You are set apart because you believed the truth, which is the word of Jesus, that he is the Son of God. You are now a special person and you are to bring glory to God by knowing his word and obeying it.

### Dig Out The Answers
1. What is the truth that sets Christians apart?
2. Why did God make you special?

**In Your Own Words:** Write down what you learned.

**My Prayer:** Dear Father, I thank you that you have set me apart to bring others to know Jesus by obeying you in all things. Amen.

**Today's Wise Words:** God has set me apart to live for Jesus and tell about him.

## READ
### John 17:20-23

**Day 318**

# Jesus Prays for His Church

Today's passage is about Jesus' prayer for all Christians. Isn't this wonderful! Before you were born Jesus knew you would follow him and he had prayed for you. And not just for you, but anyone who'll decide to become a Christian. Jesus had you in mind when he prayed for all those who would come to believe in

him. Jesus prayed that the Father would make all Christians one. Christians act as one when we love one another. When Christians love one another, the people in the world take notice and come to believe that Jesus is truly the Son of God. Wouldn't you want many people to come and know Jesus? Wonderful! Then ask the Holy Spirit to help you love other Christians.

**Dig Out The Answers**

1. Why did Jesus ask God to make Christians one?

2. List things you are going to do to show your love for other Christians.

**In Your Own Words:** Write down what you learned.

**My Prayer:** Dear God, teach me to love other Christians, so that those in the world will know that Jesus is the Son of God.

**Today's Wise Words:** I must be one with all Christians.

334

# The Church to See Jesus' Glory

**READ**

John
17:24-26

**Day 319**

Jesus also prayed that God would bring all Christians to heaven to see his glory. And one day, when the trumpet shall sound, all believers will be caught up into heaven with Jesus. Hallelujah! Jesus also prayed that those who follow him would know that he is one with them.

We are one with Christ Jesus because his love lives in us. The more we know about Jesus by reading the word and obeying it, the more his love grows in us. Just know this, that you are one with Christ Jesus if you have accepted him as Lord and Savior.

**Dig Out The Answers**
1. What did Jesus ask God in the prayer?
2. How did we become one with Jesus Christ?

**In Your Own Words:** Write down what you learned.

**My Prayer:** Dear God, I thank you that I am one with Jesus because his love lives in me. Amen.

**Today's Wise Words:** I am one with Jesus and one day I'll see his glory.

## READ

**Matthew**
**26:36-39**

**Day 320**

# Jesus in Gethsemane

Jesus had just finished praying for himself, his disciples, and all those who'd later come to believe in him. The last supper was finally over. Jesus took his disciples to a garden called Gethsemane, outside Jerusalem's city wall. Jesus and his disciples had gone there many times. Jesus was as human as you and me. See how sad and troubled he was because of all that he was about to suffer. He took his three best friends farther into

the garden to keep watch with him. Even Jesus needed his friends when he was sorrowful. You also need your friends and your friends need you, too. Ask Jesus to give you good friends who will be there for you when you need them. Don't forget to ask that you will be there for your friends, too, when they need you.

Jesus was never tired of praying. Remember, he had just finished praying at the last supper, and here in the Garden he was praying again. Jesus was eager to do what his Father wanted – to die for our sins. That was a painful thing, but Jesus was willing to do it.

**Dig Out The Answers**
1. Was Jesus ever tired of praying? What does that teach you?
2. Was Jesus willing to do what God wanted? What does that teach you?
3. Why did Jesus take along his three best friends to pray?
**In Your Own Words:** Write down what you learned.

**My Prayer:** Dear God, teach me to pray often. Also, teach me to do what you want for my life, and give me good friends, in Jesus' name. Amen.

**Today's Wise Words:** Even Jesus needed his friends.

# READ

**Day 321**

## Jesus and His Best Friends

Jesus was still praying in the Garden. Jesus returned to see that his three best friends were fast asleep. They couldn't keep watch with him. But Jesus was not angry with them. He understood that they were sleepy, and very sad. Jesus shows us how to be good friends even when we feel sad or troubled. We should not blame our friends for not helping us the way we think they should. Jesus knew better. God is the only one who is able to help us through all our problems. It is good to have friends, but best to have Jesus who'll never sleep. Jesus finished praying and was soon ready to leave the Garden with his friends. What happened next?

### Dig Out The Answers
1. What made Jesus a good friend in the story?
2. Why does Jesus make a better friend than any else?

**In Your Own Words:** Write down what you learned.

**My Prayer:** Dear God, teach me to be a good friend like Jesus even when I am sad. Amen.

**Today's Wise Words:** Jesus was a good friend to his disciples even when he was sad.

337

## Jesus Is Arrested

**Day 322**

Jesus had barely finished talking to his disciples when a crowd stormed into the garden, armed with swords and clubs. And guess who was leading them? You guessed right. Judas Iscariot, the betrayer. He was not even ashamed. He kissed Jesus on the cheeks, singling him out as the one to arrest. Jesus had asked to let his disciples go free. There and then, the men seized Jesus and took him away to the chief priests, elders and teachers of the law. Jesus' disciples deserted him. They were afraid. But Jesus had prayed, so he was ready to face what was ahead. Prayer helps us do God's will.

**Dig Out The Answers**

1. Jesus had prayed and was prepared for the suffering ahead. It is good for you to prepare to do what God wants by _____ first.

**In Your Own Words:** Write down what you learned.

**My Prayer:** Dear God, teach me to pray like Jesus, so I'll always be prepared to obey you even in difficult times.

**Today's Wise Words:** Jesus was prepared to die because he had prayed.

# READ  Jesus Protects His Disciples

Jesus made sure that the disciples were not arrested along with him. Remember they were still in the Garden. Jesus told those who were about to arrest him, in a commanding tone, to let his disciples go, and they did. The officials had to obey Jesus. Jesus did not lose any of his disciples. Jesus wants you to know that he'll

always protect you just as he did for the disciples. You are in his hands, and very safe, and nobody can touch you. Jesus was willing to suffer so his disciples would escape. As a disciple of Jesus, do you know you have also escaped with your life because Jesus chose to suffer for you? All those who trust in Jesus have escaped with their lives because Jesus died in their place. What a wonderful Savior! The disciples escaped with their lives, so they'd tell others about Jesus after his resurrection. Jesus protects you, so you will continue to live for him, and then others may come to know him too.

### Dig Out The Answers
1. Why didn't the soldiers arrest the disciples as well? Is Jesus able to protect you too?
2. List the reasons Jesus allowed the disciples to escape with their lives.

**In Your Own Words:** Write down what you learned.

**My Prayer:** Lord Jesus, thank you that you suffered so I will escape with my life and live for you. Thank you that I am safe because you protect me. Amen.

**Today's Wise Words:** Jesus chose to suffer so I would live.

339

# Whatever the Reason, Don't Do the Wrong Thing

**Day 324**

Peter wanted to defend Jesus. He wanted to fight against those who had come to arrest him. What did he do? He aimed his sword at the servant of the high priest and WHAM! struck his ear. Do you think he did the right thing? Of course not! Do you know they could have arrested Peter for striking the ear of the servant of the high priest?

But Jesus had asked those about to arrest him to let his disciples go free.

No matter how awful you feel, remember to ask the Holy Spirit to help you do the right thing. The right thing that Peter could have done was to pray and keep calm. That's good advice. When you are not sure what to do in a particular situation, just pray and be calm. This will prevent you from doing the wrong thing.

Was it wrong for the chief priests to arrest Jesus who went around doing good? Yes. And sometimes others don't treat us right either. But would it be right for you to treat them nastily in return? No.

**Dig Out The Answers**
1. Was it right for Peter to strike the servant's ear?
2. What should he have done instead?
**In Your Own Words:** Write down what you learned.

**My Prayer:** Pray that God will help you do the right thing even when you don't feel like it.

**Today's Wise Words:** Pray and be calm when you don't know what to do.

## Jesus Does the Right Thing

Today's story teaches us to be kind to those who hurt us. That's what Jesus did. When one of his disciples struck the ear of the servant of the high priest, Jesus touched his ear and healed him. The story we read yesterday gave us the name of the disciple who did this. His name was Peter. Jesus did not panic like his disciples because he trusted his Father and knew that even when he died, the Father was going to raise him again from the dead.

What we know about God helps us trust him when we are in trouble. Jesus knew all that was going to happen, and had told the disciples about it already. There was no way he would have fought with a sword. That's why it's important to read the Bible to know all that God is able to do for you. Always remember that God is able to get you out of any trouble. Trust him and you will do what is right even when you find yourself in a tight spot.

**Dig Out The Answers**

1. Why did Jesus heal the servant's ear? What does this teach you?

2. What helps us trust God and do what is right in difficult situations?

**In Your Own Words:** Write down what you learned.

**My Prayer:** Dear God, teach me more about you, so I can trust you and do what is right even if I find myself in a tight spot, in Jesus' name. Amen.

**Today's Wise Words:** Know God. Trust Him. Do what is right.

341

# Jesus Is Taken To The High Priest

Jesus was taken to the high priest, where the chief priests and teachers of the law had all gathered. They wanted someone to accuse Jesus of a crime. Jesus never sinned and so they found it hard to find someone to accuse him of a crime. The chief priests and leaders were bent on putting Jesus to death. Isn't that awful – to kill somebody who never wronged anyone but only did good things. All the things people were accusing him of were a bunch of lies.

Those speaking against him did not understand what Jesus meant by destroying the temple and building it in three days. Jesus said that a long while ago. He was referring to his body that would be crucified but raised back to life on the third day. Do you remember we learned from the Sermon on the Mount to be happy when people tell all kinds of evil lies about us? They did it to Jesus, first, but Jesus remained calm just as he had taught. Peter now followed at a distance and went right into the palace where Jesus was to be tried. It is not good to follow Jesus at a distance. You will discover that soon.

### Dig Out The Answer
1. People told all kinds of evil lies about Jesus. What Jesus taught on the Sermon on the Mount came true even in Jesus life. This teaches you that Jesus teaches the truth. So what should you do with the teachings of Jesus?

**In Your Own Words:** Write down what you learned.

**My Prayer:** Dear God, help me trust you when people tell evil lies about me.

**Today's Wise Words:** Jesus' teachings are all true.

# The High Priest Questions Jesus

**Day 327**

Jesus was still in the palace of the high priest. The high priest wanted Jesus to say something, but Jesus kept quiet. Jesus teaches us a great lesson here. It is good to be quiet when others bunch together, trying to find fault with you because you are a Christian. Jesus was also patient during the questioning time. Likewise, we need to be patient with those who treat us badly because they don't trust in Jesus.

### Dig Out The Answers

1. What are the two good things Jesus did when questioned by the high priest?

2. Why do you think it's important to be patient and quiet when others tell lies about you, just because you are Christian?

**In Your Own Words:** Write down what you learned.

**My Prayer:** Dear God, teach me to be quiet and patient like Jesus when others treat me badly because I am a Christian, in Jesus name, Amen.

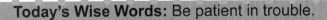

**Today's Wise Words:** Be patient in trouble.

# READ

Mark
14:61-65

## Jesus - The Messiah

Day 328

Jesus did not answer the lies told about him. But today, Jesus answered this particular question the high priest asked, 'are you the Messiah, the Son of God?' Jesus answered, "I am". Like Jesus, you should be bold to say, 'yes I am a Christian.' You must always be willing to let others know that you are a Christian by how you live. Jesus was not afraid to speak the truth about who he was and still is. What did he get for speaking the truth? They hit him with their fists, blindfolded him, beat him and decided to put him to death. Jesus had said before that they were going to do all that to him. How true Jesus' words are!

**Dig Out The Answers**
1. Was Jesus afraid to say he was and still is the Son of God?
2. Should you be afraid to say you are a Christian when asked?

**In Your Own Words:** Write down what you learned.

**My Prayer:** Dear God, teach me to be bold to say I am a Christian, even if that won't make me popular, in Jesus name, Amen.

**Today's Wise Words:** Don't be afraid to say you are a Christian.

# Peter Denies Jesus

**Mark 14:66-72**

Just as Jesus said, Peter denied he knew him. That's what happens when you follow Jesus at a distance. Peter, like all the other disciples ran away when Jesus was arrested. Of course, they were afraid to be arrested too. But Jesus understands. Jesus understands when you are afraid. And he wants you to come to him for help instead of running away. Peter followed Jesus at a distance. He was far away from where Jesus was standing for trial. Peter had mixed with the crowd. He didn't want anybody to know he was one of the disciples. Probably, if he had followed Jesus closely, he might have been bold in saying he was indeed a disciple. How do we walk close with Jesus? We walk close with Jesus by reading the Bible, obeying it and praying. To stay at a distance from Jesus is when we don't read the Bible often to find out what God wants, and also when we refuse to pray and to obey. We are happy when we walk close with Jesus. Peter was very sad when he denied he knew Jesus.

### Dig Out The Answers
1. What does it mean to walk close with Jesus?
2. What does it mean to stay at a distance from Jesus?
3. Would you stay close or at a distance from Jesus?

**In Your Own Words:** Write down what you learned.

**My Prayer:** Dear God, help me walk close with Jesus by reading the Bible, obeying it and praying. Amen.

**Today's Wise Words:** Walk close with Jesus

# Jesus Is Taken To Pilate

The chief priests and the leaders of the Jews did not have power to put Jesus to death. The Romans ruled the Jews at the time, and they had the power to put Jesus to death. That's why the Jewish leaders sent Jesus to Pilate. Pilate was the Roman Governor who ruled that part of Israel. Pilate questioned Jesus. Just like we read yesterday, Jesus was always ready to say who he was and still is – the King. Pilate saw that the Jewish leaders wanted Jesus killed because they envied him. Envy is when you want what someone else has. They were also jealous of Jesus. Sometimes, we all behave like the chief priests and teachers of the law. We say mean things to each other because we are jealous of something he or she has. We wished they didn't have this or that. A friend brings a cool new game to school, and because you are jealous, you say it's boring. Another friend gets a perfect score on his test, and you go, 'he thinks he knows everything'. That's jealousy. Jealousy may lead to other evil things. Tell God to help you not to be jealous of members of your family or friends.

## Dig Out The Answers
1. Why did the chief priest and teachers of the law want Jesus put to death?
2. Is it good to be jealous of family and friends? What should you do?

**In Your Own Words:** Write down what you learned.

**My Prayer:** Dear God, teach me not to be jealous of others. Help me pass nice comments about others and what they have, in Jesus name, Amen.

**Today's Wise Words:** Don't be envious or jealous of others.

**READ**

John
18:33-38

Day 331

Today's passage teaches us to search for TRUTH till we find it. Jesus is the truth, as you know by now. Pilate talked to Jesus.

Jesus told Pilate he was indeed a king but his kingdom was not of this world. He told Pilate that he came into the world to tell about the truth. Pilate got a little interested and asked Jesus, 'what is truth'? Did Pilate wait for an answer? No. He was more concerned about the crowd out there who wanted to have Jesus killed.

Pilate missed the truth. Probably, he was afraid to know the truth. Or maybe, he didn't care to know the truth. Or he loved his position as governor better. But Jesus wants all to know the truth. Jesus is the truth. It is this truth that saves us. Pray for people who are running away from the truth, that they'll come to know Jesus, the TRUTH. Praise God, you haven't missed the truth. Jesus is the TRUTH and lives in your heart if you've asked him to.

**Dig Out The Answers**
1. What is truth? Who is the truth?
2. You shall know the truth, and the _____ shall set you free.
**In Your Own Words:** Write down what you learned.

**My Prayer:** Pray that the Holy Spirit will make people seek Jesus who is the truth.
**Memory Verse:** *"Then you will know the truth, and the truth will set you free." John 8:32 (NIV)*

**Today's Wise Words:**
Jesus is the TRUTH.

347

# The Crowd Follows Evil Advice

**READ**
Mark
15:6-14

Day 332

Pilate realized Jesus was innocent. He had done nothing wrong. Pilate usually freed one prisoner chosen by the people during the Passover Festival. There was a very bad prisoner named Barabbas, who had killed others during a riot. Pilate was sure they'd have this good man, Jesus, released rather than Barabbas. But, Oh, what a shock he received. The chief priests told the crowd to ask for Barabbas' freedom. They were so envious and jealous, they'd rather have

Jesus crucified. What terrible things envy and jealousy lead people to do. The crowd just listened to the bad advice of the chief priests. Be careful of joining the crowd to do evil. Think before you act if you happen to be part of a crowd.

## Dig Out The Answers

1. Did the crowd do the right thing?
2. The crowd did the wrong thing because they listened to bad advice. How do you tell a good advice from a bad one?

**In Your Own Words:** Write down what you learned.

**My Prayer:** God, let the word of God make me wise so I can tell good advice from bad ones, in Jesus name. Amen.

**Today's Wise Words:**
Don't join the crowd to do evil

## READ
### Mark 15:15

**Day 333**

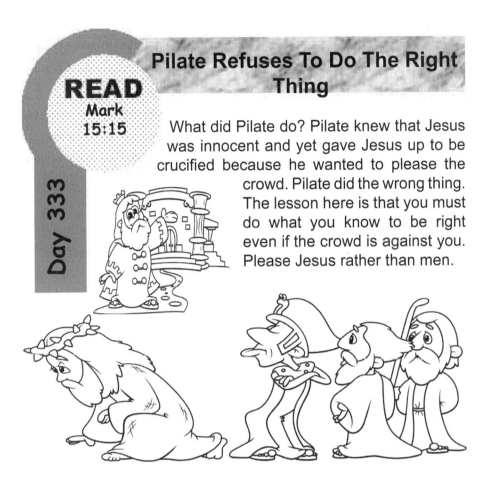

What did Pilate do? Pilate knew that Jesus was innocent and yet gave Jesus up to be crucified because he wanted to please the crowd. Pilate did the wrong thing. The lesson here is that you must do what you know to be right even if the crowd is against you. Please Jesus rather than men.

**Dig Out The Answers**

1. Why did Pilate give Jesus up to be crucified?

2. Is it good to please people rather than God? What should you do?

**In Your Own Words:** Write down what you learned.

**My Prayer:** Dear God, give me power to do what pleases you at all times, in Jesus name, Amen.

**Today's Wise Words:**
Please God rather than men.

# Judas Dies

Sin or wrongdoing may look attractive, but it leads to death for those who never say sorry to God. And this is what happened to Judas. Judas saw the horror and wickedness of his act. The money he wanted so much did not look attractive anymore. He now hated it and took it back to the chief priests. He told them he had done wrong by betraying Jesus. Judas went to the chief priests. Who do you think he should have gone to say sorry to? Of course, God! Only God has the power to forgive sins.

The chief priests couldn't care less. You'd think they'd help Judas after he'd helped them arrest Jesus, but they just mocked him. That's what the devil does. He leads people to sin, and when they are caught, he laughs and mocks. The devil made Judas feel that his sin could not be forgiven. That's another lie the devil tells people. But that's not true. If you ask God to forgive you, he is ready to forgive all your sins. Judas believed this lie and thought that it is was better for him to die. Judas lost all hope. The devil doesn't give hope. He destroys our hope. Hope is the comfort we enjoy in times of trouble because we have placed our trust in God. Judas went and hung himself. If he had gone to God in prayer, God would have forgiven him and given him hope.

**Dig Out The Answers**
1. What is the big lie the devil put into Judas' head?
2. Does God forgive any sin once you tell him you are sorry?
3. Who gives hope?
**In Your Own Words:** Write down what you learned.
**My Prayer:** Dear God, thank you for the hope I have because of Jesus. I know that you'll forgive any sin I commit once I sincerely come to you and say I am sorry, in Jesus name.

**Today's Wise Words:** God gives hope, but the devil destroys our hope.

# READ

## The Soldiers Mock Jesus

**Mark 15:16-20**

**Day 335**

Today you read what the soldiers did to Jesus. Pilate had released Barabbas, but Jesus was to be flogged and crucified. At the high priest's house they had spat on his face and struck him with their fists. Jesus' face was swollen and bloody by then.

The soldiers took over. The soldiers were usually given charge of criminals that were to be crucified. So, Jesus was in their charge, now. See the pain they inflicted on Jesus who had done no wrong. They put a scarlet robe on him, and a staff in his hand. They twisted a crown of thorns and pressed it down his head till blood oozed out. They made fun of him, bowing and spitting on him. Now, they grabbed the staff from his hand, hitting him on the head till his face and head were so crushed. You couldn't recognize him if you knew him. Jesus suffered all this so you'd be saved. Remember how much he suffered for you and praise him.

**Dig Out The Answers**

1. Why did Jesus have to suffer like this from the hands of soldiers?

**In Your Own Words:** Write down what you learned.

**My Prayer:** Dear God, teach me to appreciate Jesus for suffering for me.

**Today's Wise Words:** Jesus suffered all that for me.

351

**READ**

Mark 15:21-32

**Day 336**

Jesus was now on his way to be crucified. He was too weak to carry his own cross all the way. The soldiers forced a man called Simon to carry Jesus' cross. When they got to Golgotha, where he was going to be crucified, they took of all his clothes. Then they nailed him to the cross. The soldiers divided his clothes among themselves. Two robbers were crucified along with Christ, one on his right, the other on his left.

Those who passed by did not take pity on him. They insulted him, and challenged him to come down from the cross if he were really the Christ. But the people insulting him did not understand that Jesus was not on the cross to save himself, but all people born and yet to be born. Jesus didn't have to die because he never sinned. And Jesus wouldn't walk away from the cross because he loves us so much. He was willing to pay for our sins. Jesus obeyed God rather than men. Praise the name of Jesus. Jesus teaches us in today's story not to let what others say stop us from doing what God tells us to do.

**Dig Out The Answers**

1. Did Jesus pay attention to the insults heaped on him? Why?
2. Should the annoying things others say stop you from doing what is right?

**In Your Own Words:** Write down what you learned.

**My Prayer:** Dear God, help me do what is right even when others want to stop me by what they say, in Jesus name.

**Today's Wise Words:** Jesus did not mind the insults as he hung on the cross.

# READ

## Jesus Forgives

**Luke 23:32-34**

**Day 337**

What did Jesus do when he was being crucified? He asked God to forgive those crucifying him, because they had no idea what they were doing. Jesus gave us all an example of true love. Jesus even loved his enemies who were nailing him to the cross and prayed for them. Likewise, pray to God to help you forgive those who treat you badly.

Jesus, in all his suffering did not forget to show mercy or kindness. No matter how sad or hurt you feel, remember to be kind like Jesus. The Holy Spirit gives you power to do so.

**Dig Out The Answers**

1. What did Jesus do for those who crucified him?
2. What do you learn from Jesus' action?

**In Your Own Words:** Write down what you learned.

**My Prayer:** Pray that you will be kind even when you are hurt or sad.

**Today's Wise Words:** Jesus prayed for his enemies.

## One Criminal Had A Change of Mind

**READ**

Luke
23:39-43

Day 338

Today's story teaches us that Jesus can save even those who are close to dying. You read in the gospel of Mark, that the criminals who were crucified with him also heaped insults on him. But, one of them soon had a change of mind. This criminal knew that he deserved to die because he had done wrong things. He realized that Jesus was the Christ and a king. Jesus had done no wrong. So, he turned to Jesus and asked him to remember him in his kingdom. Jesus was ready to accept this sinner into his kingdom. Jesus promised him he would be in Paradise that very day. Paradise is heaven. Pray that criminals in prison cells will all come to know Jesus just like the criminal in today's story.

**Dig Out The Answers**

1. Did Jesus forgive the criminal who put his faith in him?

2. Will Jesus forgive criminals who are in prison right now if they come to him?

**In Your Own Words:** Write down what you learned.

**My Prayer:** Pray for criminals to come and know Jesus.

**Today's Wise Words:** It's never too late to give your life to Christ.

354

# Jesus Provides For His Mother

Jesus teaches us in today's passage to take care of our parents when we grow up. Jesus' mother, his aunt, his disciple John, and Mary Magdalene, stood near the cross where Jesus hung. Jesus' mother did not desert him like the rest of the disciples. Though Jesus was himself suffering as he hung on the cross, he did not forget his mother. He had to find a good person to take care of his mother after his death. John, one of his disciples was one of his best friends. He too did not desert Jesus, but stood near the cross.

Jesus asked John to take care of his mother after his death. John was such a faithful friend. He took Jesus' mother to his own home and took care of her. Jesus' father was probably dead by then. It pleases God when grown children take care of their aging parents. And also, we should be faithful friends like John, such that our friends can trust us to help members of their families when they are in need. Even before you become a grown child, there are things you can do now to help take care of your parents. List a few that you do or will soon start doing to help your parents.

**Dig Out The Answers**
1. How did Jesus show his love to his mother even as he hung on the cross?
2. What does God expect grown children to do for their parents?
3. What can you do now to help take care of your parents?
**In Your Own Words:** Write down what you learned.
**My Prayer:** Dear God, help me take care of my parents when I grow up. Also let me help out with chores at home, so my parents can take a break, in Jesus name, Amen.

**Today's Wise Words:** Jesus took care of his mother.

355

# READ

## Darkness At Jesus' Death

Jesus was about to die but his was no ordinary death. Jesus was crucified at about nine in the morning. At noon darkness came over the whole land for three hours. It cleared at three in the afternoon. When the darkness cleared, Jesus cried out to God, using words found in Psalm 22, verse 1. It is good to speak the word of God when you pray. Jesus teaches us that here. That's why it is important to memorize Bible verses. Jesus cried out to God in a loud voice because at that moment he was paying for our sins.

**Dig Out The Answers**
1. What came over the whole land at noon? How long did the darkness last?
2. What did Jesus do when the darkness disappeared?

**In Your Own Words:** Write down what you learned.

**My Prayer:** God, teach me to pray using the words in the Bible just as Jesus did. Amen.

**Today's Wise Words:** Jesus prayed using Bible verses.

# Jesus' Last Cry

Jesus cried out with a loud voice before he died. Jesus' loud cry was a cry of victory over sin, the world and the devil. Hallelujah! And what followed? The curtain in the temple was torn in two. In the Jewish temple, there was a curtain that separated a place called the Holy from the Most Holy Place. Only the high priest was allowed into the Most Holy Place, and

he did that only once a year when he offered a sacrifice for the sins of all Jews. Apart from the high priest anyone who dared to enter the Most Holy place died.

What was so important about the curtain being torn in two? This is what it means – from that time on all who want to can come to God through Christ. There's no need for priests to go to God on your behalf anymore.

When Jesus died, there was also an earthquake. Tombs broke open, and many holy men were raised back to life. Did you hear of such things ever happening at the passing away of an important person? All this shows that Jesus is really the Son of God, who came to die for our sins.

**Dig Out The Answers**
1. List the things that happened when Jesus died?
2. Do you need a priest to pray to God for your sins to be forgiven? Why?
3. You go into the presence of God through _____
**In Your Own Words:** Write down what you learned.
**My Prayer:** Dear God, I thank you that I can now come straight to you through Jesus Christ. Amen.

**Today's Wise Words:** I don't need priests to ask God for forgiveness on my behalf.

## It Is Finished

**READ**

John
19:28-30

**Day 342**

Yesterday, we read that Jesus cried with a loud voice and then died. In today's passage, we read what Jesus actually said when he cried out loud. 'It is finished', Jesus spoke for the last time. What did Jesus mean? Jesus had finished all the work God sent him to do on earth. God sent Jesus to come and die to save us from sin and

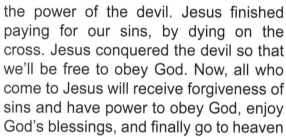

the power of the devil. Jesus finished paying for our sins, by dying on the cross. Jesus conquered the devil so that we'll be free to obey God. Now, all who come to Jesus will receive forgiveness of sins and have power to obey God, enjoy God's blessings, and finally go to heaven when they die. Praise the name of Jesus!

**Dig Out The Answers**
1. What did Jesus do to pay for your sin?
2. What did Jesus do to conquer the devil so he'll not have power over you?

**In Your Own Words:** Write down what you learned.

**My Prayer:** God, thank you that Jesus died to pay for my sins, and conquered the devil so I can live for you alone. Amen.

**Today's Wise Words:** Jesus died to pay for my sin, conquered the devil and gave me power to live for him.

# The Centurion Believes

The darkness and earthquake frightened the centurion and his soldiers. They knew then, they had crucified an innocent man. It dawned on them that Jesus was no ordinary man. They realized that Jesus was indeed the Son of God. God opened the eyes of even those who nailed Jesus to the cross, to see that Jesus *is* His Son.

God loves everybody and wants to save one and all. Never think that somebody is so bad that he cannot be saved. God is willing to save all who come to him through Jesus Christ.

### Dig Out The Answers
1. What made the centurion and soldiers say that Jesus was the Son of God?
2. Why do you think Jesus is the Son of God?

**In Your Own Words:** Write down what you learned.

**My Prayer:** Thank God that you know that Jesus is the Son of God.

**Today's Wise Words:** Jesus, the Son of God is able to save the worst of sinners.

# Jesus – King of The Jews

Today's passage teaches us that Jesus was still king when he died on the cross. When a criminal was crucified in those days, they usually wrote his crime and fastened it to the cross. 'Thieves' was probably fastened to the crosses of the two criminals who were crucified with Jesus. And that would be true because one of them admitted to Jesus that he was a bad man and needed salvation. But see what sign Pilate had fastened to Jesus' cross 'King of the Jews'. Do you think anybody should be killed because of that? Jesus did not commit any crime so they couldn't write anything but that. This was written in three languages commonly spoken in Israel in those days – Aramaic, Latin and Greek. This way most people could read the sign.

Remember that this took place during the Passover Festival when many Jews had come to Jerusalem from all parts of Israel and other countries. Jesus wants all the people of the world to know that he is the King, the Christ, the Son of God, who alone saves man from sin. Jesus wants people to read the good news in their own languages so they'll understand and believe. Pray for all those missionaries who are working hard to write the Bible in different languages around the globe.

**Dig Out The Answers**

1. Why should the Bible be written in languages spoken around the world?

2. What can you do for those writing the Bible in different languages around the world?

**In Your Own Words:** Write down what you learned.

**My Prayer:** Dear God, I thank you for missionaries busy learning different languages so they can write the Bible in those languages. Let those who read the Bible in these languages come to Jesus to save them. Amen.

**Today's Wise Words:** Jesus is King.

# READ

## John 19:31-37

# Jesus Actually Died

This passage teaches us that Jesus actually died, and you must believe this always. If anyone should tell you that Jesus didn't die, tell the person to read this passage in the Bible. As said before, the devil wants people to believe that Jesus didn't die. If Jesus didn't die for our sins then none of us can go to God. But this is not true. Jesus died for our sins so we can be God's children. The crucifixion took place on Friday, so the following day, Saturday, was the Sabbath. The Jews were not allowed to do regular jobs or chores on the Sabbath. They were supposed to go the temple and worship God. Dead bodies were not supposed to hang on crosses on the Sabbath either. It took a long time for a crucified person to die and the Jews didn't want them hanging out there on the Sabbath. They asked Pilate to let the soldiers break their legs, so they would die sooner and be buried before the Sabbath. The soldiers broke the legs of the two criminals, but when they came to Jesus, he was already dead, so they didn't break any of Jesus' bones. All this happened to Jesus as was written in the Old Testament (Exodus 12:46, Numbers 9:12 and Psalm 34:20). Be sure of this, every word of God will come true. Be happy that all God has planned for your life will come to pass just as everything written about Jesus in the Old Testament came true.

## Dig Out The Answers

1. Did everything that was written about Christ Jesus in the Old Testament come true?

2. Does it mean everything God has planned for your life will come true if you walk with Jesus? Write this lesson in a journal.

**My Prayer:** Dear God, thank you Jesus actually died. And thank you that just as everything written about Jesus came true, so will all the things you have planned for my life come true.

**Today's Wise Words:** God's plan for my life will come to pass.

## Jesus Is Buried

**READ**

John
19:38-42

Day 346

Today's story teaches us that God is able to make us bold to do what he wants us to do. Joseph of Arimathea was a secret disciple of Jesus because he feared the Jews. He was a rich man. Nicodemus was the guy who came to Jesus at night. And Jesus taught him about what it means to be 'born again'. Remember he was a ruler of the Jews? He was also a secret disciple. Both Joseph and Nicodemus were very important people and yet they were disciples of Jesus.

Though they were secret disciples for a while, their love for Jesus finally drove away their fear of the Jews. While Joseph went to ask Pilate's permission to get Jesus' body off the cross for burial, Nicodemus was busy preparing a mixture to embalm Jesus. When they had embalmed Jesus, they laid him in a new tomb nearby. God is able to make you bold to stand for Jesus just like he did for Joseph and Nicodemus. Remember, the love of Jesus in your heart will always drive out fear and shame, so you can live and serve him. The love of Jesus is more powerful than shame and fear.

**Dig Out The Answers**
1. What drove the fear of the Jews out of Joseph and Nicodemus?
2. What did they do to show their love to Jesus?
3. The love of Jesus in your heart is greater than ___ and ____.
4. What would you do to show your love to Jesus?
**In Your Own Words:** Write down what you learned.

**My Prayer:** God, thank you that the love of Jesus in my heart is greater than fear or shame, so help me show my love to you at all times, in Jesus name, Amen.

**Today's Wise Words:** The love of Jesus is greater than fear and shame.

362

# Guards At The Tomb

Today's story teaches us that God's word is so powerful that those who hear never forget, even Jesus' enemies. The chief priests suddenly remembered that Jesus had said he would rise again on the third day. They had to be sure that, that wouldn't happen. They asked Pilate to seal the tomb as well as send a large number of soldiers to guard it, afraid the disciples of Jesus might come and steal the body and say that he had risen. The chief priests were afraid of the words of Jesus. They'd seen and heard how he raised Lazarus from the dead.

Though they hated him, they were afraid of his words. His word is truth and it always comes true. Do you know that the word of God does not leave the heart of any person who hears it? The Holy Spirit uses the word of God people hear to convince them to come to Jesus. That's why it's so important to tell your friends about Jesus. The words you speak about Jesus will remain in their hearts whether they come to Jesus or not.

Now that the tomb is sealed and being guarded, would Jesus still rise from the dead?

**Dig Out The Answers**
1. Why is the word of God so powerful?
2. What does the Holy Spirit do with the word of God people hear?
3. Why were the chief priests afraid of Jesus' words?
**In Your Own Words:** Write down what you learned.
**My Prayer:** God, I thank you that your word is very powerful. Thank you that the Holy Spirit uses the word of God to convince people to come to Jesus. He also uses the word of God in me to change me so I can bring glory to you, in Jesus name, Amen.

**Today's Wise Words:** The word of God is powerful.

## He Has Risen

**READ**

Matthew
28:2-4

Day 348

God is more powerful than any person or thing in the world. You must know this. What happened on the third day at the tomb of Jesus? The third day would be Sunday. Remember that the tomb was sealed along with a large number of soldiers guarding it. There was a violent earthquake as an angel of the

Lord came down from heaven. What did he do? He rolled away the stone from the tomb and sat on it. That easy! It's always this easy for God to help us when we bring our problems to him. The guards who were supposed to guard the tomb were so afraid, they became like dead men.

**Dig Out The Answers**
1. Was anything able to stop Jesus from rising from the dead and out the tomb?
2. What does this teach you about the power of God?

**In Your Own Words:** Write down what you learned.

**My Prayer:** Thank you God for showing your power by raising Jesus from the dead. Help me trust you with all my problems. No problem is ever too difficult for you, in Jesus name.

**Today's Wise Words:** God raised Jesus from the dead.

### READ

**Matthew 28:11-15**

**Day 349**

Today's story teaches us never to accept money or gift to lie for someone. The frightened guards fled the tomb as soon as their legs could carry them. They told the chief priests all about the earthquake and the angel. The chief priests didn't want others to know the truth that Jesus actually rose from the dead miraculously. See what they did. They gave the guards money so they would spread the lie that Jesus' disciples stole his body

while they slept. This lie spread very quickly among the Jews at the time and people still believe this lie. The devil is the father of lies, and he still whispers into the ears of people this lie, that the disciples of Jesus stole his body away. But you know that Jesus rose again from the dead. The guards themselves saw everything. Nobody has ever laid eyes on Jesus body or his bones. Jesus is in heaven right now and praying for you. Jesus lives in your heart by His Holy Spirit.

### Dig Out The Answers

1. Why did the chief priests give the guards money to spread a lie?
2. Did Jesus actually rise from the dead? How do you know?

**In Your Own Words:** Write down what you learned.

**My Prayer:** God, help me never to accept money or gift to tell a lie for someone, in Jesus name, Amen.

**Today's Wise Words:** Never accept a gift or money to tell a lie for someone.

# The Stone Rolled Away

Mary Magdalene, Mary the mother of James, and Salome decided to go visit the tomb. They were going to anoint Jesus' body with spices. This was what was done to dead bodies during the time of Jesus. They were still sad about Jesus' death. But then, they remembered that there was a big stone at the entrance of the tomb. They were not strong enough to roll the stone away. But there was another problem that they didn't know about. And that was – there were lots of soldiers guarding the tomb. But see what God did. When they got to the tomb the problem they knew about – rolling away the stone had been solved. We know who did it from yesterday's story – the angel from heaven. The problem they didn't know about – the soldiers guarding the tomb had run away from fear of the angel. The soldiers for sure would have driven the women away from the tomb. God will not only solve the problems you know about, but even the ones you don't know about. God does this for all who follow Jesus with all their hearts. There are many problems around you that you can't see or know about. But everyday, God delivers you from them. Today, thank God for all the problems he delivers you and your family from, because you trust in Jesus.

**Dig Out The Answers**

1. Write down the problem the women discussed on their way to Jesus' tomb?
2. Write down the problem that the women didn't know about?
3. How did God solve problem one and two? What does this teach you?

**In Your Own Words:** Write down what you learned.

**My Prayer:** God, I am very grateful that you don't only solve the problems I know about, but those I don't even know about.

**Today's Wise Words:** God solves problems I know about and the ones I don't.

366

## Jesus Lives

Today's story tells us other women went along to the tomb with Mary Magdalene, Mary the mother of James and Salome. Joseph of Arimathea, and Nicodemus had already wrapped Jesus' body in spices. Yet still, these women brought more spices to the tomb, the first day of the week, because they loved Jesus and had to be sure that he was given a perfect burial. What does this teach you? Don't let what others do to show their

love for Christ stop you from doing the same for him. For example you may hear of somebody giving up his bike or allowance for a missionary in a far country. This shouldn't stop you from giving up your bike or allowance for another missionary elsewhere. You don't have to worry about doing the same thing if you want to show your love to Jesus. Yesterday, the women found out that the stone had been rolled away from the tomb. Today's story tells us that they entered, but they did not find Jesus' body. They didn't know that Jesus had risen just as he said.

**Dig Out The Answers**

1. Can you think of the number one reason the women took along spices to Jesus tomb?

2. Should the way others show their love to Jesus stop you from doing the same?

**In Your Own Words:** Write down what you learned.

**My Prayer:** Pray that God will help you show your love to Jesus, even if what you plan to do has been done already.

**Today's Wise Words:** Be ready to give to Jesus even though others may have done so.

## READ

**Day 352**

# Jesus Keeps His Word

The women stood there wondering what had happened to Jesus' body. While they stood wondering, two men suddenly appeared beside them. They were angels. Their clothes gleamed like lightning. The women were very afraid but the angels told them the good news – "Jesus has risen from the dead". Then the women remembered that Jesus had said he would rise again.

Jesus keeps his word. Jesus has promised all who believe in him that they will live together with him in heaven. Believe him, for Jesus is able to do all that he promises. Maybe you can write some of the things Jesus promises in the Bible down in your notebook. Read Matthew chapter 6, verse 33, and Matthew chapter 28, verse 20, and write down the promises you find there. Whenever you read them, remember that Jesus will keep every one of them.

### Dig Out The Answers

1. What did the women remember after the angel had spoken to them?
2. Write down two things that Jesus promises to all who follow him.

**In Your Own Words:** Write down what you learned.

**My Prayer:** God, I thank you that Jesus keeps his promises. Help me trust him everyday. Amen.

**Today's Wise Words:** Jesus keeps his word.

# Peter and John Believe

When the women saw that the stone had been rolled away from the tomb, Mary Magdalene hurried away to go and tell the disciples. Meanwhile, the other women stood wondering when two angels appeared to them as we read in yesterday's story. Mary Magdalene told Peter and John that Jesus' body had been taken away. Peter and John decided to go and check it out. They came to the tomb and found the strips of linen Jesus had been wrapped in lying there. Peter and John were not afraid to go into the tomb.

This teaches us not to scare ourselves with monsters and foolish fancies as we follow Christ Jesus. There's nothing to fear when Christ Jesus is your Lord and Savior. John and Peter both believed that Jesus had truly risen from the dead. Had they seen Jesus yet? No. They realized that Jesus rising from the dead was a miracle. Jesus didn't have to unwrap himself from the strips. He just slipped out of them. Likewise when Christ comes again you will also slip out of your natural body and be given a glorious body. Hallelujah!

**Dig Out The Answers**
1. Were John and Peter afraid to enter the tomb? Why?
2. Should you allow your imaginations about the graveyard to scare you? Remember Jesus had been to the grave and he walked out of that place without any harm, so you need not be afraid of graveyards, or monsters in the dark. Jesus is more powerful.
**In Your Own Words:** Write down what you learned.
**My Prayer:** Lord God, some people think the grave is the scariest thing in the whole wide world, but I know Jesus conquered it, so thank you for giving me courage when I am afraid, in Jesus' name. Amen.

**Today's Wise Words:** Jesus conquered the grave. I don't have to fear anything.

## Jesus Appears to Mary Magdalene

**READ**
John
20:10-18

Day 354

Mary Magdalene teaches us in today's story to seek Jesus without getting tired of it. We seek Jesus by reading the Bible daily, obeying it, praying and doing God's work. Mary Magdalene stayed behind even when Peter and John left the tomb. She wanted to find out what had happened to Jesus. She stooped to look into the tomb and saw two angels. Was she happy? No. She was not looking for angels. She was looking for Jesus. She asked the angels where she could find Jesus' dead body. Remember, we are not to seek angels or things, but Jesus alone.

The next moment, Jesus was standing behind her. She couldn't recognize him until Jesus called out her name. Oh what joy! She finally saw Jesus, the risen Jesus! Mary Magdalene was the first to see Jesus because she searched for the whereabouts of Jesus without getting tired. Jesus rewards all who seek him with all their hearts. Those who seek Jesus always get to know more of his love, his power, miracles, joy, and many other blessings.

### Dig Out The Answers
1. Why wasn't Mary Magdalene happy when she saw two angels in the tomb?
2. You are to seek only _____, because he is your Savior and Lord.
**In Your Own Words:** Write down what you learned.
**My Prayer:** Dear God, I thank you for teaching me to seek Jesus only and nothing else, because he is my Savior and Lord.

**Today's Wise Words:** Jesus rewards those who seek him with all their heart.

370

# Seek Jesus Early

This proverb is a promise from God. God kept this promise to Mary Magdalene. Those who seek God eagerly find him. And people who are eager start early. Mary Magdalene sought for Jesus early and with all her heart, so she was the first to see him. Just as Mary was the first to see the risen Jesus, God is also willing to do something special in your life if you keep seeking him everyday. God keeps his promises. Be sure to seek Jesus, reading the Bible, obeying, praying and doing God's work. Even as you do these things, expect God to bless you in a special way.

Do you know that grown-ups who became Christians while they were children avoided so many teenage problems as well as other grown-up ones? How? Because they studied God's word and obeyed it, so they became wise and made wise choices. Children who seek Jesus early are wise.

### Dig Out The Answers

1. What does God promise those who seek him early with all their hearts?
2. What was Mary Magdalene's reward for seeking Jesus?

**In Your Own Words:** Write down what you learned.

**My Prayer:** God, help me seek Jesus everyday, so I can be wise and receive a reward from you. Amen.

**Today's Wise Words:** Seek Jesus early.

## READ    On the Road to Emmaus

Luke 24:13-16

After Jesus appeared to Mary Magdalene, he appeared later that same day to two other disciples on their way to Emmaus. What were the two disciples discussing as they went along? They were talking about Jesus, how he taught with authority; how he healed the sick; performed miracles; that the chief priests and Jews had him crucified; and

now they heard he had risen from the dead. As they talked, Jesus joined them but they didn't recognize him.

You, too, are to talk about Jesus whenever you meet another Christian friend. What happens when you do that? Jesus joins your conversation even though you don't see him. Isn't this wonderful! The things we learn about Jesus from God's word, or from church, should excite us so much that we always want to talk them over with friends. When you meet another young person who is a Christian, try discussing what you know about Jesus. Jesus is always present when we talk about him with our Christian friends.

**Dig Out The Answers**

1. What were the two disciples talking about on their way to Emmaus?

2. What should you talk about when you meet another Christian friend?

**In Your Own Words:** Write down what you learned.

**My Prayer:** Dear God, teach me to discuss your word with other Christians whenever we meet, because it pleases you, in Jesus' name. Amen

**Today's Wise Words:** Chat with other young people about Jesus.

# Jesus Joins the Two Disciples

## READ

Luke
24:17-27

**Day 357**

When Jesus is present, he makes us understand his word better. As we read yesterday, Jesus joined the two disciples on their way to Emmaus though they didn't recognize him. Jesus joined the conversation by asking a question, as we read in today's passage. They were sad at first, but managed to tell him all that had happened to the one they had thought was the Christ. How funny – talking to Jesus about himself! What did

Jesus do after hearing all that they had to say about him? He explained to them that Jesus had to suffer so he could enter into his glory. Jesus also explained all that had been written concerning him by Moses and the prophets of old. This is what happens when we talk about Jesus. The Holy Spirit comes in and helps us understand God's

word better. Do you want to understand God's word better? Then keep talking about it with your Christian friends.

**Dig Out The Answers**
1. What did Jesus do for the two disciples?
2. What does the Holy Spirit do when you discuss God's word with others?

**In Your Own Words:** Write down what you learned.

**My Prayer:** God, I thank you that your Holy Spirit helps me understand your word whenever I discuss it with my Christian friends.

**Today's Wise Words:** The Holy Spirit helps me understand God's word better.

373

# The Two Disciples Host Jesus

The two disciples enjoyed listening to Jesus explain the word of God to them so much they invited him to stay the night with them. This action by the two disciples teaches us also to be so thrilled listening to God's word that we want to hear it over and over again. They were more than happy to have Jesus stay the night.

Are you happy when Christian families stay a few nights in your home? Or would you be sad if your parents brought a foster kid home to stay? Jesus encourages us to want to have Christian workers stay a few days in our homes when they have to.

What can you as a child do to show Jesus' love to Christian workers who may stay the night in your home? Preachers, pastors, gospel singers, missionaries, children's/youth choirs are all Christian workers who travel around and may need a place to spend a few nights. Would you help Dad and Mom get their room ready? Could you help set the table for supper? Would you empty their laundry baskets? Would you chat with them or play with their children? God blesses us when we show such kindness to other Christian workers.

**Dig Out The Answers**
1. Why do you think the disciples asked Jesus to stay the night?
2. Would you encourage your parents to host Christian workers in your home if it were announced in your church one Sunday?

**In Your Own Words:** Write down what you learned.

**My Prayer:** Dear God, help me encourage my parents to host Christian workers in our home, and teach me to help out cheerfully, in Jesus' name. Amen.

**Today's Wise Words:** Enjoy listening to God's word. Enjoy hosting Christian workers.

374

# The Two Disciples Recognize Jesus

**READ**
Luke
24:30-35

**Day 359**

The two disciples were good hosts. Once Jesus was in their home they served him supper. When it was time to eat, Jesus took the bread and broke it as he usually did. There and then the disciples recognized who he was – Jesus! Would you recognize Jesus if he came to your home? Nobody could fool the two disciples about Jesus, because they had walked with him, they had eaten with him and watched how he gave thanks at every meal. They had listened to him, been taught by him, and obeyed him. So they could recognize him.

Jesus never changes. He is the same yesterday, today, and forever. When you walk with Jesus you'll also know him. You know Jesus by reading the word of God, obeying it and praying. If Jesus came to you, he would speak the way the Bible speaks about him. Jesus would show the same kindness, compassion, gentleness, power, and all that you read about him. When you know Jesus this way, nobody can fool you by pretending to be Jesus. The disciples were overjoyed, even though Jesus disappeared. They couldn't hold the news any longer. They had to tell the rest of the disciples. So off to Jerusalem they went with the good news.

**Dig Out The Answers**
1. Why did the two disciples recognize Jesus?
2. How would you also recognize Jesus if he came to your home?
**In Your Own Words:** Write down what you learned.
**My Prayer:** Dear God, let your Holy Spirit teach me more about Jesus through your word, so I'll know him and see him in all that I do, in Jesus' name.

**Memory Verse:** Hebrews 13:8 "Jesus Christ is the same yesterday and today and forever." (NIV)

**Today's Wise Words:** I know Jesus when I walk with him.

# Jesus Appears to His Disciples

We are still continuing the story from yesterday. The two disciples told the eleven about the good news – the Lord had risen!

While they were still talking Jesus appeared in the room where they were.

Jesus rose again from the dead with a special body. His body now had a special ability to appear and disappear. Jesus said to them, "Peace be with you". Whenever Jesus is with us, he brings us peace. Whenever you are frightened, remember that Jesus is with you and you'll have peace. The disciples were all frightened because they thought he was a spirit. Jesus proved to them that he was not a spirit. He still had a body with bones and flesh, even though it was a much more special body now. He showed them the nail marks in his hands and feet. He also ate the broiled fish he asked for to prove that he wasn't a spirit.

Jesus really did rise from the dead and when he comes back all Christians in the grave will rise up.

### Dig Out The Answers

1. What does Jesus bring us when we are frightened?
2. What did Jesus do to prove that he wasn't a spirit?
3. What could Jesus' special body do?

**In Your Words:** Write down what you learned.

**My Prayer:** God, I thank you that Jesus actually rose from the dead with flesh and bones.

**Today's Wise Words:** Jesus' resurrected body was flesh and bones

376

# Jesus Explains His Death and Resurrection

**Luke 24:44-49**

**Day 361**

Jesus was still with his disciples as we read yesterday. He realized that his disciples did not understand all that had happened to him, so he explained the Scriptures to them. Scriptures is another word for the Bible. Jesus pointed out to them that what Moses, the Prophets, and the other Scriptures spoke about him must all be fulfilled. Do you know that so many passages in the Old Testament talk about Jesus' coming into the world, his sufferings, dying and rising to save us? Moses wrote the first five books of the bible. You've also heard about prophets like Isaiah, Jeremiah, Daniel, Jonah, Ezekiel, Joel and the others. Jesus was willing to teach the disciples to understand that he suffered, died, and rose again, so all who come to him will receive forgiveness and be saved from their sins. Isn't this wonderful! Whenever you don't understand something you read in the bible, ask the Holy Spirit to teach you. Now that Jesus is in heaven, the Holy Spirit is the one who teaches us the word of God. Jesus also told them to remain in the city until the coming of the Holy Spirit who'd give them power.

**Dig Out The Answers**

1. What did Jesus do to show that he wants us to understand the word of God?
2. Who teaches us the word of God now?
3. Why did Jesus have to suffer, die and rise again?

**In Your Own Words:** Write down what you learned.

**My Prayer:** God, I thank you that Jesus wants me to understand the Bible, so he sent the Holy Spirit to help me. Amen.

**Today's Wise Words:** Jesus wants me to understand the Scriptures.

## READ

John
20:24-29

**Day 362**

# Jesus Appears to Thomas

Thomas was not with the disciples when Jesus appeared to them the first time. Thomas wouldn't believe what the other disciples told him about Jesus. Thomas wanted to be sure that it was the same body he saw crucified on the cross that had come back to life. Thomas missed out on the blessing of seeing Jesus the first time because he was not with the other disciples.

Do you know that you miss out on God's blessings if you fail to meet with other Christians for fellowship at church services or Sunday school? Always look forward to meeting with other Christians so you'll be blessed.

A week later Jesus appeared to his disciples when Thomas was around. Jesus told Thomas to stop doubting and believe. Jesus tells all of us the same thing – stop doubting and believe! Have you been asking God to do something for you? Do not doubt, keep praying and God will answer you. Thomas saw Jesus. It was the same Jesus who had hung on the cross. Thomas believed at once and called Jesus, "My Lord and my God". Those who know Jesus call him Lord *and God*. You are very blessed and so are all Christians who did not see Jesus physically, his sufferings, dying, and resurrection – and yet we believe!

**Dig Out The Answers**
1. Why did Thomas miss Jesus' appearance to the disciples the first time?
2. What does this teach you?
3. Jesus doesn't want you to _____, but believe.
**In Your Own Words:** Write down what you learned.

**My Prayer:** Tell God to help you believe in Jesus more and more each day.

**Today's Wise Words:** Jesus is my *Lord* and my *God!*

378

# READ

John
21:1-14

Day 363

## Jesus and Peter

Jesus had now risen from the dead and appeared to the disciples two times. In today's story, he appeared to his disciples a third time. The disciples had fished the whole night but caught nothing. Jesus, standing on the shore, told them to cast their net to the right side of the boat and they would find fish. They did not know it was Jesus and yet they obeyed. And when they did, they caught so many fish! Sometimes Jesus brings us help by using other people. It may be your little sister or big brother. You must be humble and patient to listen to them just as the disciples listened to the stranger at the shore who happened to be Jesus. Do you know that Jesus is with you even when you have difficulty completing your homework or chores, and he is there to help you out? Immediately, John (who calls himself "the disciple whom Jesus loved" because he doesn't want to name himself in his own book) realized it was Jesus. Would you recognize Jesus if he came to your school, or your neighborhood park, your soccer game or music class? John knew it was Jesus because everything Jesus says comes true. As soon as they obeyed, they caught lots of fish. When you allow Jesus to lead you in all you do, you will succeed. Only Jesus has perfect knowledge, so he knows exactly what you need to do to be successful. It is good to talk to Jesus about your plans. It is good to listen to him as you pray. Jesus puts good ideas into your head to help you in all you do.

**Dig Out The Answers**
1. Why do you have to talk to Jesus about your plans?
3. What did Jesus do in today's story to show that he has perfect knowledge? **In Your Own Words:** Write down what you learned.
**My Prayer:** Tell Jesus about your plans and ask him to lead you in all you do.

**Today's Wise Words:** Jesus has perfect knowledge.

# Peter Still Dear to Christ Jesus

**READ**

John
21:15-19

**Day 364**

You remember that Peter denied Jesus three times when Jesus was being tried at the High Priest's palace. Peter was ashamed and sad and wept bitterly. Jesus had earlier warned Peter he would deny him, but Peter thought he'd never do such a thing. Jesus had also prayed for Peter that his faith would not fail. And look what happened! Peter's faith did not fail. What did Peter do to show that he'd repented? After weeping bitterly about denying Jesus he came back to the disciples. Peter was with the disciples when Mary Magdalene came with the news that Jesus' body had been taken. Peter was with the disciples when Jesus appeared to them the first and second times. Those who truly repent of their sins always come back to fellowship with other believers. Judas did not seek fellowship with the other disciples. His was not a true repentance.

When we repent of our sins, Jesus asks us one question, "Do you love me"? Jesus asked Peter this same question. Peter told Jesus he loved him, and through the grace of God, he served Jesus the rest of his life. Through Peter and the other disciples, Jesus founded his church on earth. All who love Jesus have grace to serve him like Peter even if they do wrong things sometimes.

**Dig Out The Answers**
1. Peter denied Jesus. What did he do to show that he repented of his sin?
2. What are those who love Jesus able to do after they repent?
**In Your Own Words:** Write down what you learned.

**My Prayer:** God, thank you for the grace you give me to love and serve you whenever I say I am sorry for my sins, in Jesus name.

**Today's Wise Words:** Love Jesus and fellowship with other believers

# Jesus Is Taken up into Heaven

**Acts**
**1:1-11**

**Day 365**

Jesus finally leaves the earth for heaven as you read today. Jesus finished everything God asked him to. What a wonderful job he did! He preached the good news of the kingdom, performed miracles, healed the sick, suffered and died for our sins. Then he rose again from the dead and gave us hope that one day we would also rise again and be with him in heaven, forever. As Jesus was being taken into heaven, two angels stood beside the disciples. They told them Jesus was coming back the same way he ascended into heaven. Now you know where to look as you expect Jesus' second coming – into the heavens. Jesus is not coming back as a baby anymore. He is coming back as the King of Kings and Lord of Lords. Hallelujah! Well done for reading all about the life of Jesus.
May the Lord truly bless you!

**Dig Out The Answers**
1. What did the two men in white tell the disciples as Jesus ascended into heaven?
2. What did Jesus tell the disciples to wait for?
3. Who would give the disciples power to be witnesses in Jerusalem, Judea, Samaria and to the ends of the earth?
**In Your Own Words:** Write down what you learned.

**My Prayer:** Thank God that Jesus finished all his work on earth. Also thank him for helping you finish your work well too, while you are alive.

Memorize the verse in 'Today's Wise Words'.

**Today's Wise Words:** *"This same Jesus, who has been taken from you into heaven, will come back in the same way you have seen him go into heaven." Acts 1: 11b (NIV)*

## Bibliography
### (Recommended for Further Study)

McGee, Vernon J. *Through the Bible with J. Vernon McGee: Matthew – Romans.* Vol. 4, Nashville, Tennessee: Thomas Nelson, Inc., Publishers, 1983.

Henry, Matthew. *Matthew Henry's Commentary on the Whole Bible.* Vol. 5, McLean, Virginia: MacDonald Publishing Company.

Doll, F., Singer, C., and Stoll, A. M. *Toward Easter.* San Mauro, Italy: Editions Du Signe, 2001.

Cura, M., Doll, F., and Stoll, A. M. *Advent Christmas 2002.* San Mauro, Italy: Editions Du Signe, 2002.

Youth For Christ (USA). *Practical Christianity.* eds. LaVonne, N., Beers, R., Barton, B. et al., Carmel, New York: Guideposts®. 1987.

The Regina Press. *Blessed Are You: The Beatitudes For Children.* ed. Murphy, W and C. P., New York: The Regina Press, 1982.

Kohlenberger III, John R., and Wescombe, N. *The Amazing Book.* Vol. 1, Portland, Oregon: Multnomah Press. 1991.

Cook Ministry Resources. *Praise & Worship – Year One, Preschool.* Colorado Springs, Colorado: Cook Ministry Resources. 1997.

Gospel Light. *My God and Me – Leader's Guide.* Ventura, California: Gospel Light. 2002.